IMAGES
of America

AIKEN'S SPORTING LIFE

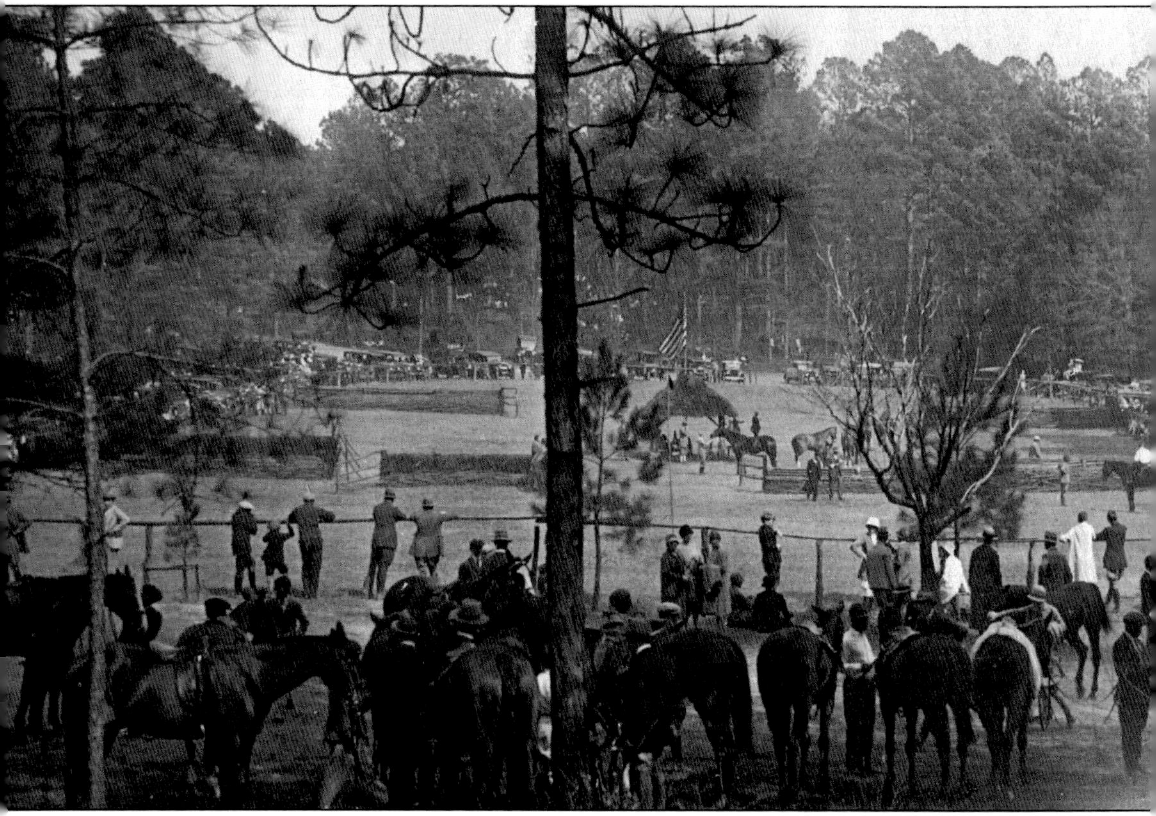

Aiken is known chiefly for three things: beautiful tree-lined streets, the Savannah River Site, and as a resort town resplendent with horses, golf, and hospitality. At the very heart and soul of what makes Aiken a special place are the Hitchcock Woods. (Peter Brainard.)

On the Cover: Pictured here is Louise Corcoran Eustis Hitchcock, master of the Aiken Drag hounds in the Hitchcock Woods. Rosalie Sellar Brainard and Alix Dolan Toland were whips for the hunt. Brainard's love of Aiken shows in the many photographs of Aiken's sporting life she preserved, many of which can be found within this book. (Peter Brainard.)

IMAGES
of America

AIKEN'S SPORTING LIFE

Jane Page Thompson, foreword by
Linda Knox McLean, MFH Aiken Hounds

ARCADIA
PUBLISHING

ISBN 978-1-4671-1497-4

Published by Arcadia Publishing
Charleston, South Carolina

Printed in the United States of America

Library of Congress Control Number: 2015941807

For all general information, please contact Arcadia Publishing:
Telephone 843-853-2070
Fax 843-853-0044
E-mail sales@arcadiapublishing.com
For customer service and orders:
Toll-Free 1-888-313-2665

Visit us on the Internet at www.arcadiapublishing.com

To Celestine Eustis, whose forethought safeguarded Aiken's Pinelands for the future, and Mark Thompson, horseman husband, whose patience and love mean everything.

Contents

Foreword

Aiken has a unique past, from the days when the train first brought settlers from the coast to the building of the vast Aiken hotels and the influx of Northern visitors who were enchanted by the climate and soft footing for their horses. Aiken has made its mark.

Today, we are looking at a vibrant town with a diverse population. We are an All-America City and are growing and changing while still appreciating our unique past.

When I moved to Aiken full time, 22 years ago, I was struck by how welcoming Aiken is and how easy it was to be a part of this community rather than a visitor to it. As I became a part of this town, it became a part of me; I feel privileged to call Aiken home.

This book is a labor of love for Jane Page Thompson. She began work on it three years ago and has spent countless hours unearthing photographs from Aiken's past and present. A good many have never been seen before. With single-minded determination, she has researched the background of each shot in order to give us a broader view of our town and the events that have given Aiken its unique character. All of the author's proceeds from this book will go to the Hitchcock Woods Foundation. That generosity of spirit defines Jane Page in everything she does. I am proud to call her my friend and proud to call Aiken my home.

—Linda Knox McLean, MFH Aiken Hounds

Acknowledgments

The South Caroliniana Library at the University of South Carolina has been a main source of photographs. Thanks to Beth Bilderback and the staff at Caroliniana. All images, unless otherwise noted, appear courtesy of the South Caroliniana Library.

Peter Brainard, in memory of his late wife, Rosalie Dolan Sellar Brainard, contributed many of her family photographs. The use of these is a true gift for the Aiken Horse Show 100th and tribute to the memory of a fine sporting lady.

All images from Courtney Conger, Lucy Tower, Bettina Ruckelshaus, Linda Knox McLean, Thomas Bossard, Nick Bridges, Amber Asbill Jackson, Elizabeth Carey-Gregory, Beth Sauerborn, Todd Lista, Cathy Cram, Lisa Hall, Glenn Thompson, Sandra Thomas, Teddy Milner, Ashley Seawell, and the Aiken Standard and Historical Museum are noted with the name in parentheses.

Content and grammar review was provided by Sandy and Bill Tucker, Elliott Levy, Nancy Wilds, and Linda Knox McLean. Thanks to James Riley and Howell Printing for their technical skills. For their kindness, Paula Blessing and Marion Blocker and all of my Realtor colleagues and real estate clients at Aiken Properties who have been understanding and supportive deserve thanks. Thanks to the editors and staff at Arcadia Publishing for their hard work, and thanks to the Hitchcock Woods Foundation.

INTRODUCTION

Aiken, South Carolina, has become a thriving Southern town because of industry and the traditions of equine sport and golf that keep Winter Colony residents returning decade after decade. It began as a tourist destination for coastal dwellers and is now a winter festival destination. Aiken's Gilded Age occurred from 1892 to 1942, when American high society just *had* to spend Easter in Aiken. In 1950, the federal government came in and, in a 310-square-mile area, built a nuclear laboratory operated by DuPont. This project uprooted villages and quadrupled the size of the county seat, Aiken, in 18 months.

The 10,000 or so site workers and subcontractors became interested in the horse sports of Aiken and picked up where the Gilded Age left off. Then, in the 1970s and 1980s, Canadians started returning to this charming town for foxhunting and became a welcome addition to the local demographic. The world-famous Willcox Inn in Aiken flies both the US and Canadian flags out front.

The Aiken Horse Show is a 100-year-old tradition that reaches out across the country, bringing many home to Aiken for the horse riding as much as for the golf the next Sunday over in Augusta. The Aiken Hounds celebrated their 100th season in 2014, and Aiken Prep School, now Mead Hall Episcopal School, celebrates 100 years of private education in Aiken. A town where women have made their mark in sports, politics, and society, Aiken has been the must-do stop on the road to the White House for over a century, a training ground for the Olympics, and the start to many happily-ever-afters, in which heroines really do marry Prince Charming.

A veritable gathering place of food moguls, culinary figures such as Jack Seabrook, Martin Ritter, Lou Piancone, Russ McCall and the Ganzis all came for driving, polo, or foxhunting. The last three decades have seen international polo and Olympic three-day events and World Cup carriage driving come to Aiken. All the while, Aiken's Triple Crown of steeplechase jumping, harness racing, and polo has had 30,000 spectators captivated for the last century.

Walking down the sidewalk in Aiken on a spring evening, one can hear Japanese, French, German, Argentinean, and British accents because major corporations such as Bridgestone, Owens Corning, AGY, and MTU Diesel bring industry to Aiken. Horses bring polo greats, Olympic medalists, and world champions, and professional golfers, athletes, and their fans come together in this small Southern town with roots that run deep for sporting and living.

Along with Hunt Week and the Triple Crown, Juilliard in Aiken, now Joye in Aiken, is another example of how this little town reaches to the famous New York icon, which brings its best down to perform at the behest of Pulitzer Prize–winning authors and Grammy-winning musicians who call Aiken home. International real tennis players flock to the Aiken Tennis Club to challenge a ranked world champion—now that is the life in Aiken.

As with every Southern town, there are various perspectives that go along with the visitors who make it famous, and the vivid telling of the past by Jim Gaver, John Ashhurst, Lucy Tower, and Bettina Ruckelshaus has allowed great stories of the characters who made up Aiken's history come to light or "swell," as the town still does in winter. Lifelong friendships, powerful industrial alliances, advantageous marriages, and great love affairs have always been a part of the heartbeat of this charming town. Aiken is one of those places that gets under your skin and becomes a part of you as much as you become a part of it. Cole Porter captured that best in his classic inspired by Aiken's residents, *Anything Goes*.

Divine guidance and inspiration from the works of Harry Worchester Smith, Julian Peabody, Celestine Eustis, Kay Lawrence, Dorothy MacDowell, and Emily Bull can be found within these pages. The sentiment of generational commitment that keeps people returning to visit or compels residents to stay is in the air and said to be in the water.

Elliot Levy, the retired curator of the Aiken County Historical Museum, has more stories to tell about Aiken than the scope of this work would allow. He recounts the history of jazz greats who came to Aiken and got their start in nightclubs and hotel ballrooms, the great golfers, female and male, who paved the way for future athletes and their successes, and the mixing of cultures and backgrounds. Aiken is truly a dynamic network of interconnected lives and experiences that make living life brighter.

Often space limits the history we want to tell. In this book, highlighting the roles of those who may have been in the shadows or have been edited out of history was a key objective. And as with any lofty undertaking, one may overlook, make a mistake, or slip, but as John Ashhurst reminds us, "Everything that happens in Aiken happened for a reason!"

One

Aiken is Calling

Hotels, Healing Air, and Horses Keep Luring People Back

From the time of the Cofitachequi and Yuci, the Silver Bluff along Savannah River and the surrounding pine forests have been a refuge. Between 1520 and 1540, Lucas Vazquez de Ayllon and Hernando de Soto explored the area. In 1660, Henry Woodward established treaties with the tribes near Pinelands Crossroads for the British, and by 1730, George Gaulphin had established his trading post. In 1781, Fort Dreadnaught was sacked by colonists led by Henry "Light-Horse Harry" Lee (father of Robert E. Lee) and Andrew Pickens. In 1791, Revolutionary War soldier Ephraim Franklin was granted Coker Spring for his service to the army. In 1814, Harry Schultz founded Hamburg Town to compete with Leroy Hammond's Ferry Post. The rivalry between these two merchants along the river garnered the attention of William Aiken of the South Carolina Canal and Rail Road Company, who chose to build a 133-mile passenger rail from Charleston to Hamburg, the longest passenger train in the world at the time. The secondary aim of Aiken and his board of directors was to establish a resort destination for Charlestonians to escape malaria in summer.

Between the 1830s and 1850s, economic stability was dependent on tourism from the railroad and jobs at Gregg Graniteville Mill, the turpentine industry, and Southern Porcelain Manufacturing Company. By the 1870s, Aiken was a bustling resort town. Visitors from New England, the Midwest, and Canada were flocking here for the climate's tonic qualities and recreational pastimes that this fashionable watering place offered. Doctors were prescribing their patients rehabilitation in Southern health resorts. Much of the Aiken fervor is credited first with the waters from Coker Spring, said to keep the consumer returning, and, second, with the society that Celestine Eustis began when she brought her niece to Aiken. In 1882, six-year-old Louise fell in love with horses and riding in the turpentine air around Aiken, and Eustis seized on the investment opportunity that the town presented.

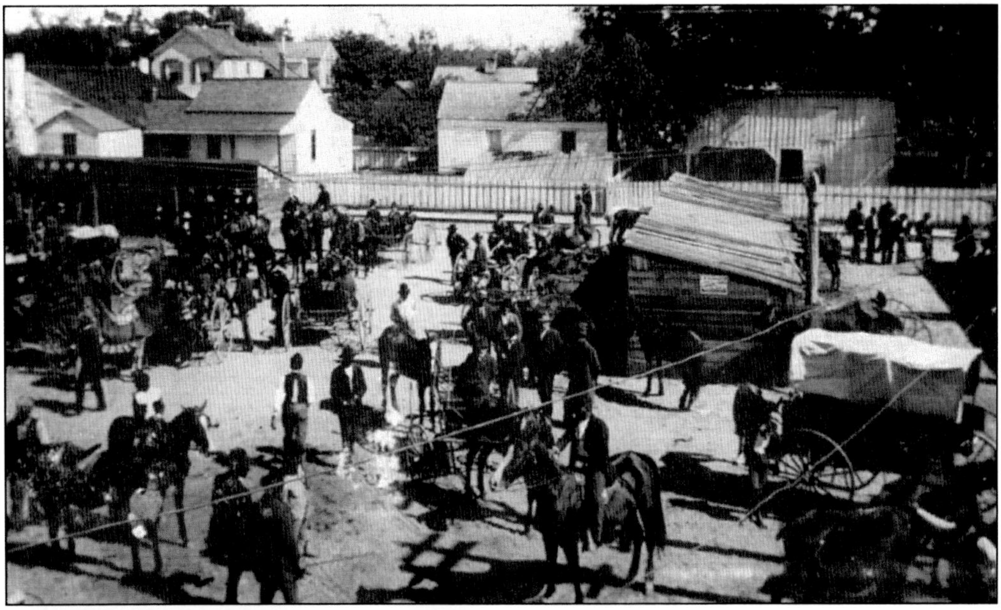

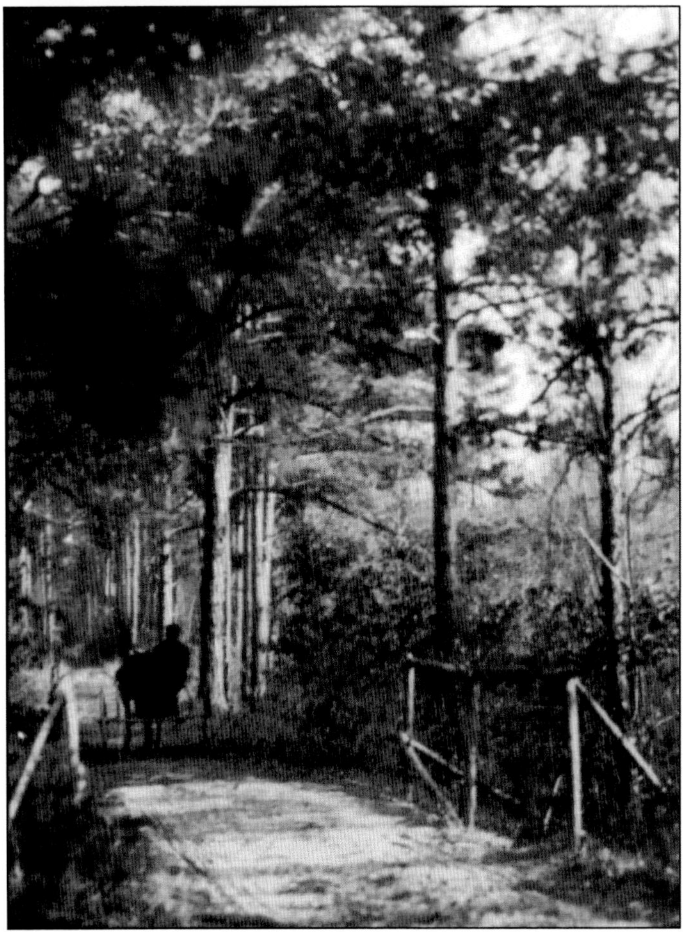

Pictured here is a horse-trading day. The Savannah River trading posts have long attracted successful merchants and travelers seeking clean water and a safe place to rest. Originally called Pineland Crossroads and Coker Spring, Aiken attracted horses from the start, and much of the city's continued success is owed to the buying, selling, and riding of the noble beasts. (Aiken County Historical Museum.)

Pineland trails, now part of Aiken's Hitchcock Woods, provided shade for travelers moving through the area on their way to cross the Savannah River or moving north off of the coast. These pine forests permeated the air of Aiken with bracing clean refreshment that doctors have lauded since the 1830s.

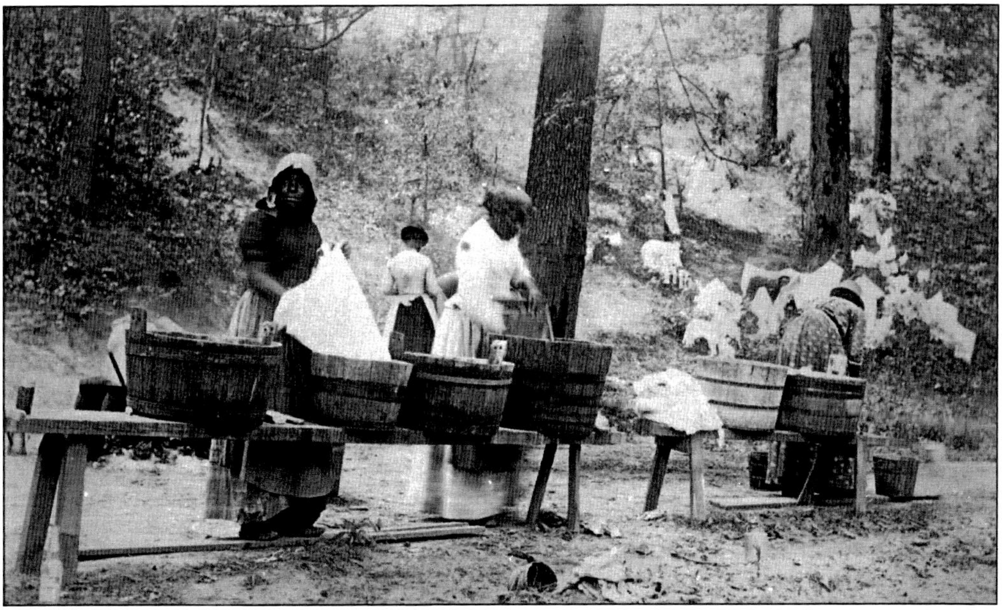

Coker Spring on washing day was a busy locale. Had it not been for the clean freshwater spring, Aiken may never have been founded. The 280 acres surrounding Coker Spring were a Revolutionary War service grant to Ephraim Franklin, who later donated a portion to the railroad company.

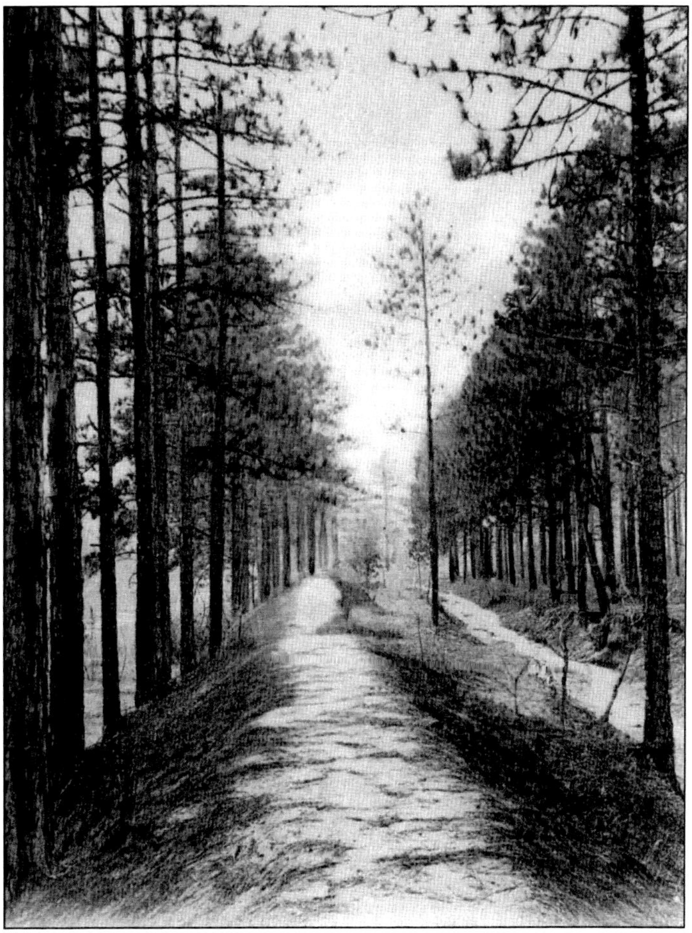

Devil's Backbone is the primary trail leading from South Boundary Avenue into the Hitchcock Woods and down through Memorial Gate. Horatio Allen's engineering feat that saved the railroad company 14 miles of track was an inclined plane, a visual reminder in the woods of the melding of science and nature that has long served Aiken well.

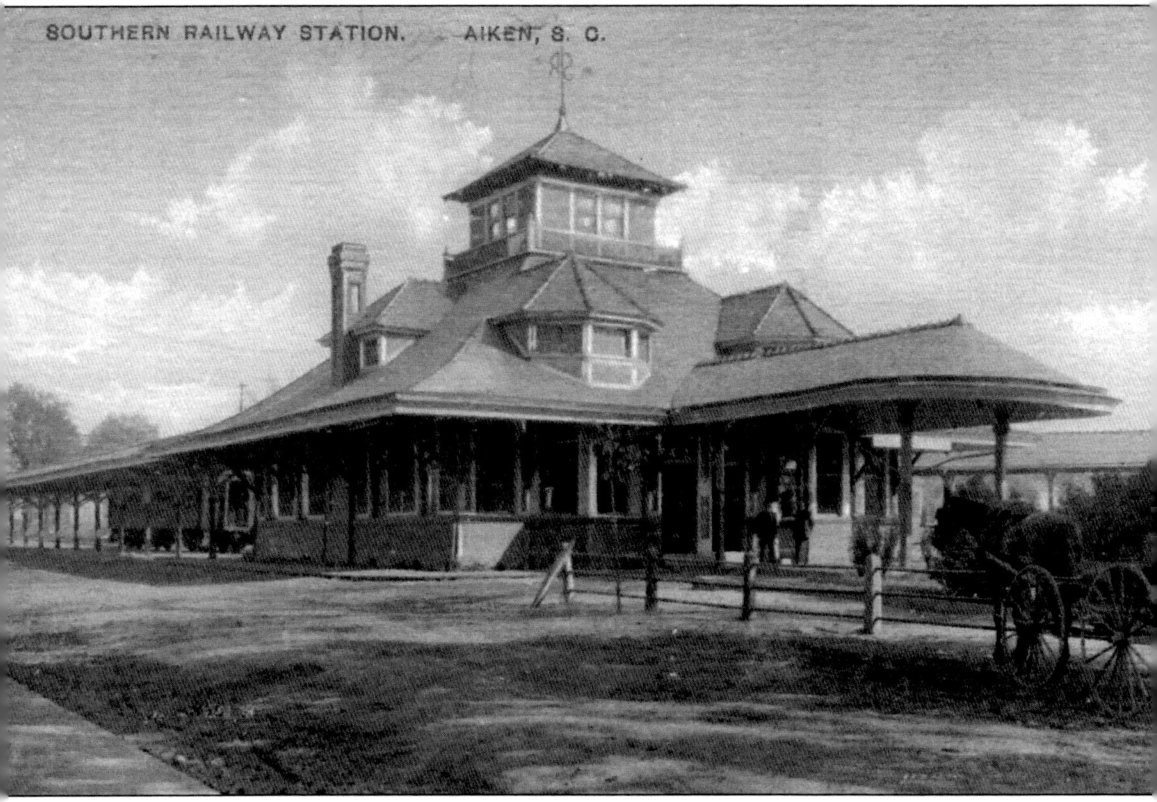

In 1827, William Aiken and the South Carolina Canal and Rail Road Company began planning for the 133-mile passenger train route to deliver Charlestonians to the high bluffs north of the coast to avoid malaria. Collaborations with land owners along the route allowed the railroad to promote a planned town with a large hotel as its focal point. Some land acquisitions would come easily, while others required a bit more negotiation, with a marriage in the mix. On December 19, 1835, Aiken received its official charter in the Barnwell District. The town was designed within a two-mile grid around 27 core blocks, with Union Street and Railroad Avenue (now Park Avenue) as the center axis. The original station building had been simple, but in 1899, the Southern Railway erected an elegant station to welcome wealthy visitors to Aiken.

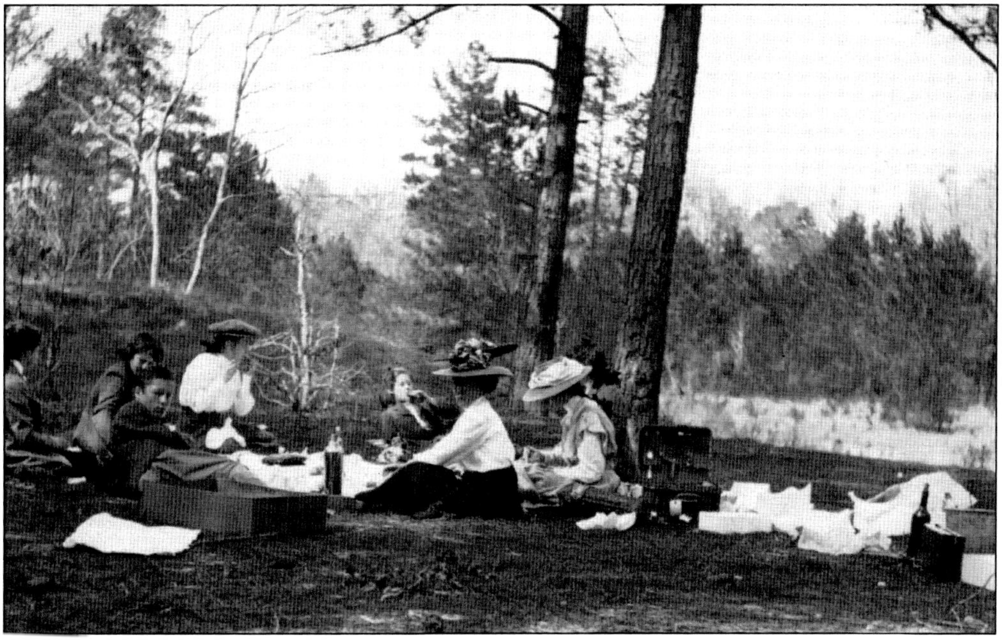

Alfred Dexter, an engineer with the railroad company, spent his days planning the city and enjoying the company of local belles, primarily Sara Williams. Dexter's love for Sara led to a mutually beneficial business arrangement with her father, William Williams. And so it began, a tradition of love affairs anchoring Aiken's future social and economic development.

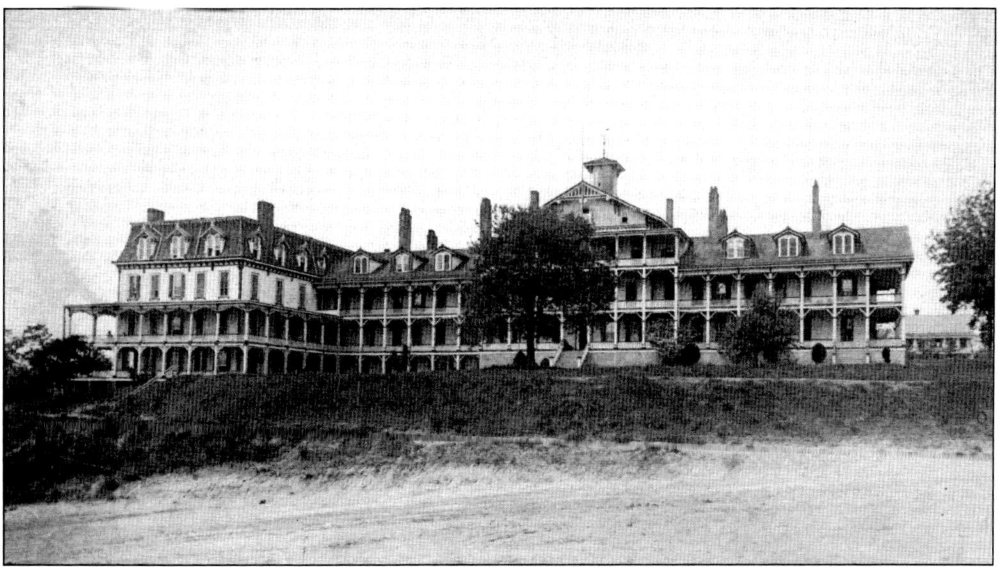

Highland Park Hotel, built in 1866, was the world's largest wooden structure at the time. The hotel and its grounds boasted ladies' and gentlemen's billiard rooms, a bowling alley, one of the country's first lawn tennis courts, a golf course, and well-appointed salons for gathering. The first proprietor was B.P. Chatfield of Connecticut, and over the years, the hotel attracted guests from British royalty to industrial magnates, movie stars, and US presidents.

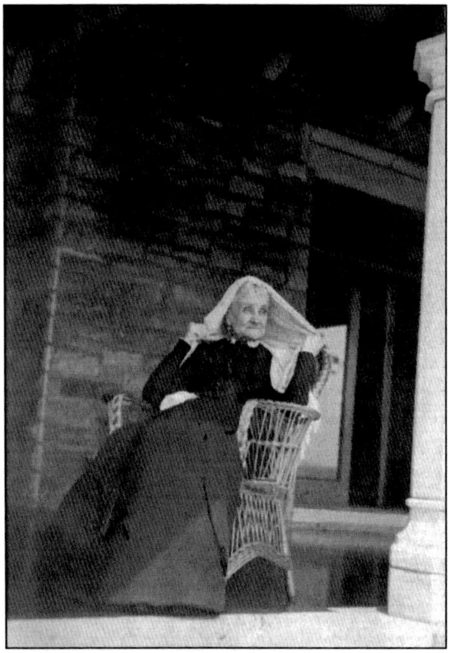

Celestine Eustis was born in New Orleans, the daughter of George Eustis, owner of the Pontchartrain Railroad and benefactor of Tulane University. Her Creole roots took her to France, where she owned Villa Louisianna in Cannes. In the late 1890s, she started a real estate company in Aiken with W.C. Whitney. She held joint custody of her niece and nephews with their maternal grandfather, W.W. Corcoran, for whom she served as hostess during many of his soirees in Washington, DC. Celestine wrote a cookbook, *Cooking in Old Creole Days*, preserving the recipes that delighted her guests on multiple continents. On February 1, 1921, the *New York Times* reported, "Miss Celestine Eustis had a fainting spell while riding her horse in Aiken." Only 10 days later, all social events were cancelled, and the entire town mourned her passing. (Both, Brainard.)

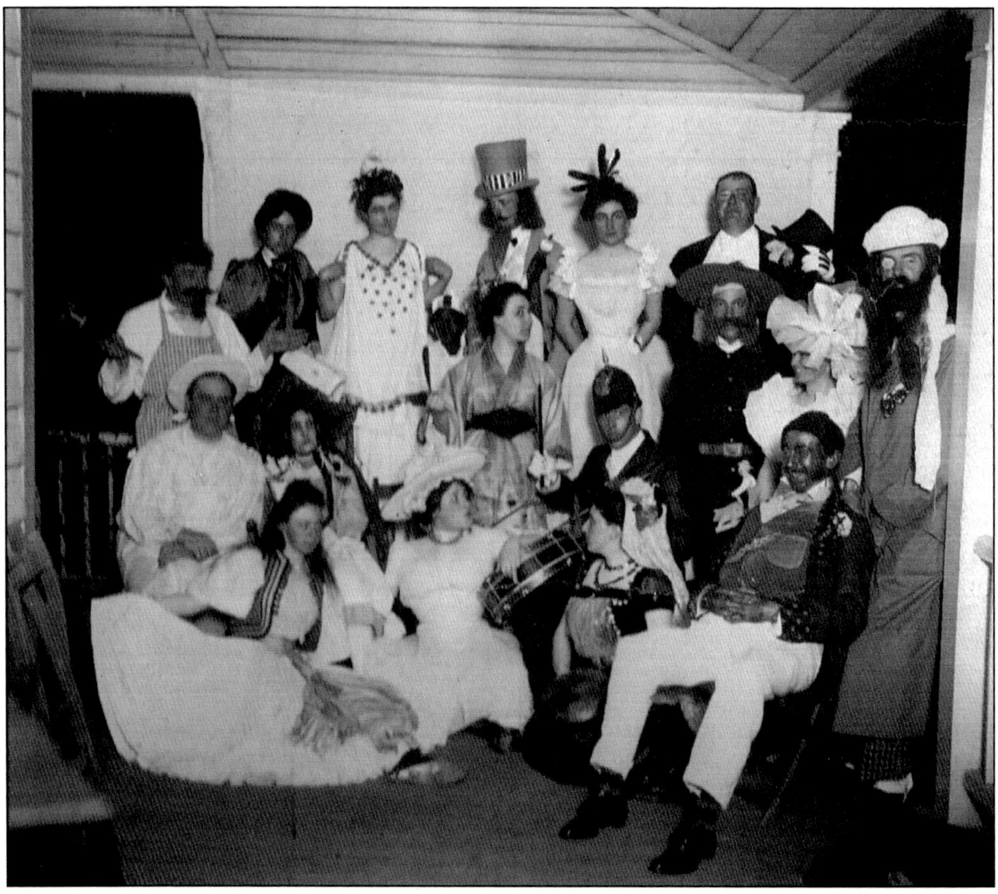

Carriage rides in the countryside around Aiken were doctor's orders for some, while for others, a drive to Beech Island meant a visit with fellow Harvard alum James Henry "Harry" Hammond at his family plantation, Redcliffe. Hammond is the originator of the phrase "Cotton is king," used in a speech to the US Senate in 1858. The road to Beech Island, known today as Silver Bluff, rolled down toward the river. The Hammond and Billings families were a large part of the marketing and publicity for Aiken.

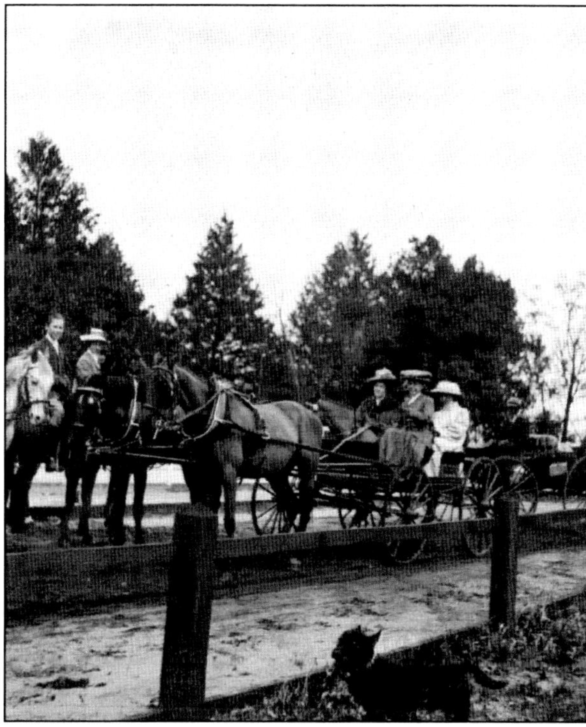

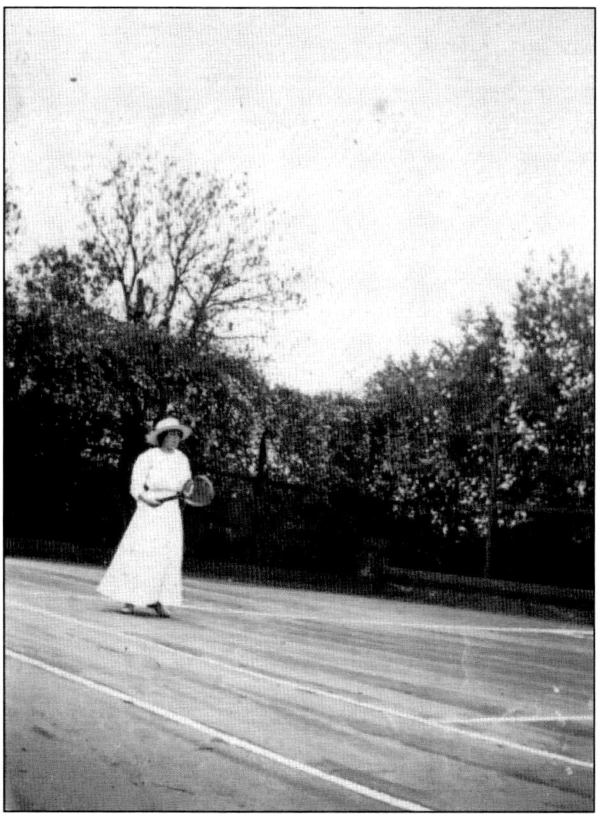

Patsey Carroll enjoys a game of tennis at Highland Park Hotel. While Aiken originally served as a summer retreat from its founding in 1835, by 1898, the future of Aiken would rest with the Winter Colony. The Winter Colony was a collection of prep school and Ivy League heirs whose fathers made their fortunes during the Industrial Revolution.

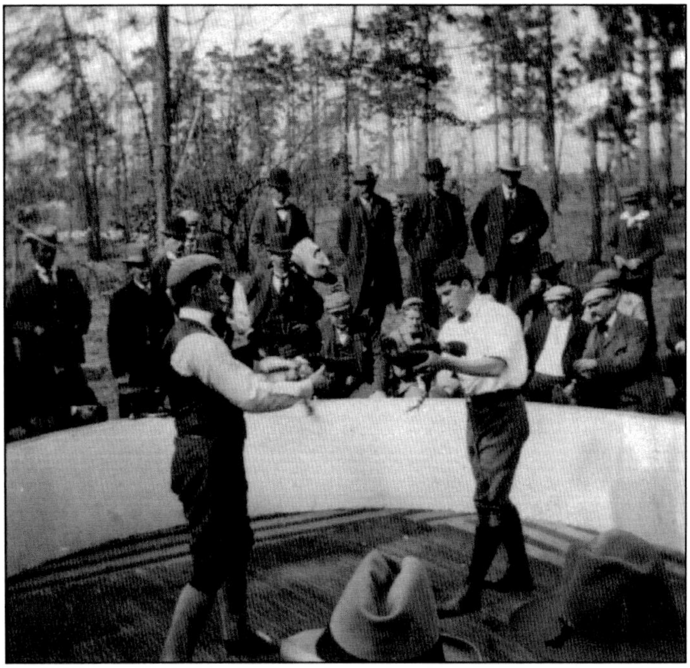

The University of South Carolina's mascot is aptly named, given the prominence of cockfighting as a pastime through the 19th century. Cocks bred for fighting in Aiken were of the highest caliber, much like the stallions that were bred for horse racing. Wagering on fights served as revenue for farmers who struggled to pay their taxes and freedmen who worked to establish their households during Reconstruction.

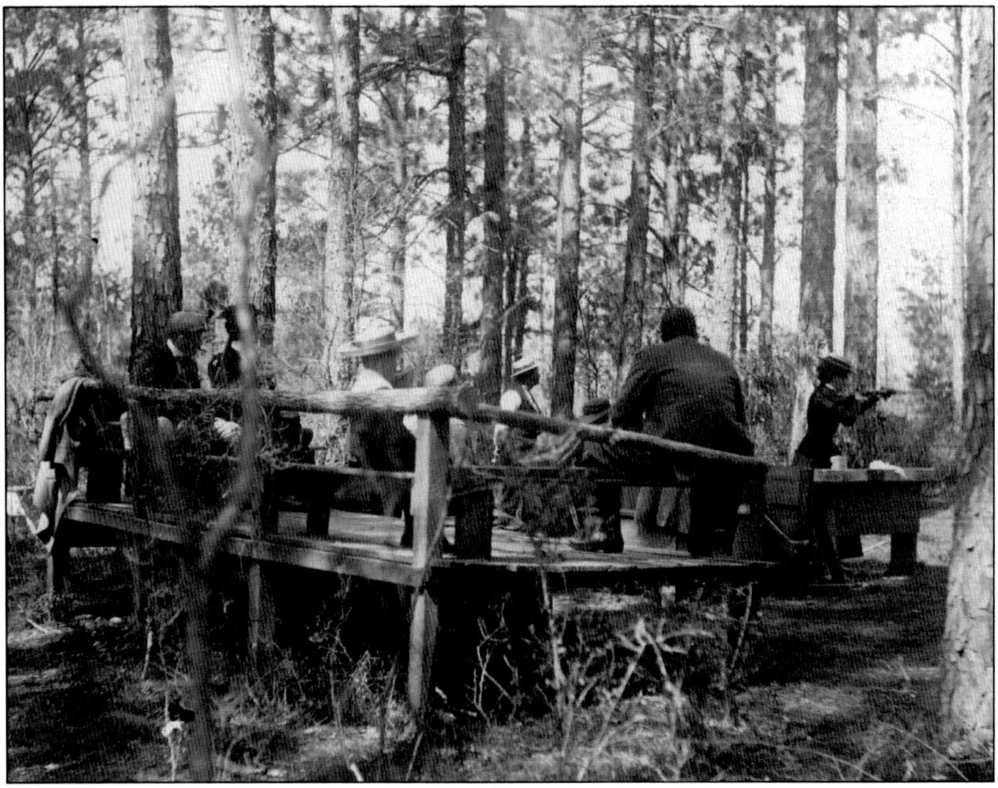

Marketing of the "Sports Center of the South," included bird hunting, an outdoor activity encouraged for both sexes. The area offered dove, quail, pigeon, and partridge preserves for the guests at the various hotels that filled Aiken.

Eleanor Phelps tees off at Aiken Golf Club. The Phelps family contributed much to the early years of Aiken's Winter Colony and has remained connected to Aiken through golf, tennis, polo, and the Camellia Society. Today, the Phelps estate, Rose Hill, is an inn with restaurant and wedding venues.

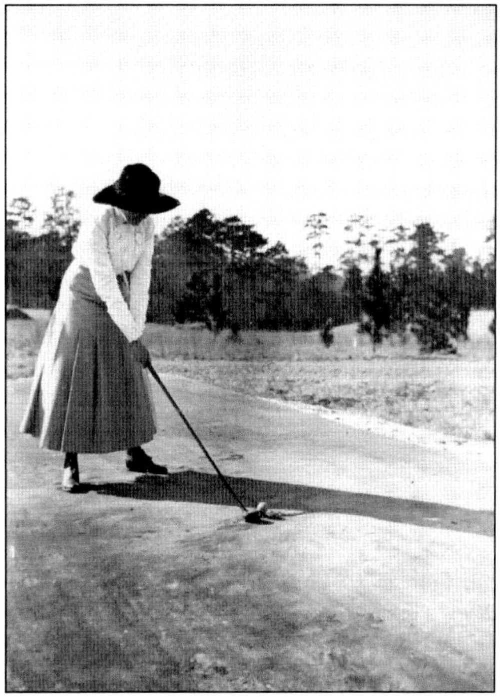

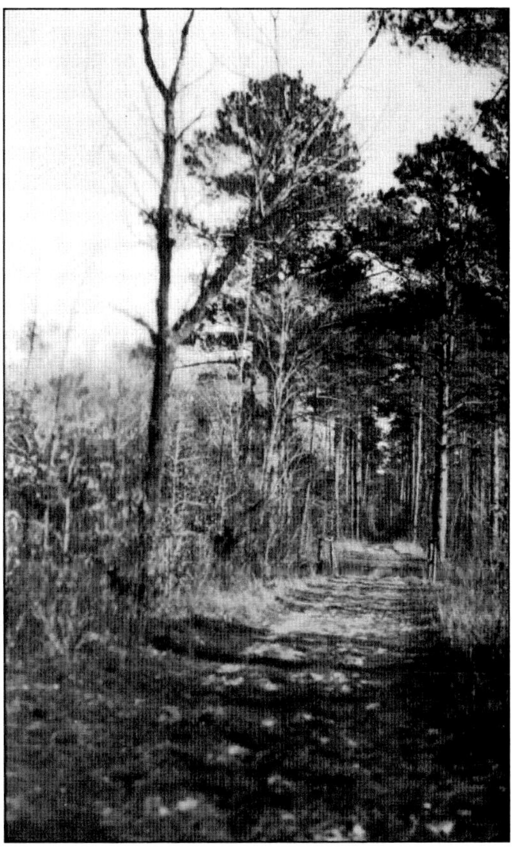

While wealthy visitors established their estates along Whiskey Road and the wide boulevards of town, a few cabins and cottages remained within the 8,000 acres of pine forest, 2,100 of which are now the Hitchcock Woods. The trails, like Cathedral Aisle pictured here, cut for recreational enjoyment, arc shaded pathways for horse and rider, carriage drivers, and walkers to enjoy to this day.

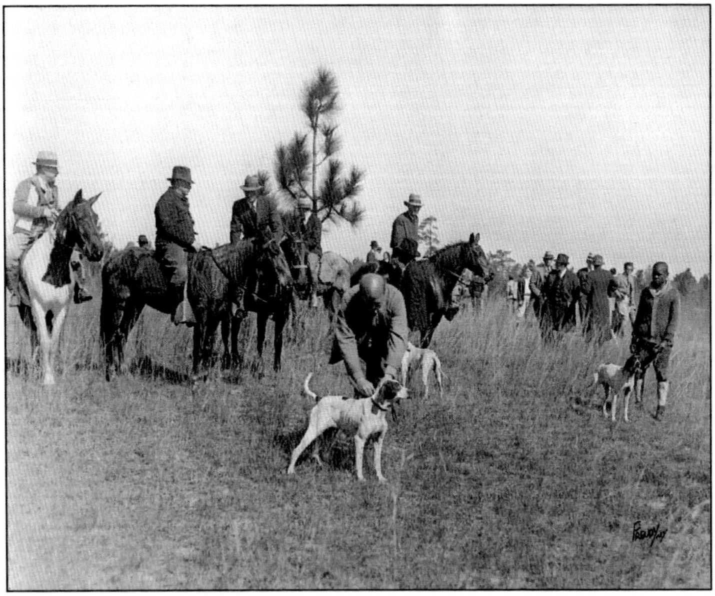

Francis "Frankie" Hitchcock would gather folks at his brother Thomas's home, Mon Repos, by 5:00 a.m. to prepare for a day afield. Frankie was one of the founders of Westminster Kennel Club and an integral part of writing their breed standards. Second and third generations of hound men are still in the area promoting healthy care of canine partners in sport. Bird dogs and foxhounds from Aiken still compete at the national level.

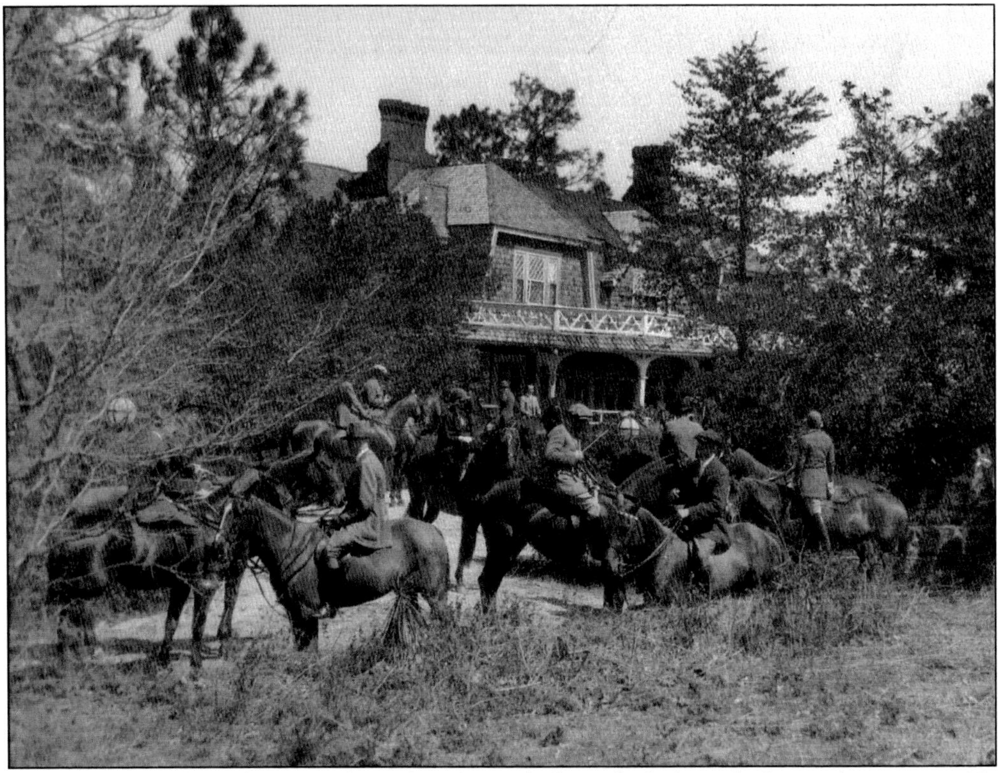

Rita and Alexandra Dolan were also early risers to the hounds, foxhounds that is; this unstoppable mother-daughter duo was on horseback as often as in heels. Also among the first sporting families of Aiken, they donated land for the Hitchcock Woods and supported the sporting activities that made Aiken a draw for the outdoor enthusiast. In this view of a fox hunt from their home, it is clear that Aiken's riding attire was much more relaxed when compared to the formality of Virginia or hunts farther north. (Brainard.)

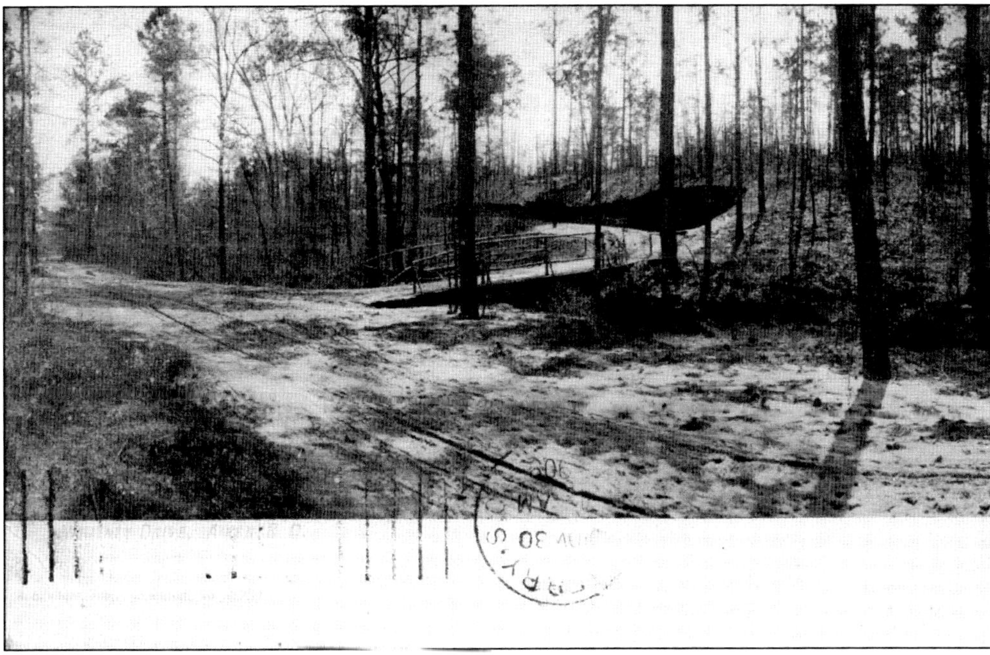

A sign of the widespread popularity that Aiken celebrated, photographers and periodicals captured the open, welcoming feel that Aiken offers visitors. No single event in Aiken embodies all that drew the early settlers, the Charlestonians in summer, the Winter Colony, and even the federal government, more than the Aiken Horse Show. Celebrating 100 years in the Hitchcock Woods, this classic event showcases foxhunters and children, silver foxes, sidesaddle, and gentlemen riders. Harkening back to its early years, it is one of two times annually that motorized vehicles are allowed in the woods. Once at the show ring, the tent and tailgates welcome exhibitor and spectator alike. (Below, Brainard.)

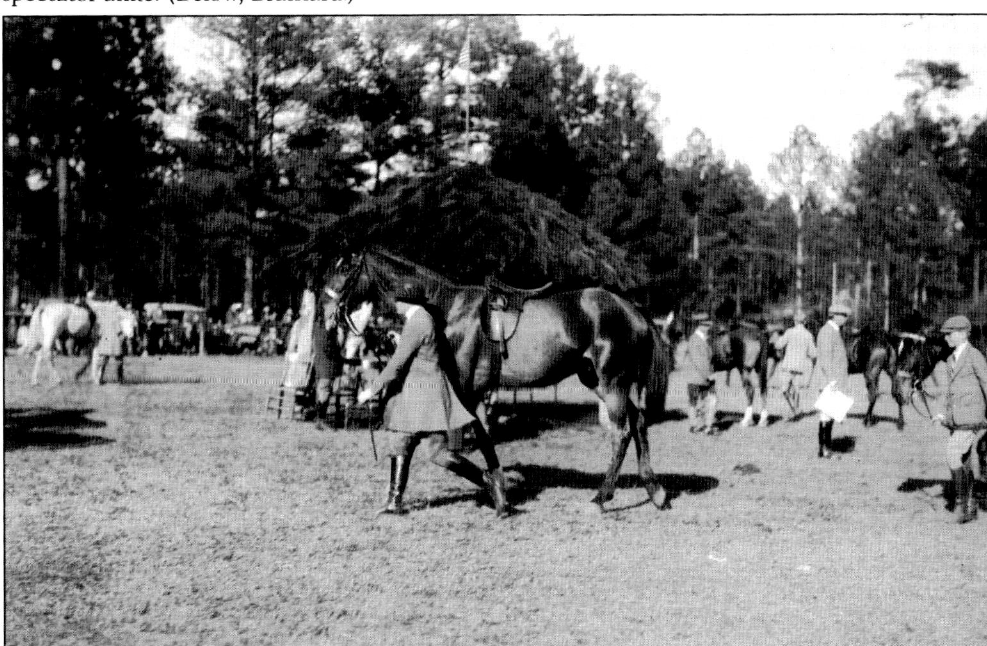

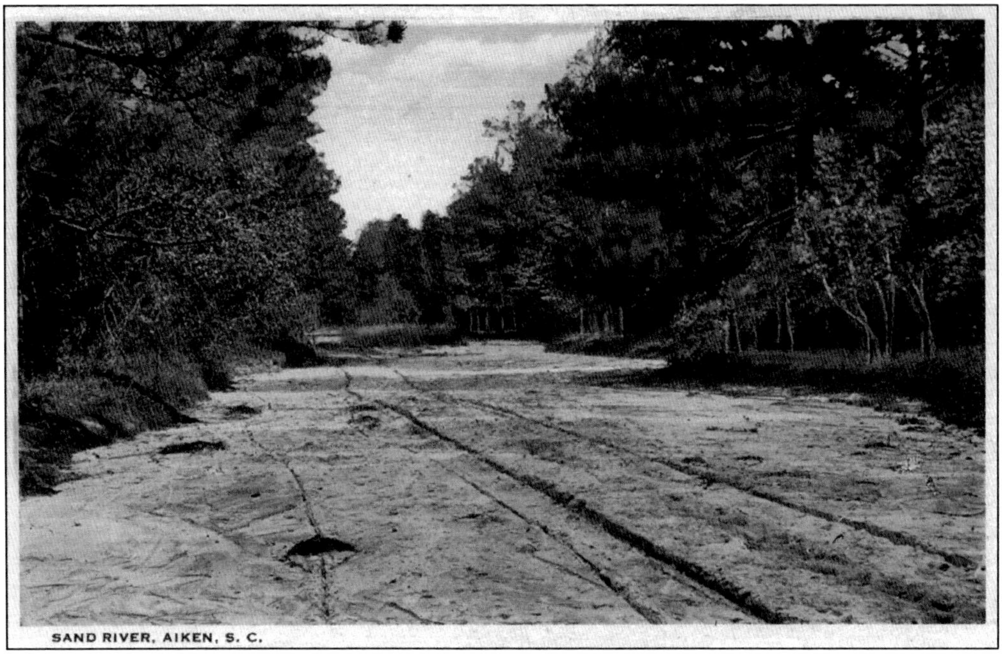

Sand River has been a landmark dating back to Indian times, and explorer journals reference "the river of sand near the flowing spring under the tall pines." Sand River is still a vital landmark within the woods. George Gaulphin married a tribal princess, Alfred Dexter married Sara Williams, and Wallis Warfield Simpson and King Edward sought refuge in Aiken. What is it about the waters or the air that brings out people's amorous side? Lover's Lane is an aptly named trail in the woods. What love affair in Aiken's history could be more influential than the city's love affair with horses? Below, Sophie Mott and Walter Phelps watch from their beloved mounts as other horses race around Whitney Track.

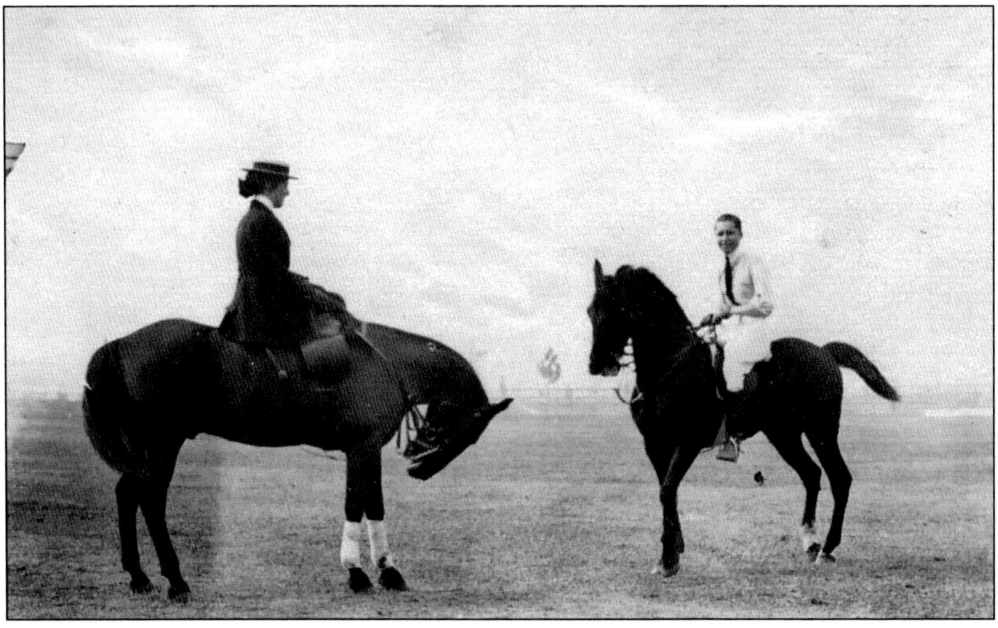

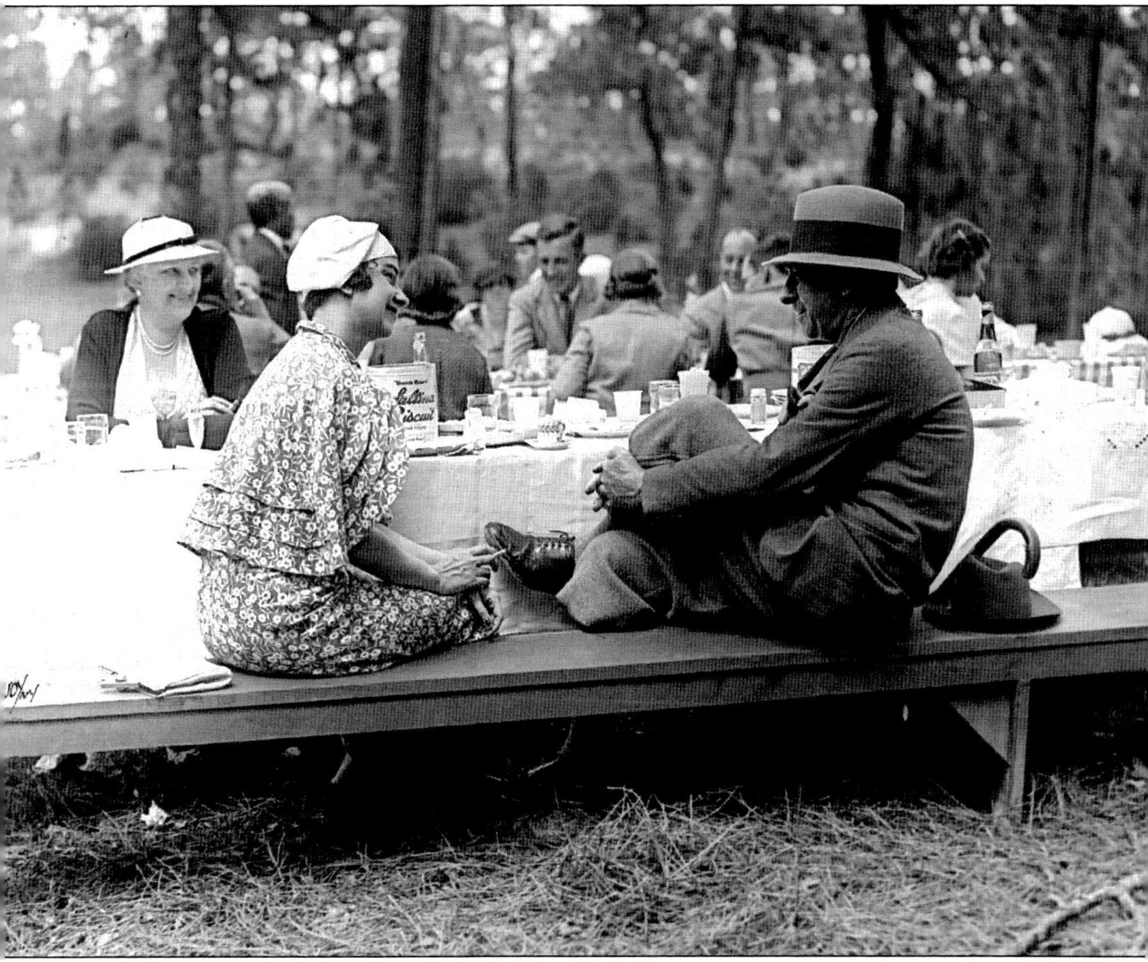

The *New York Times* reported about Aiken, "Everything happens outdoors, not a breath of fresh air is ever wasted." Here, Harry Payne Whitney entertains the ladies at a picnic at the Tea Cottage. China coffee cups and crystal champagne flutes visible among the saltines and bottled beer are more proof of the formality mixed with frivolity that Aiken represents. Prior to World War II, the magnates of industry and the queens of society made Newport, Westbury, Beacon Hill, Palm Beach, Cannes, Tuxedo, and Aiken popular. Hosting world leaders, inventors, and moguls for their sporting pursuits also afforded them opportunities to ally their interests in business and politics. Adding to the network of alliances were advantageous marriages and convenient land transactions. (Tower.)

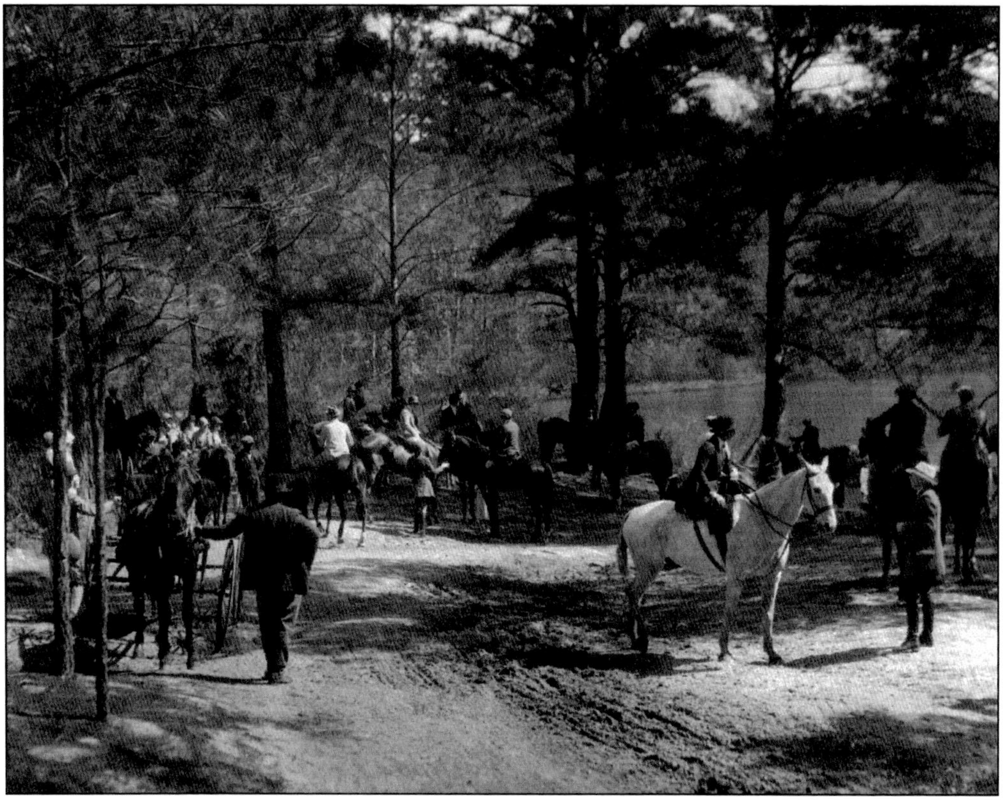

Visible in this gathering at Eustis Pond are the various mounts and riding styles of the time and the equipage available to hotel guests and visitors. Eustis Pond and Barton's Pond converged when the dam broke in 1927, and are now wetlands. A walk along Peek-A-Boo Lane toward Cathedral Aisle reminds all that times change, but the woods remain. The legacy of the Hitchcock Woods began with Celestine Eustis and W.C Whitney and remains with the Hitchcock Woods Foundation. (Brainard.)

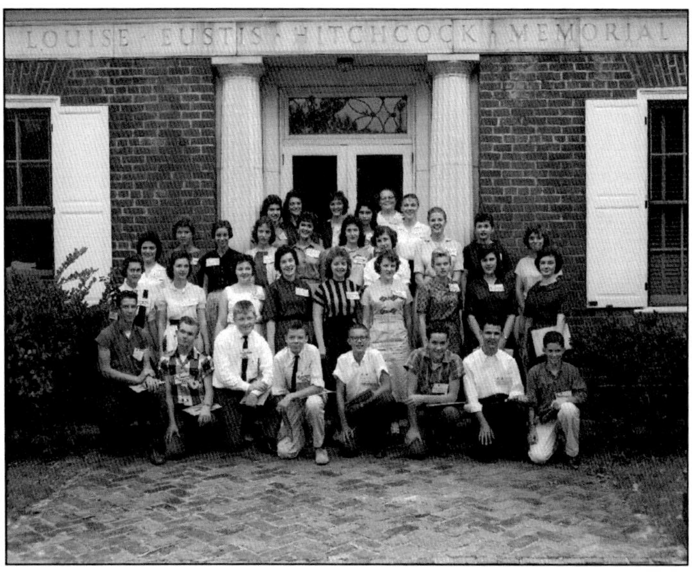

The 1959 Aiken Tuberculosis Association is pictured here in front of the Louise Eustis Hitchcock Memorial Building. This photograph demonstrates the combining of old Aiken with new Aiken, as the DuPont contract to manage the Savannah River Site brought scientists and workers to Aiken from all over the United States. They brought their commitment to charity, community health, and strong education to the sporting and social swell of Aiken.

Two

Golden Age of Sport

Hitchcock Woods Invite Three Sports a Day

In 1891, Louise Corcoran Eustis married Thomas Hitchcock, and they wintered in Aiken that year. Thomas was taken with the climate. As Thomas's father insisted that none of his children enter trade, sporting life was the only vocation left for an athletic man who married a woman who could keep pace with his own sporting interests. The next year, Thomas invited his brother Francis and close friend William C. Whitney to join them in Aiken, and the Golden Age began. By 1895, Whitney and the Hitchcock brothers had invited their boarding school and Ivy League chums to join them for the temperate winters and excellent sport.

W.C. Whitney, Louise and Thomas Hitchcock, Francis Hitchcock, and Celestine Eustis built a center for winter sports in Aiken. They purchased pine forests, formalized the polo grounds, built the Palmetto Golf Club, and secured the racing stables along Mead Avenue. In 1901, Whitney formed a foundation that would provide for the permanent use of his center for winter sports. Two years later, upon Whitney's death, Francis Hitchcock purchased all of Whitney's remaining lands and interests in Aiken. Celestine Eustis died in 1921, and Louise Hitchcock inherited from her aunt a large number of acres under the condition that the pine woods be preserved. In 1926, when Francis Hitchcock died, he left what he had acquired from Whitney to his sister-in-law Louise. Following Celestine's lead, he too provided that the woodlands be protected for the future. Following the 1934 death of Louise, Thomas "Tommy" Hitchcock Jr. and Helen Hitchcock Clark followed through and gifted the Hitchcock Woods Foundation 1,191 acres in 1939.

Today, the Hitchcock Woods Foundation manages 2,100 acres with 70 miles of trails, all open to the public. The sporting traditions of foxhunting, driving, dog walking, and horse showing still happen in these beloved woods. Known for offering visitors three outdoor sports a day, throughout its charmed history, Aiken has been a sporting center for those who love horses, golf courses, and dogs of any kind.

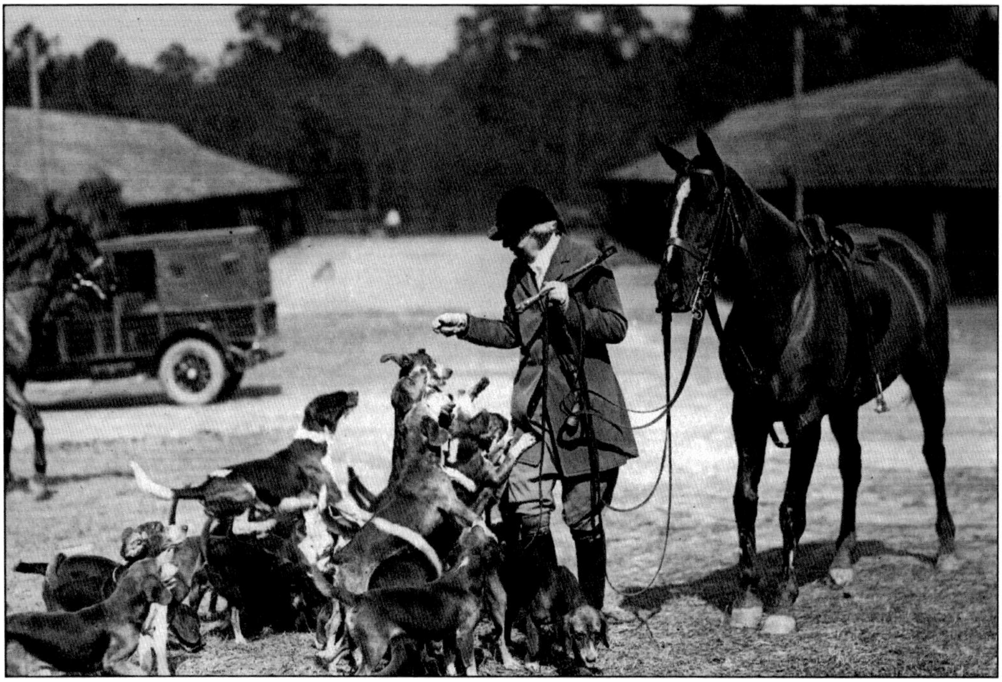

Louise Hitchcock is pictured here with her beagles in the stable yard at her Aiken home. Along with her husband, Thomas, she registered Aiken Drag, now Aiken Hounds, with the Masters of Fox Hounds Association in 1914. The hunt does not chase live quarry but follows a scent laid by humans. Originally a beagle pack before 1914, Aiken Hounds still wears the green livery reserved for hare hunting. Of the 31 masters of fox hounds that Aiken has had over the last century, 24 have been women, quite a unique dominance of female leadership for any sport. (Brainard.)

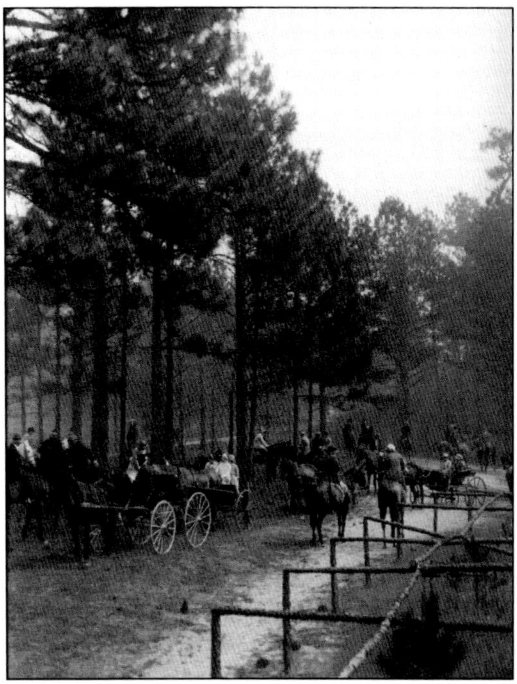

The Winter Colony had well established its core events and key locations by the early 1900s. Aiken had always been a relaxed setting for the scions of American society; there was no rush to formalize the events they enjoyed while spending time in the sleepy Southern town. The Aiken Horse Show began in 1916, even though the woods had played host to many sporting contests in the decades prior. Pictured here are the corrals placed for multiple entries, as spectators arrive by buggy for the show. (Brainard.)

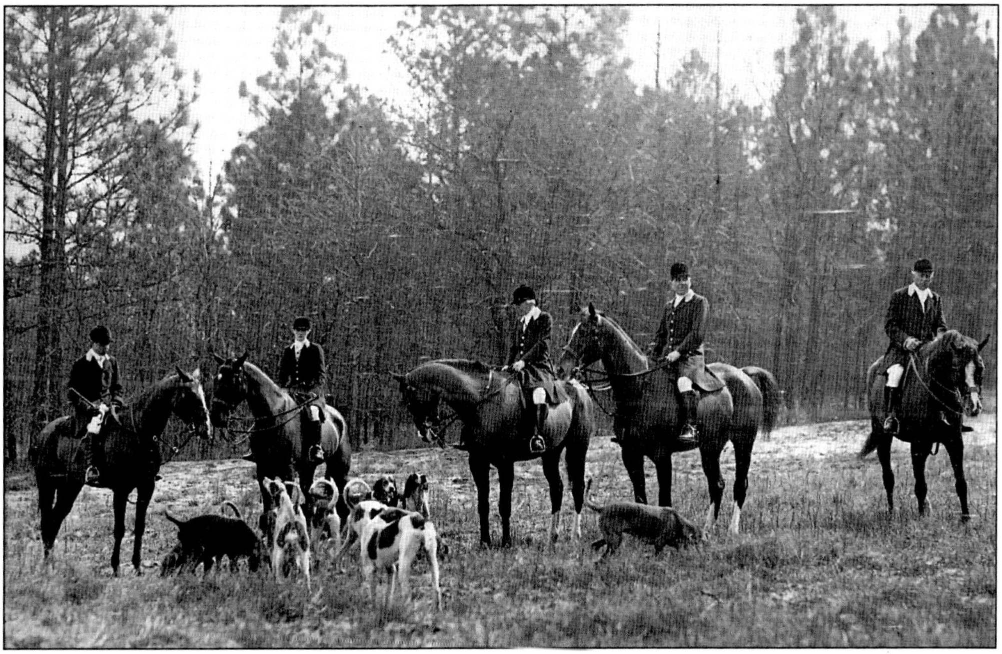

Louise and Thomas Hitchcock fostered a devotion to all things horse. They dedicated much time to mentoring young boys and girls in the many sports that they loved. Thomas and his African American racing protégé Pete Greene worked on developing great racehorses and great jockeys. Louise was dubbed the mother of American polo for her time spent training her boys. Irish sporting author Edith Somerville noted, "In Aiken the girls, with grace and courage, act as whippers-in to the hounds with the confidence of seasoned professionals." (Brainard.)

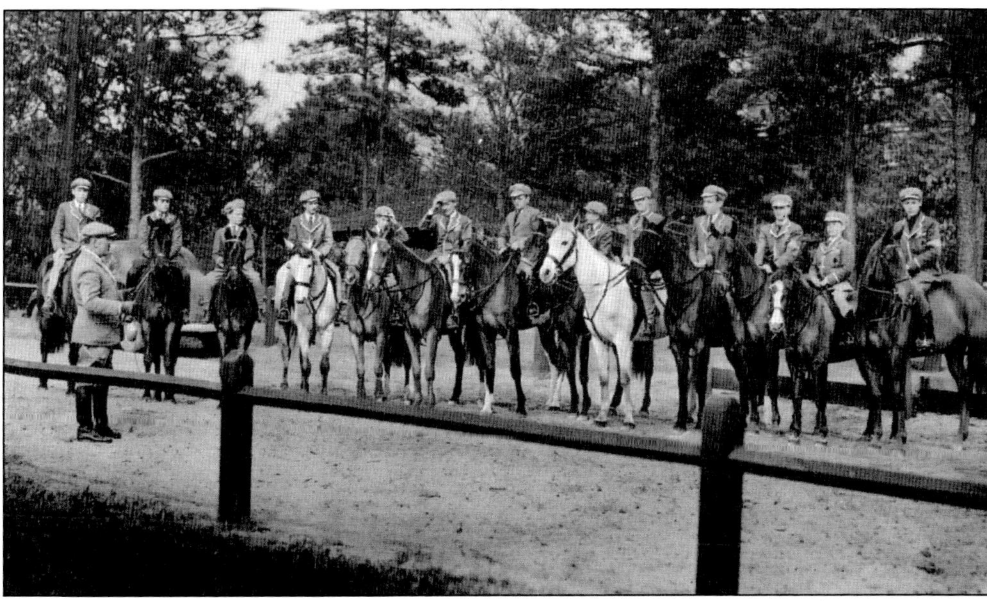

Louise Hitchcock founded Aiken Preparatory School for Boys in 1916. Later, her cousin Marie Hoffman went on to form Fermata School for Girls. Both served as an excellent source of young riders to aid with collecting hounds and beagles during hunts. Captain Gaylard and the prep school boys, pictured here, show their intensity and desire for sport. (Conger.)

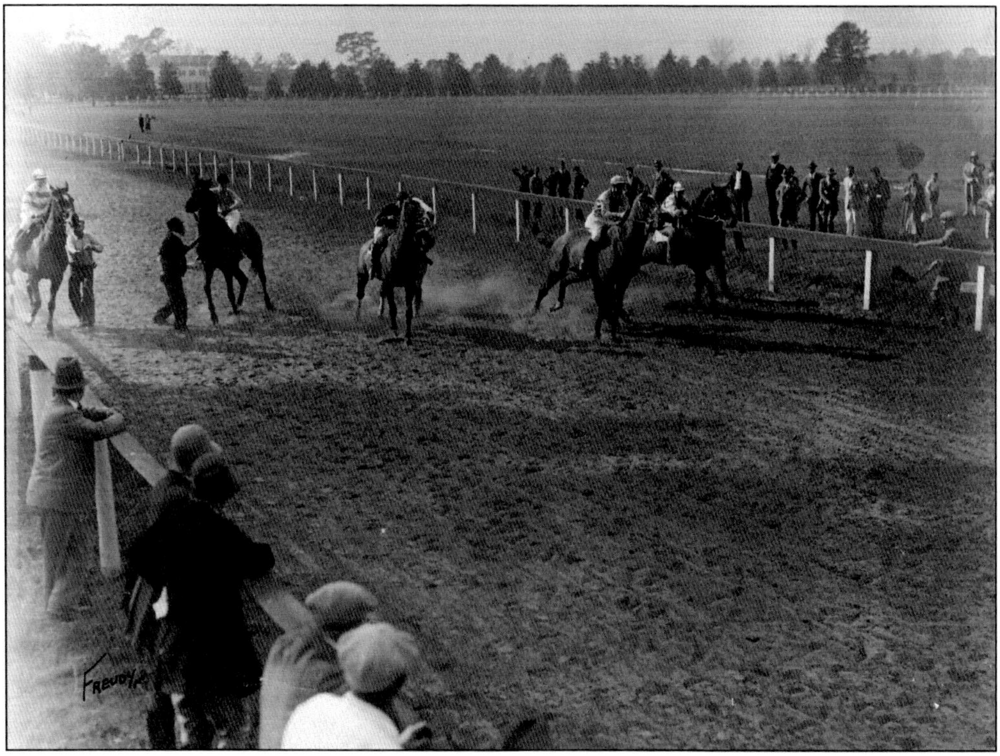

The Golden Age of sport brought Thoroughbred breeding, training, and racing to Aiken. The Ridge Mile Track, Hitchcock Track, and Cuthbert Tracks are just a few of the many early 1900s training grounds that offered good footing and strong breezing. The Aiken Trials, originally held at the Hitchcock Track around the Whitney Polo Field, were later moved to the training track built by Fred H. Post in 1941. Watching horses race and train was a beloved pastime in Aiken, and F. Ambrose Clark welcomed spectators every day. The Diana Cup, with a horse race over fences as well as on the flat, was awarded to the female rider who successfully topped both circuits.

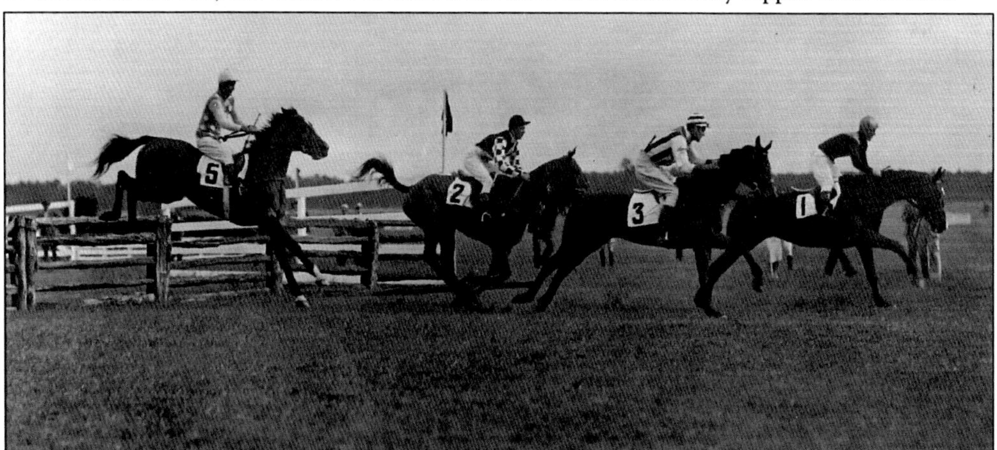

Steeplechase, or racing over obstacles, was a regular occurrence around town. The 1930 course on Powderhouse Road and Audubon Drive was the third location for such steeplechase races. Today, Aiken's Spring Steeplechase meet is the second-largest sporting event in the Central Savannah River Area, second only to Augusta National's Masters golf tournament.

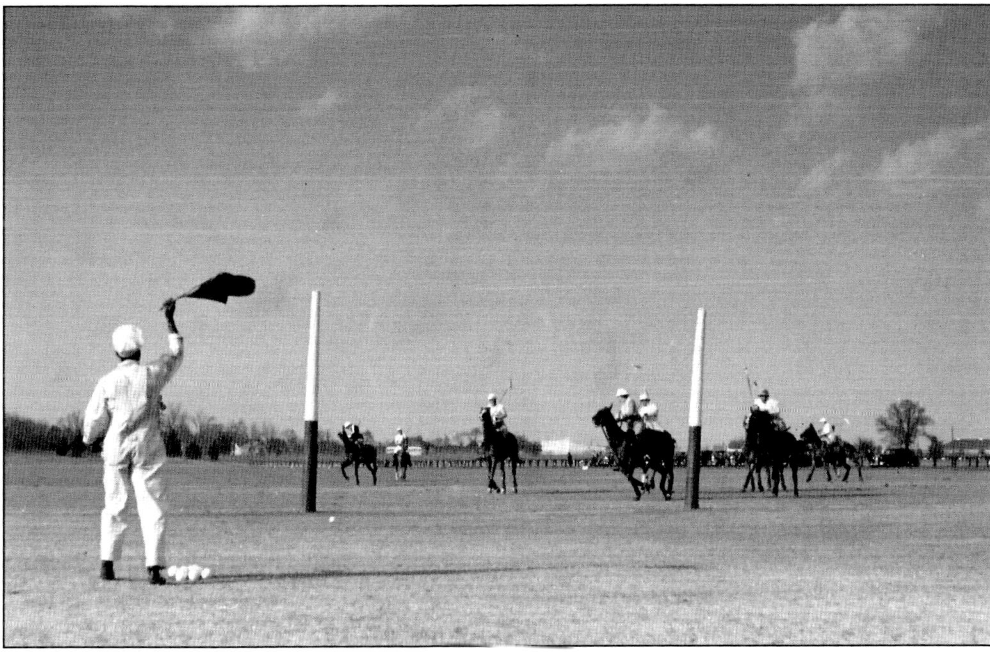

Aiken had many polo fields: Cochran Field, Mead Road Fields, Whitney Field, and Hassler's Field were among a reported 17 polo fields in town. Pictured here is the present-day location of the trotting track. James Gordon Bennett brought the sport of polo to America, and Aiken embraced it as an exhibition sport in 1882. A decade later, in 1892, Thomas Hitchcock formalized gameplay for Aiken Polo Club.

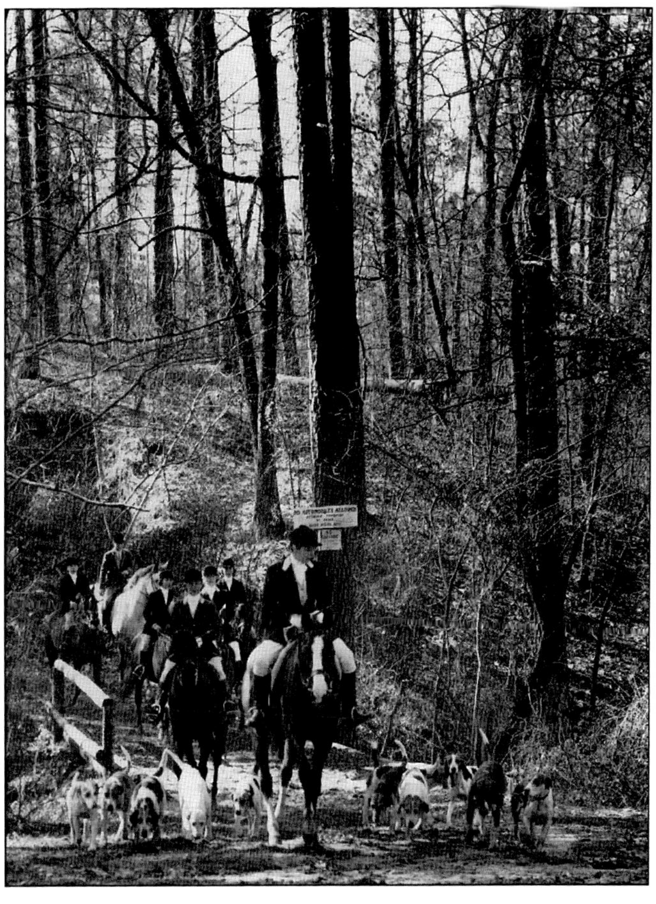

Aiken Hounds are pictured at the Laurens Street crossing, which is no longer in place. It was only three blocks from the main business intersection in downtown. Nancy Harrington, master of fox hounds (MFH) for Aiken, is followed by Lucetta Knox, returning to the kennels after a meet in 1960. (Conger.)

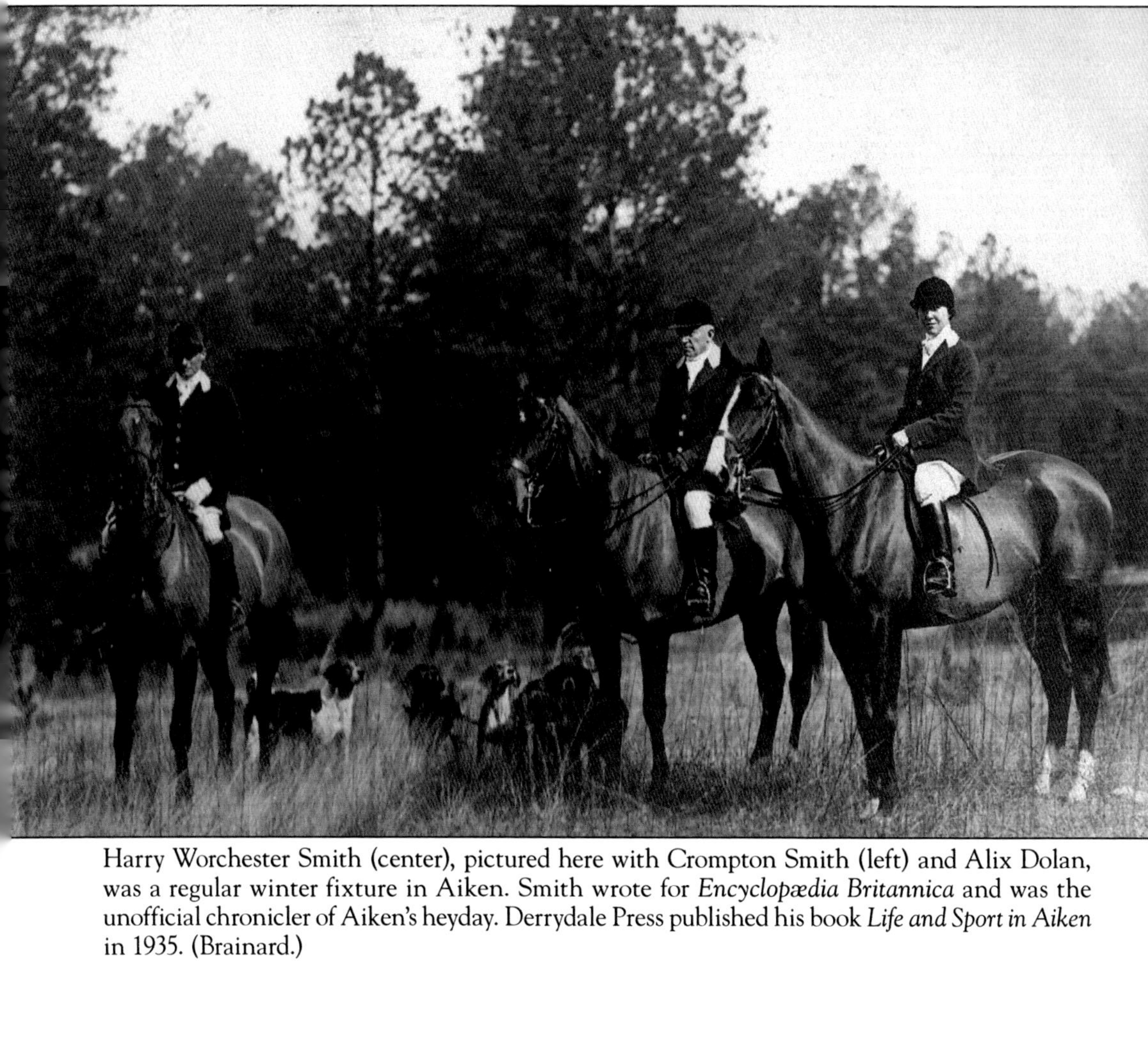

Harry Worchester Smith (center), pictured here with Crompton Smith (left) and Alix Dolan, was a regular winter fixture in Aiken. Smith wrote for *Encyclopædia Britannica* and was the unofficial chronicler of Aiken's heyday. Derrydale Press published his book *Life and Sport in Aiken* in 1935. (Brainard.)

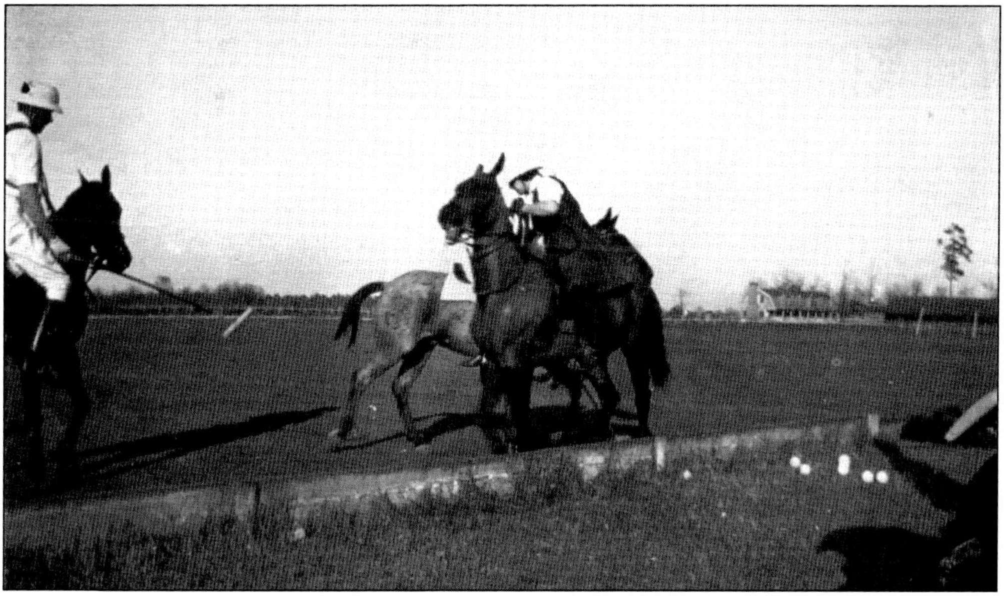

As with foxhunting, beagling, and shooting, polo was open to the ladies. Earl Hopping (left), master for Aiken Hounds, helps coach Claudia Phelps (right) during a practice along the boards in 1911. Eleanor Phelps's photograph collection was donated to the South Caroliniana Library at the University of South Carolina in Columbia.

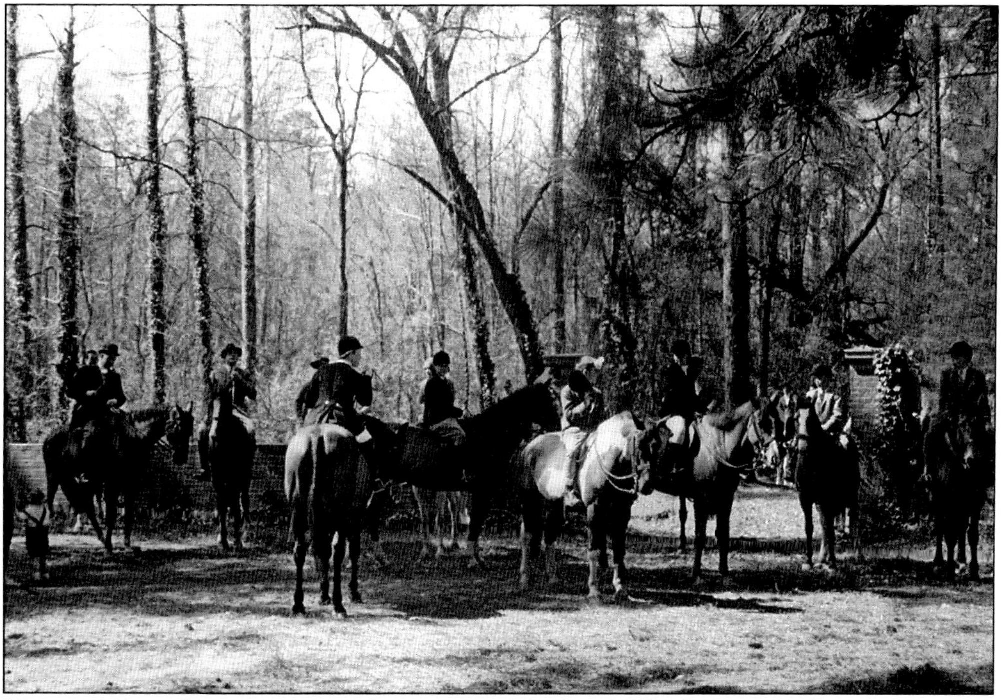

Memorial Gate, the meeting point for activity in Hitchcock Woods, has brought together young and old to pursue sport in the woods. The Aiken Hounds traditions of the children's drag, junior whips, and junior huntsmen from Aiken Prep and Fermata School have been carried on to the riders from Aiken Day School, Saint Angela Academy, and now Mead Hall School. (Conger.)

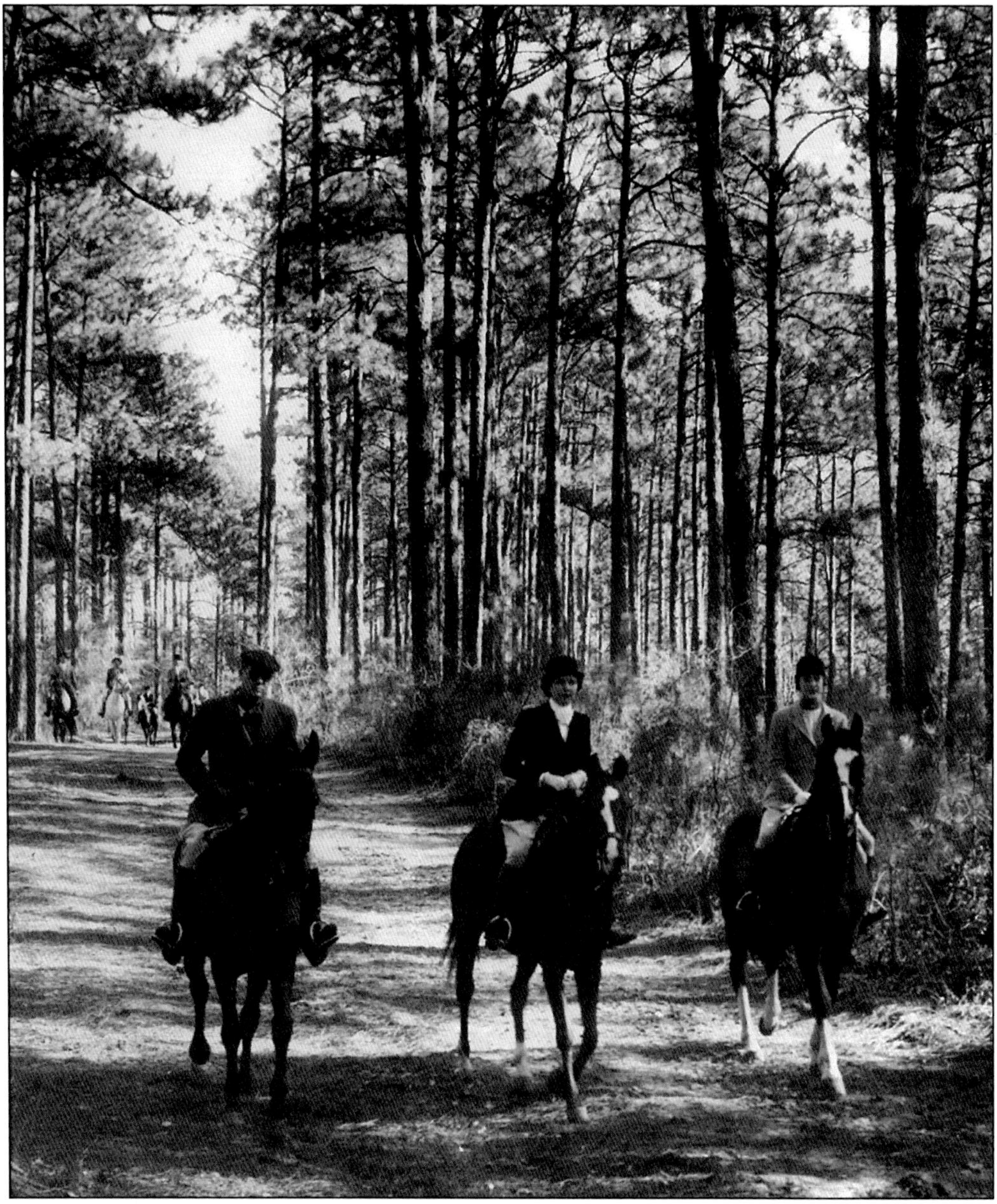

Devil's Backbone is one of the many trails in and out of Hitchcock Woods. A continuation of South Boundary Avenue, tourists have often mistakenly driven into Hitchcock Woods during the annual Aiken Horse Show in search of the Willcox Inn. They are surprised to arrive along this dirt trail at a tent filled with happy spectators and a ring full of hopeful riders instead of one of Condé Nast's top 50 small hotels in the world. (Conger.)

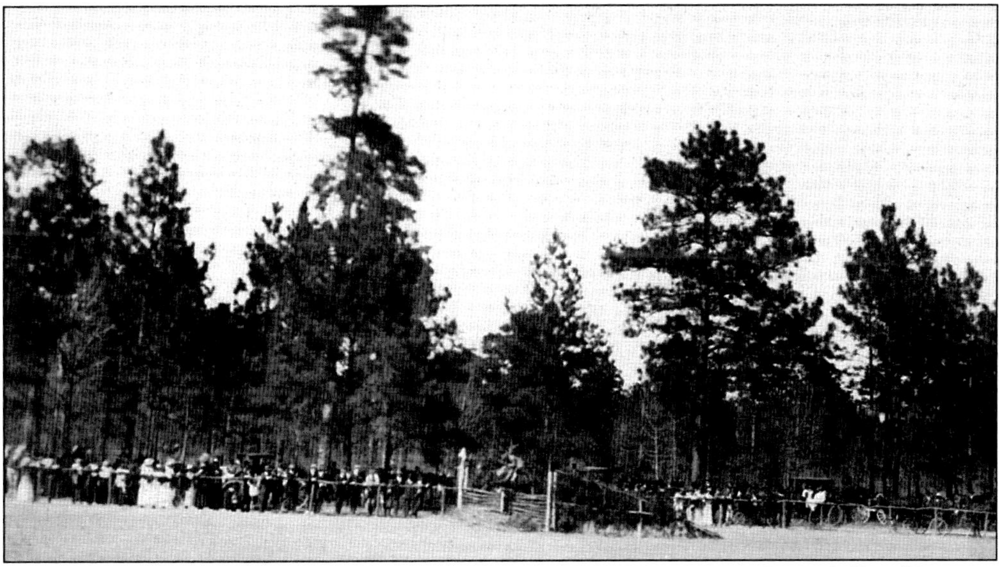

One of the early races on Ridge Mile Track over Aiken fences was a test of true skill and bravery. The jumps were between four and five feet high and had to be taken at high speed. Spectators and riders alike enjoy the thrill of the thundering hooves. The $1,000 Aiken Gold Cup was established in 1930.

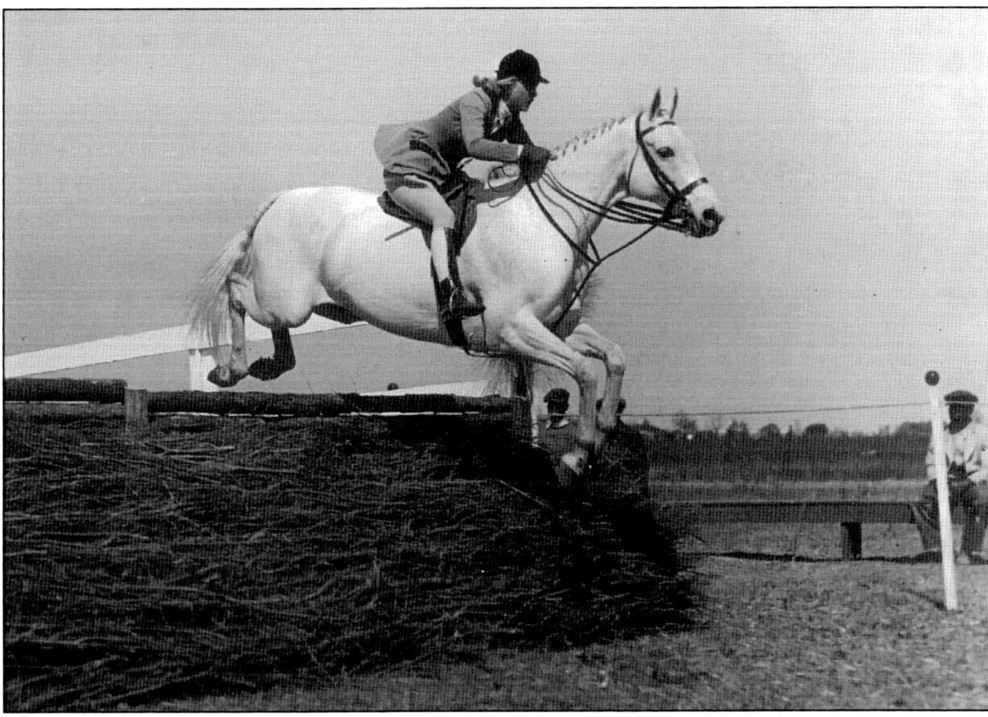

In 1930, Harry Worchester Smith proposed to the Hitchcocks an official hunter trial for the foxhunters to be timed and tested. Testing their horses much like bird hunters do their dogs and clockers do horses, it was a way to prove the suitability of mounts for potential buyers. The popularity of trials like the Aiken Hunter Trials has given way to the National Hunter Championship of America. (Brainard.)

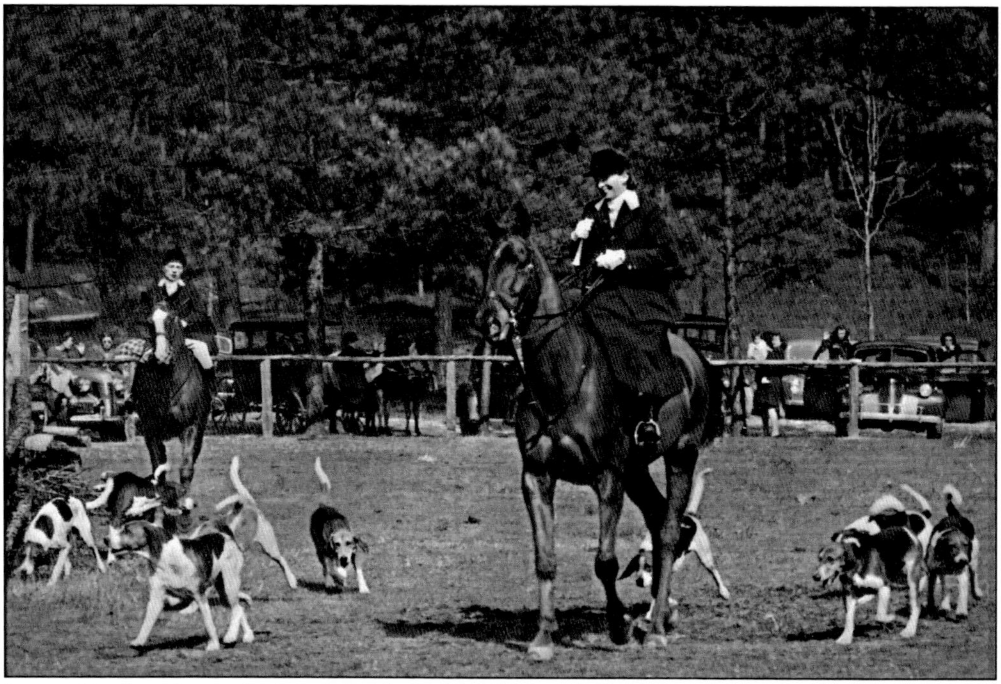

Louise Hitchcock was the first lady of society to be seen riding astride as men do; the convention was not so readily adopted by her peers. Helen Northrup Knox (right), who carried the horn for Aiken Hounds from 1940 to 1945, rode sidesaddle. (McLean.)

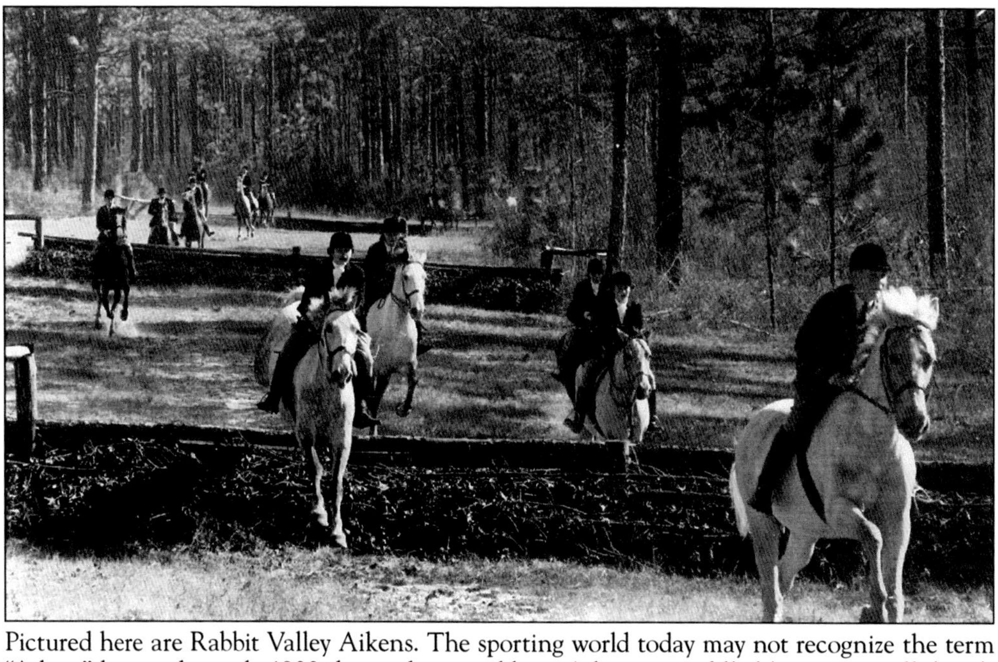

Pictured here are Rabbit Valley Aikens. The sporting world today may not recognize the term "Aiken," but in the early 1900s horse show world, an Aiken was a felled log jump stuffed with brush. These jumps are all around Hitchcock Woods. Aikens became a standard for horse shows nationwide. In the 1932 Olympic games in Los Angeles, an Aiken was among the equestrian competition's obstacles. (Conger.)

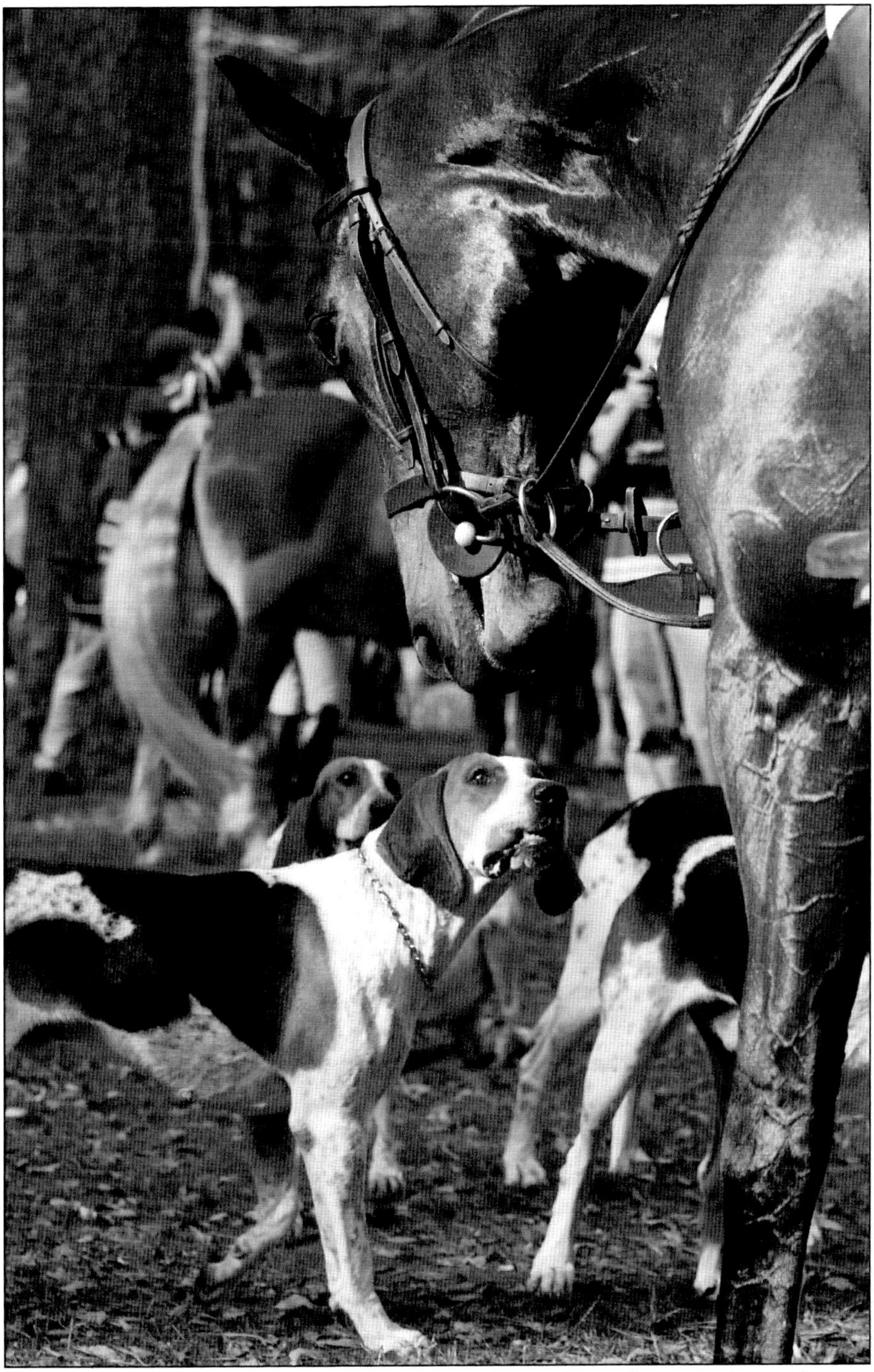

The Blessing of the Aiken Hounds is an annual tradition that welcomes riders and non-riders to Memorial Gate on Thanksgiving morning. Aiken has had a longstanding love of its dogs. Francis Hitchcock and Berkeley Sherwood Dunn, with their efforts for the Westminster Kennel Club and the Society for the Prevention of Cruelty to Animals, have been at the heart of Aiken's relationship with man's best friend. (Author's collection.)

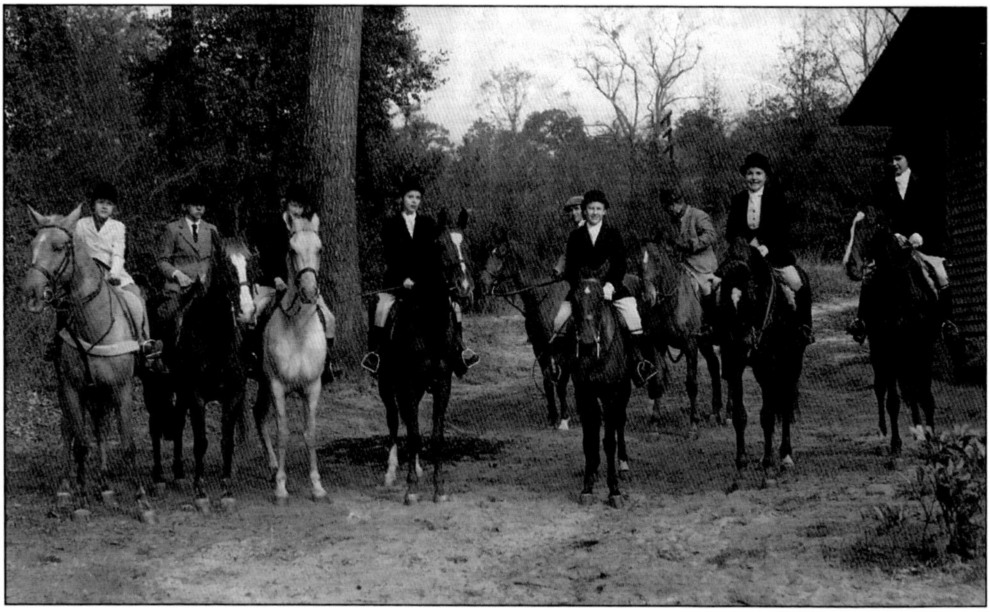

Horses leave an indelible mark; almost 60 years later, Courtney Willard (far right) recalls that she is on EscaMain in this photograph. Willard's friends pictured here in 1959 are, from left to right, (first row) Pat Minnick on Candy Man, James Benson on Chocolate, Gail Howell on Nifty, Lottie Manschalk on Ed Kilra, Anne Hopkins on Fast Company, Ruth Henderson on Long John, and Willard on EscaMain; (second row) John Hosang on Woody and James Minnick on Reno. (Conger.)

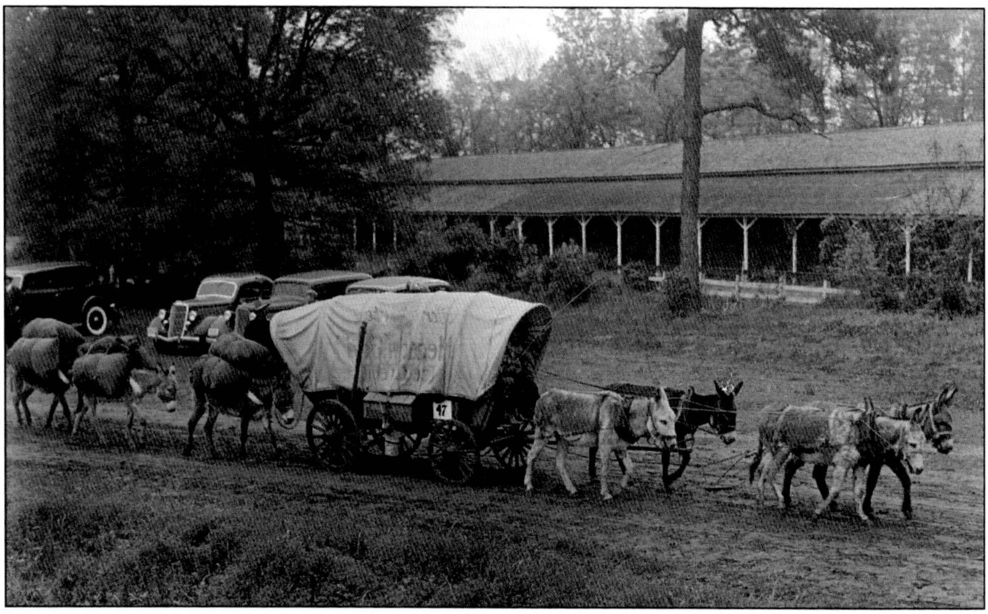

The Thoroughbred racing barns along Mead Avenue were protected by W.C. Whitney's trust in 1901. Between Whitney's death in 1904 and Aiken's centennial in 1935, F. Ambrose Clark, Averill Harriman, Oliver Iselin, and Frederick Post had added more barns for racehorses in Aiken's Horse District. The parade for the city's 100th birthday ended at the barns, as seen here. In 2015, a group led by philanthropist Jack Wetzel committed to renovate these barns.

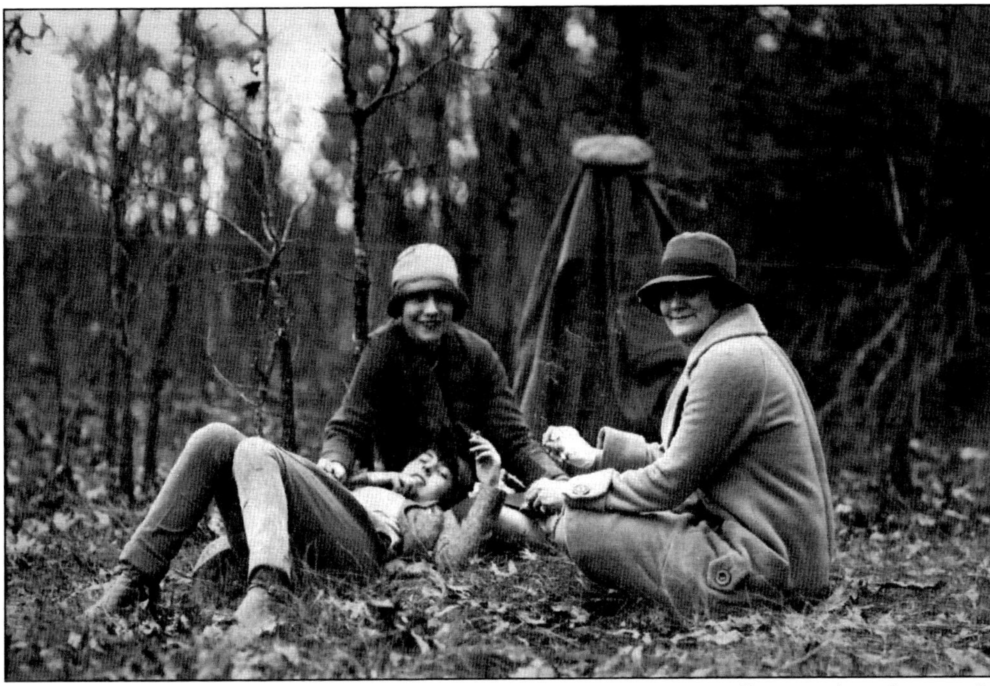

While foxhunting, racing, carriage driving, and dog training were all pursued in the woods, gathering with friends and family for a picnic is still one of the most treasured outings in an arboreal setting. The Dolan girls pictured here were at home in their woods, not quite the place for debutantes of their caliber, but that was the way of Aiken. (Brainard.)

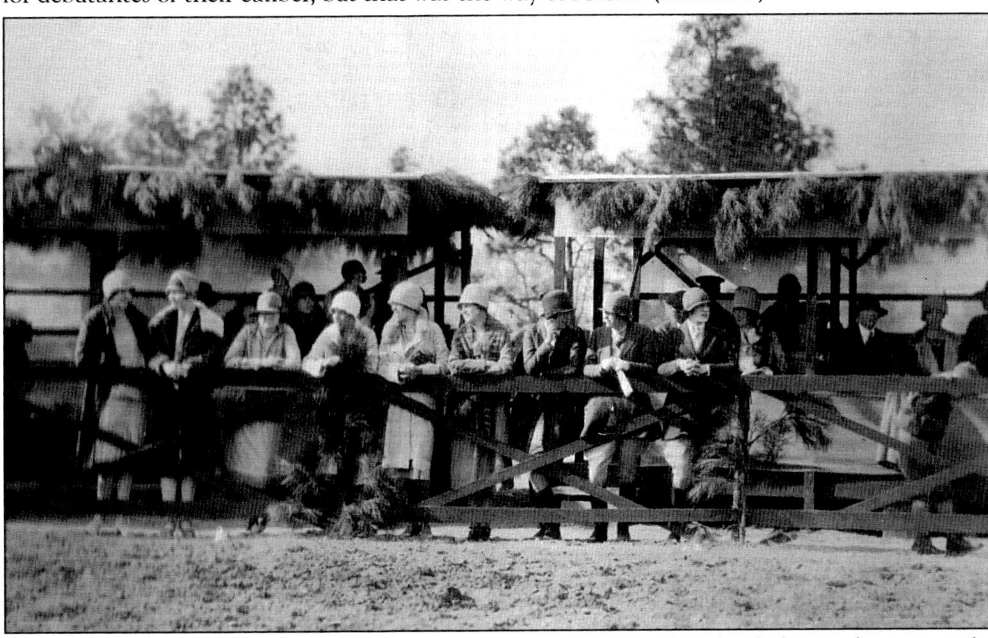

Gathered along the rail to watch a match race with pine branches for shelter, tailgating in the Golden Age of Aiken had a bit more of a refined atmosphere than the pop-up tents and grills of modern times. The ladies are collected with a relaxed anticipation that seems to be the norm when waiting for an Aiken sporting event to start. (Tower.)

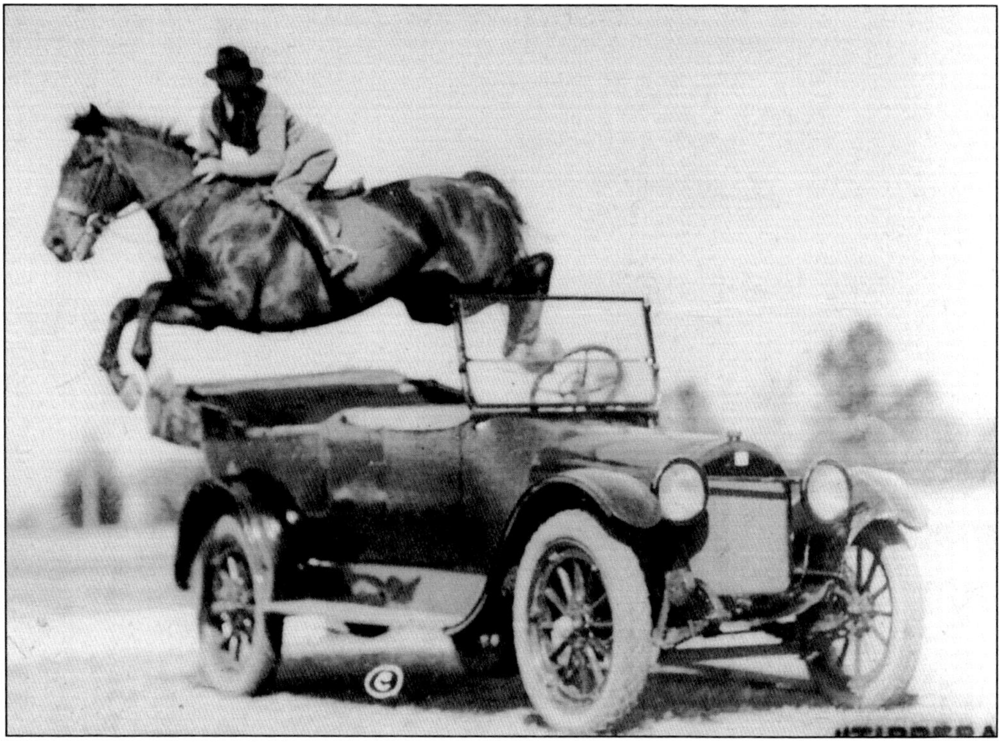

Out to prove which kind of horsepower was tops, this rider looks back over the vehicle his mount has overcome. Not a recommended jumping obstacle, but in Aiken a good wager and a good horse could easily land one clear of any car. This horse and rider combo were clearly game for anything and make the impossible look easy, as was the way of the Golden Age. (Aiken Thoroughbred Racing Hall of Fame and Museum.)

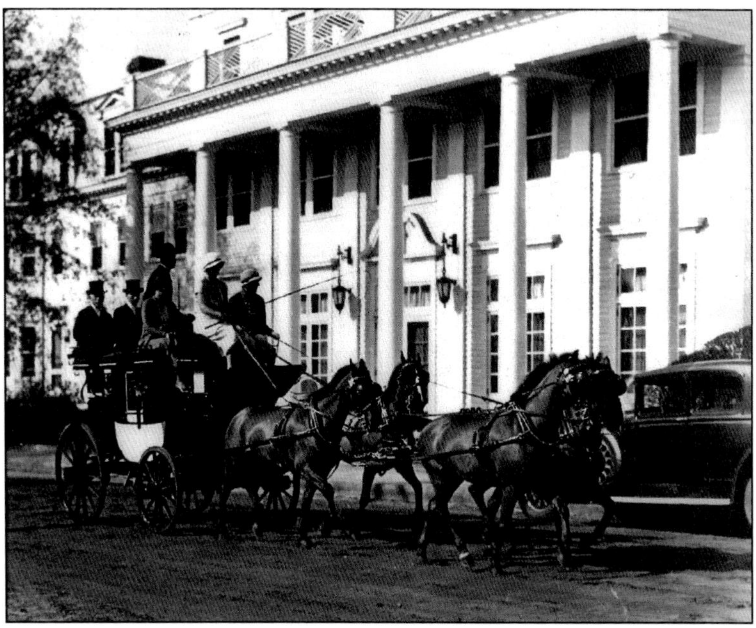

The Willcox, one of Aiken's inns from the Golden Age, still beckons travelers to stop and rest awhile. Helen Hastings, world-renowned driver, has this coach and four off on an Aiken adventure to enjoy the area. During the swells, visitors from near and far would float into town and increase the population threefold for the season.

Three

Social Life is Sport in Aiken

Southern Hospitality Meets Yankee Ingenuity

Steel magnates, railroad speculators, New York bankers, and dry-goods merchants all gathered in Aiken for the winter season starting in 1882. Much has been made about the role of the Eustis, Hitchcock, and Whitney families, who took over from the Charlestonians before them. The Rhetts, Aikens, Ravenels, Legares, Hugers, Simons, Hendersons, Crofts, and Laurens, to name a few, are some of the Lowcountry families who started the resort reputation, but it was the likes of Gertrude Vanderbilt, married to W.C. Whitney, and Madeline Astor, who took up residence after her husband, John Jay, was lost in the sinking of the *Titanic*, who cemented Aiken's social reputation. Marshall Field, Joseph Leiter, Robert Hassler, Berkeley Sherwood-Dunn, George Eustis, Thomas Dolan, Norrie Sellar, Albert Bissell, and William Wood are some of the sporting industrialists with Midwestern and Mid-Atlantic connections who joined the Aiken scene to augment the likes of the Phelps, Iselin, Grace, Bostwick, Goodyear, Clark, Knox, Niblack, Rogers, Winthrop and Howe families who were permanent fixtures. By 1935, Devereaux Milburn, Winthrop Rutherfurd, and Thomas Hitchcock considered themselves local citizens given their contribution to the centennial program.

By 1900, it was reported that if a debutante did not spend Easter in Aiken, she would never secure a suitable match. With so much to do out of doors in winter, the social life of Aiken's evenings seemed dull when compared to Boston, New York, London, and Chicago. But with the rise in popularity of jazz and the traveling acts booked into the local hotels and halls, Aiken boasted crooners and comedians of national repute. Tableaux vivants and midnight poker matches led to not only advantageous marriages but also lasting charitable pursuits. With streets named Whiskey and Easy, it is not hard to imagine the jovial approach to living brought to Aiken through the inherited Southern heritage of Louise Hitchcock and many of the mothers who married Ivy League fathers, who blended with the Yankee ingenuity of W.C. Whitney and his railroad and steel colleagues.

The Migration of Society to Aiken

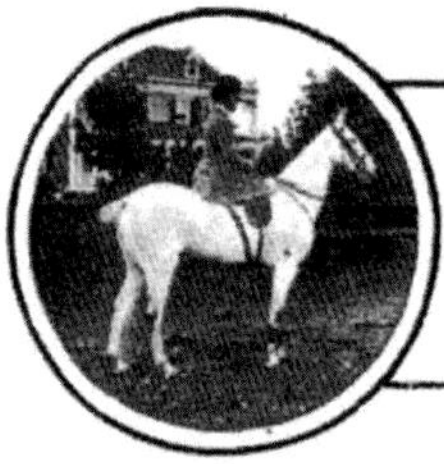

Mrs. J. L. Kernochan

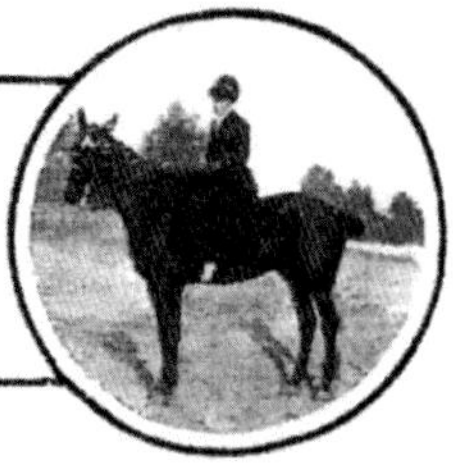

Mrs. Adolf Ladenburg

AIKEN has in prospect one of the liveliest seasons it has known in the brief years of its popularity as a fashionable winter resort for the millionaires of the East. The town is not yet over the excitement of its two great sensations—one, the opening of a twenty-thousand-dollar tennis-court by the Aiken Club, and the other the visit of Mr. William C. Whitney's racing string in the splendid stables prepared for its reception. Another event has been the completion of his mile track, which lies nearly two miles beyond his private race-track. Racing is one of Aiken's favorite pastimes, and steeplechasing and polo have ardent champions.

The houses of the Hitchcocks, Eustises, Whitneys, Hunnewells, Motts, Iselins, that of Woodbury Kane, the Mallorys, Harringtons, Sands, Travers, and others stand upon high, sloping lawns that cover a square or more of ground, and are invariably surrounded by high box-hedges. Whiskey Road is the fashionable residence street in Aiken, and is ever alive with teams and horsemen going back and forth to and from the race-tracks, polo-grounds, and golf club.

The Aiken preserves are among the finest in the country. The quail reservation alone occupies 40,000 acres, and is maintained at enormous expense. There are other reservations for deer, fox, rabbits, pigeons, wild doves, and partridges, and these furnish sport for the entire season.

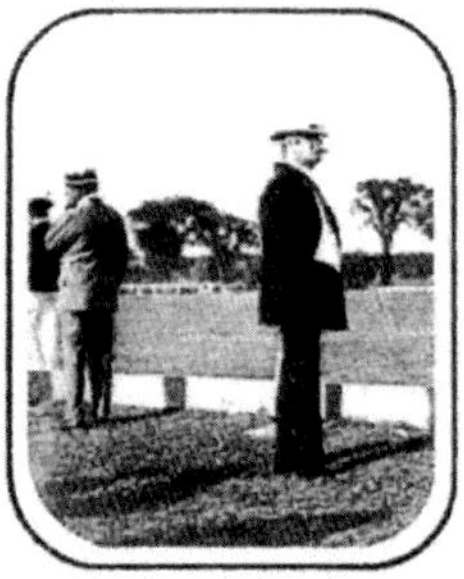

Mr. W. C. Whitney

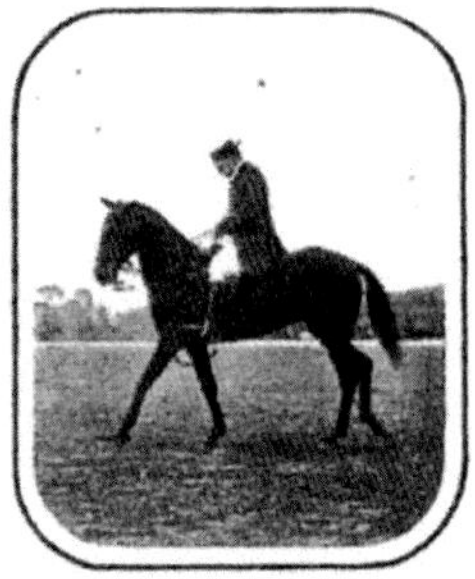

Mr. T. Hitchcock, Jr.

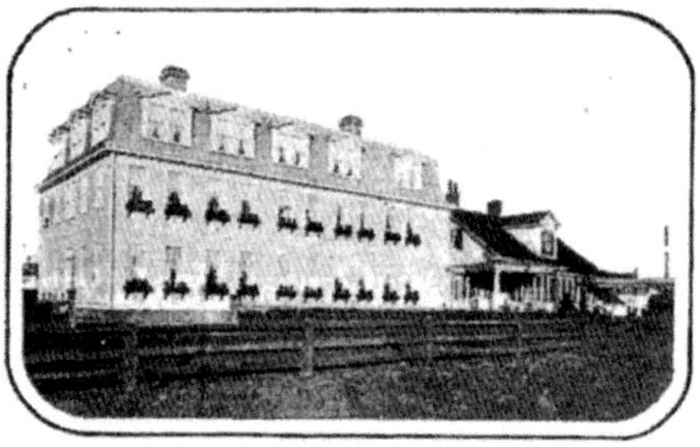

Wilcox's, the Hotel-Club of Aiken

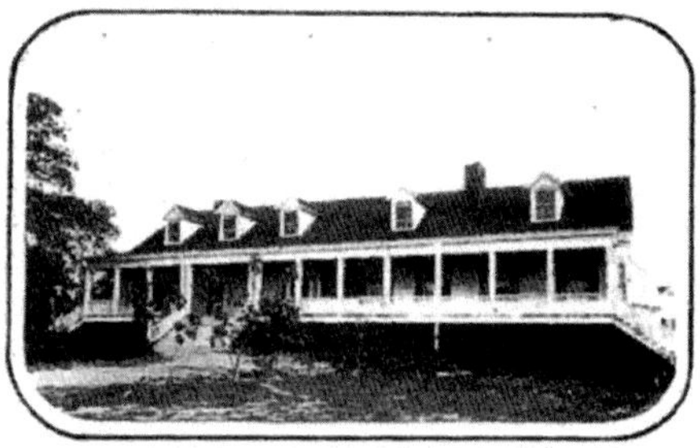

Mr. Whitney's Cottage at Aiken

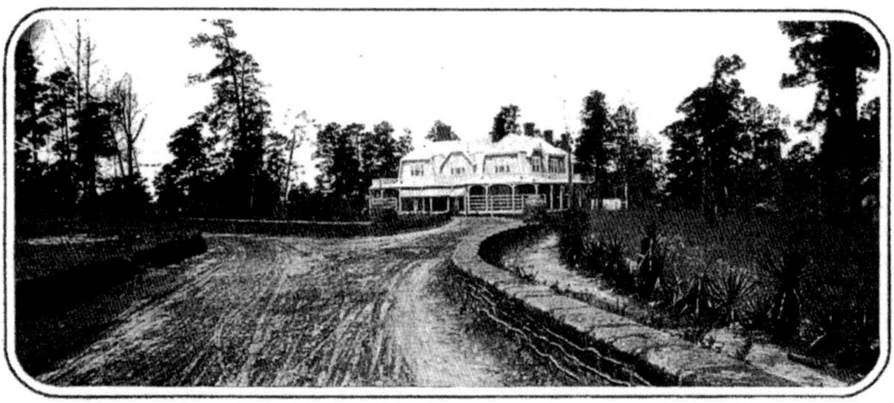

Mr. Clarence Dolan's Cottage at Aiken

The migration of society to Aiken was as much for the hospitality as for sport. The relaxed manners of Aiken allowed visitors to slough off the guarded manners of metropolitan living. The Winter Colony during its Edwardian time was happy for the reprieve of pressure that Aiken offered. (Author's collection.)

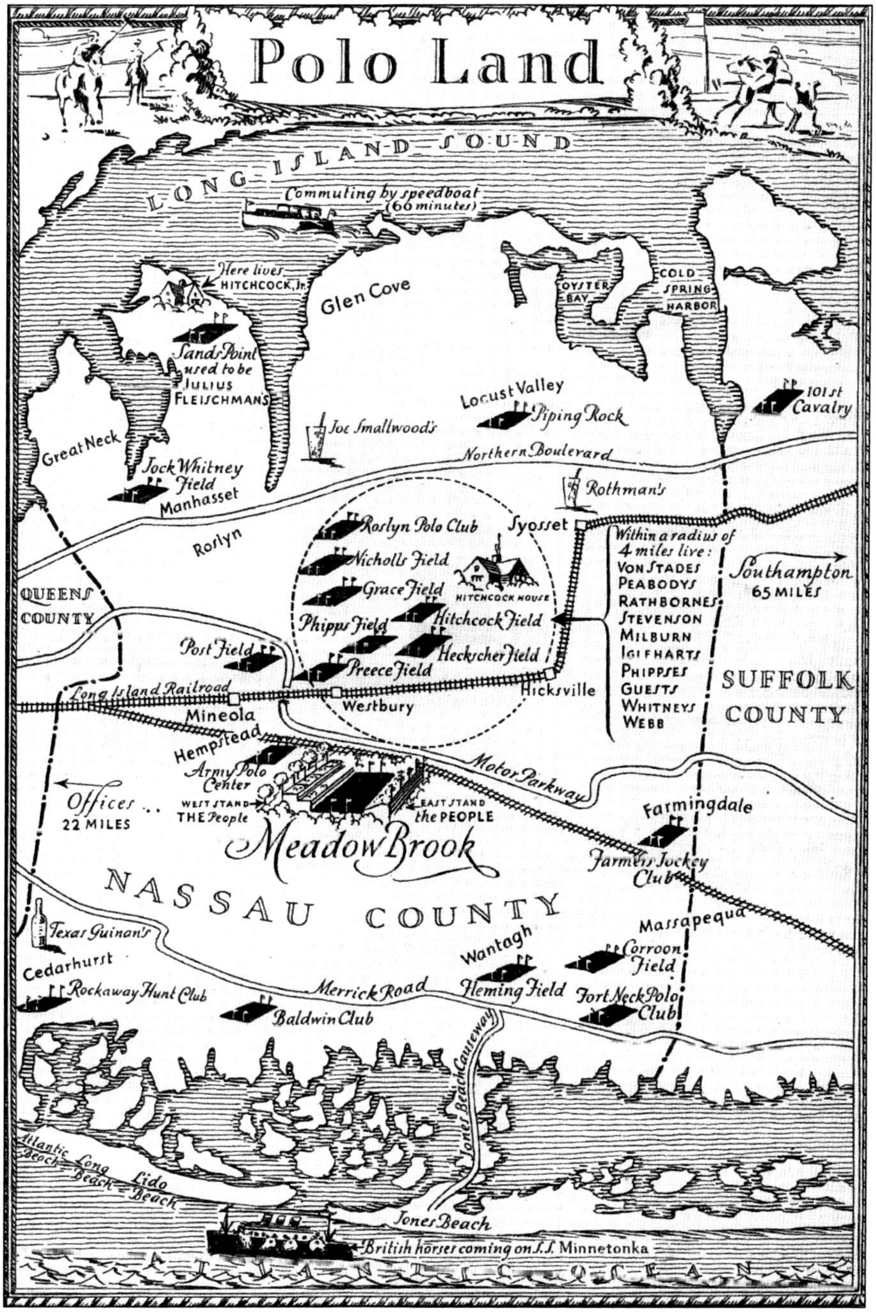

In the 1930s, Capt. Gaylard and Louise Hitchcock selected the junior Meadow Lark team for summer play. The map of "Polo Land" from whence they came to Aiken shows numerous opportunities for sport in Westbury, Long Island. Louise Hitchcock coached her boys, whose fathers were the kings of the sport of polo: Skitty von Stade, Julian Peabody Jr., Devereaux Millburn Jr., Jack Millburn, David Dows Jr., Jimmy Curtis, Marshall Field Jr., Coolidge Chapman, Charles von Stade, Nelson Brown, and Scott Trousdale. It was said of the Hitchcocks that they were the refutation of the idea that polo is for snobs; they welcomed polo and horsemanship from anyone and anywhere. (Author's collection.)

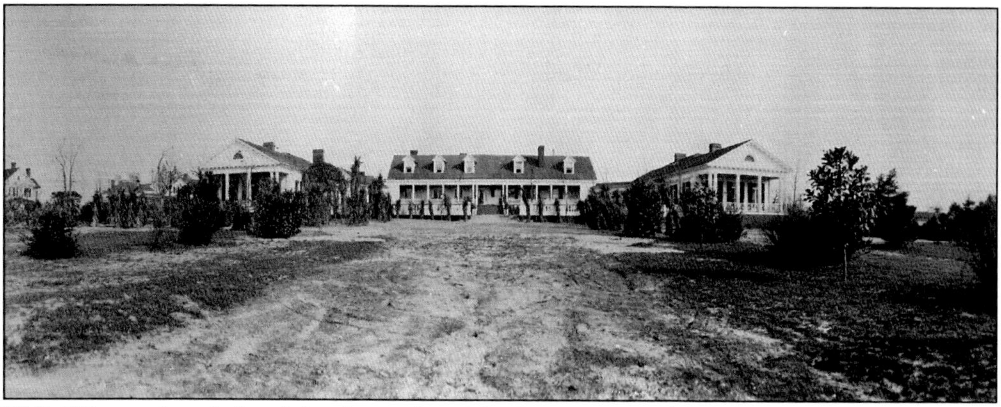

W.C. Whitney bought his Aiken home from Mrs. Joye. He remodeled the cottage into a 64-room home with 15 bathrooms and later added guest wings and a ballroom, bringing the room total to 94. He built stables and a squash court, both private residences now.

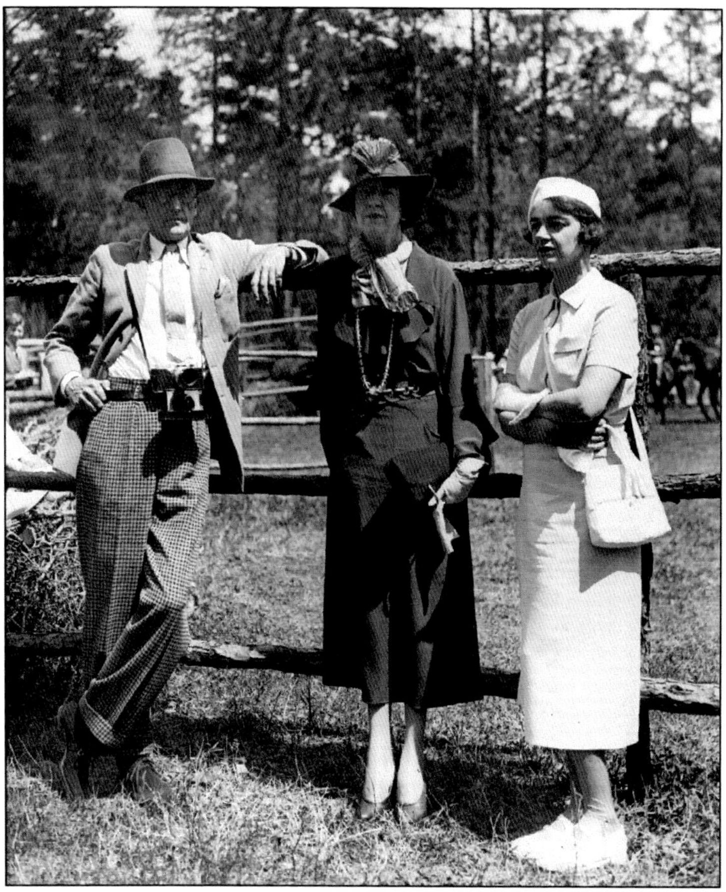

Gertrude Vanderbilt married Harry Payne Whitney. Their daughter Flora Tower's son Whitney Tower remained a force in retaining Aiken's sporting charm. Marriages have seemed to connect many of the families who spent time in Aiken. When Whitney Tower married Lucille Niblack, it connected Chicago to New York. Many of the generations of sporting families in Aiken intermarried, creating a complex web of sporting enthusiasts. (Tower.)

Wister Randolph is pictured here at Whitney Field. Polo is thought to be the first organized team sport. It is also played on bicycles and elephants, on ice and in snow, and in an arena as well. Aiken has hosted the international championship of bicycle polo on the same field where the modern sport's founders played 125 years earlier. Playing polo on bicycles was an ingenious solution to the void that World War I left in the equine world.

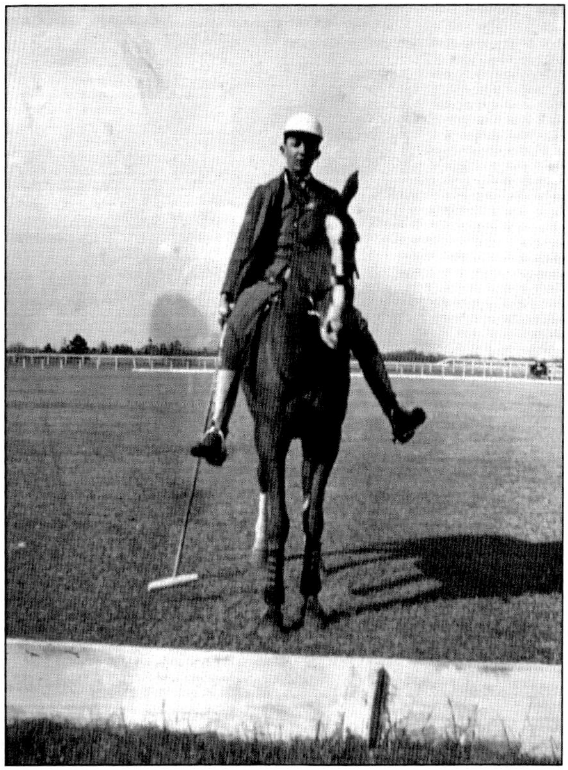

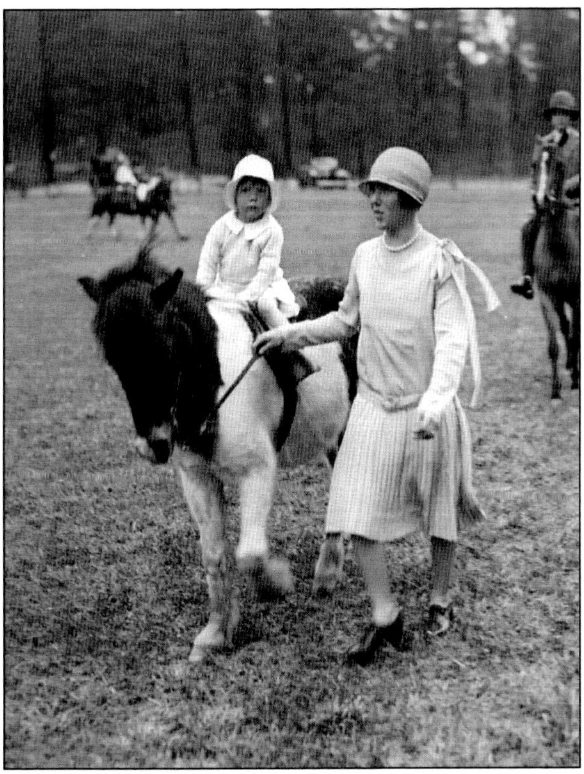

The Tolands welcome the applause of spectators at the Aiken Horse Show. One evening after the horse show, Evalyn Walsh McLean, a renowned jewelry collector, wore the 45.52-karat Hope Diamond to a casual dinner gathering at the Dolan estate, and when the formality of her dress was mentioned, she turned to the source and said, "Had I wanted to be formal I would be wearing the Star of the East." It is not surprising that Cole Porter found inspiration in the society of Aiken and included much of it in his hit musical *Anything Goes*. (Brainard.)

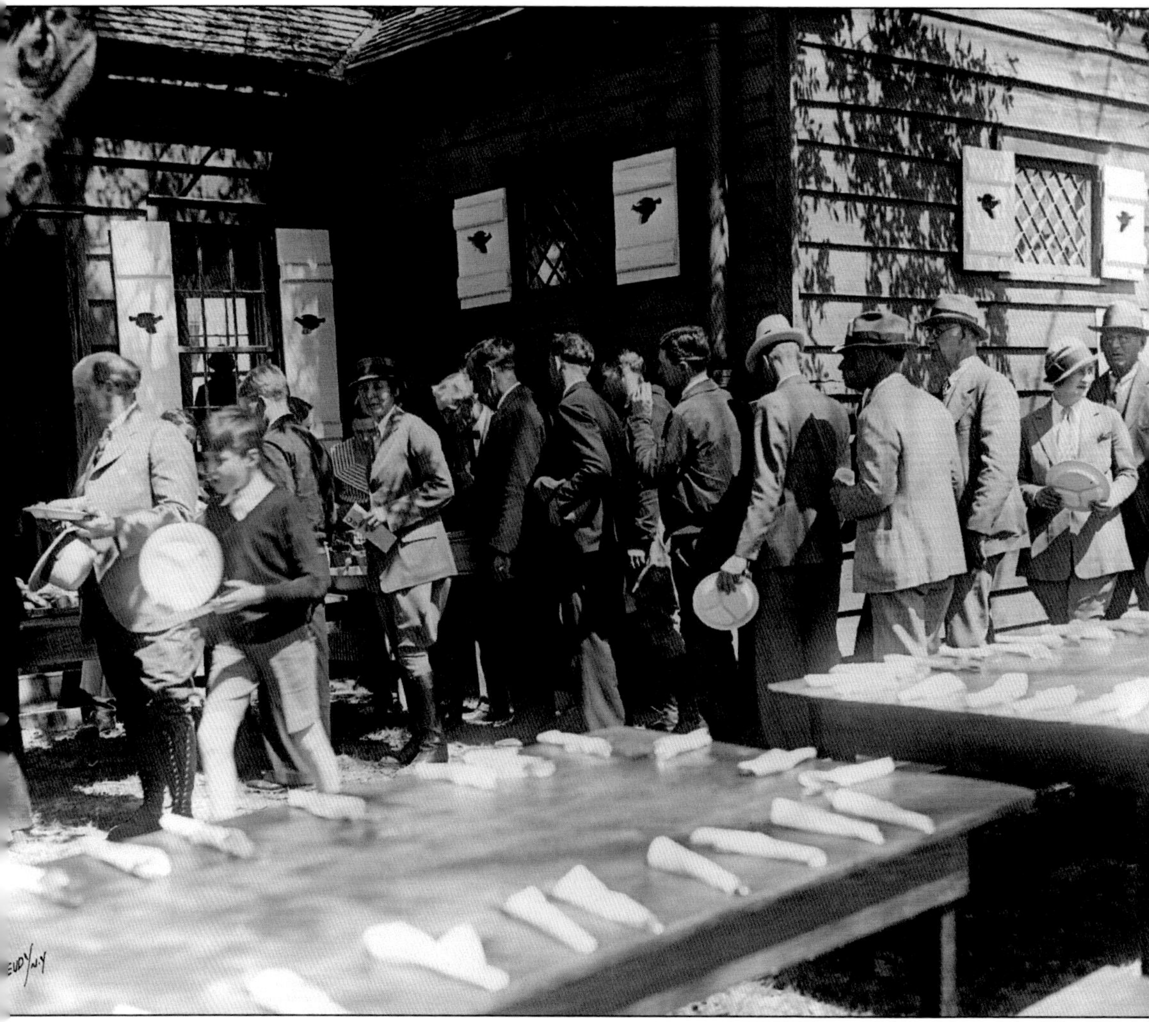

The Schutzenplotz, later bought by Francis Hitchcock, was one of the many gun clubs in Aiken. The Shutzenplotz was at the western end of the Aiken woods; it had bowling alleys, shooting galleries, and a wings preserve. Aiken Gun Club, on the east end of South Boundary Avenue, was called the Pigeon Traps and is now a private residence. Quail preserves throughout the state owned by a veritable who's who of American society hosted long weekends in pursuit of birds. The 40,000-acre quail preserve in Aiken had quite a reputation. The German family that opened the Shutzenplotz Gesellschaft hosted a three-day festival in Aiken that attracted shooters from across the globe. By 1900, it was known as Hitchcock Traps. Francis Hitchcock used this area to study the characteristics of hunting dogs for his Westminster Kennel Club. Julian Peabody's book *Gran* mentions that Francis was a founder of the Kennel Club Show and known to be a keen observer of equine bloodlines for the Jockey Club as well.

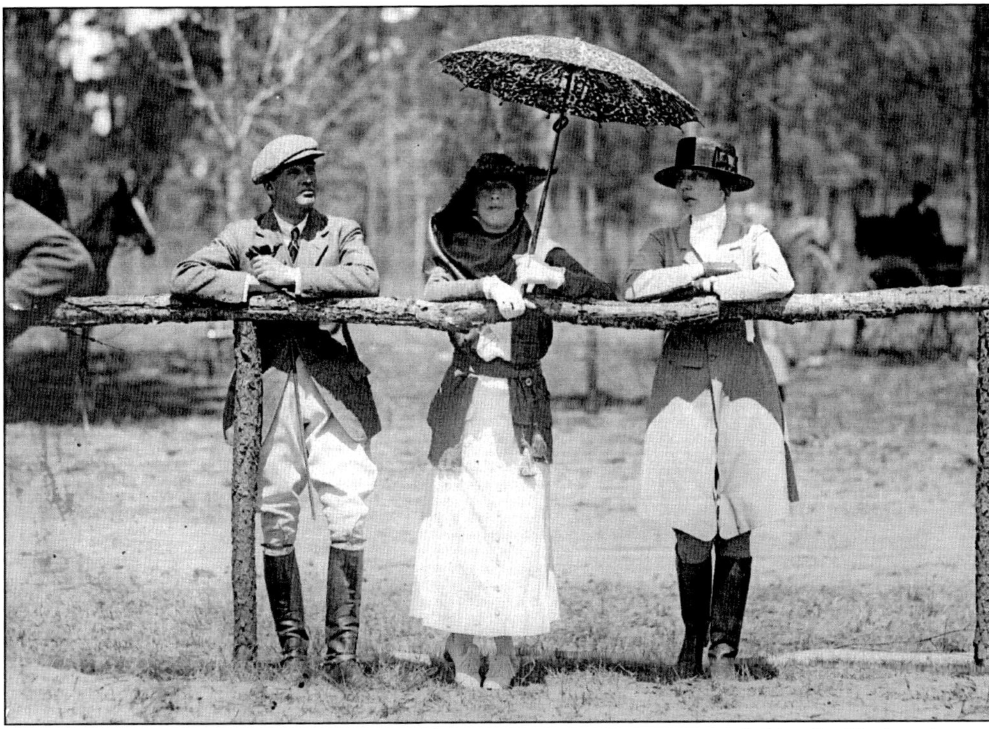

In 1916, (from left to right) Marshall Field, Mrs. W. Scott Cameron, and Claudia Phelps observe the activities at the Aiken Horse Show ringside. The 1916 inaugural of the horse show called together many sporting enthusiasts from the Midwest and the Northeast. They came to enjoy the Southern hospitality and the sporting activities presented during the winter festival and raised funds to stock the hospital that Hope Iselin gave with her poker winnings.

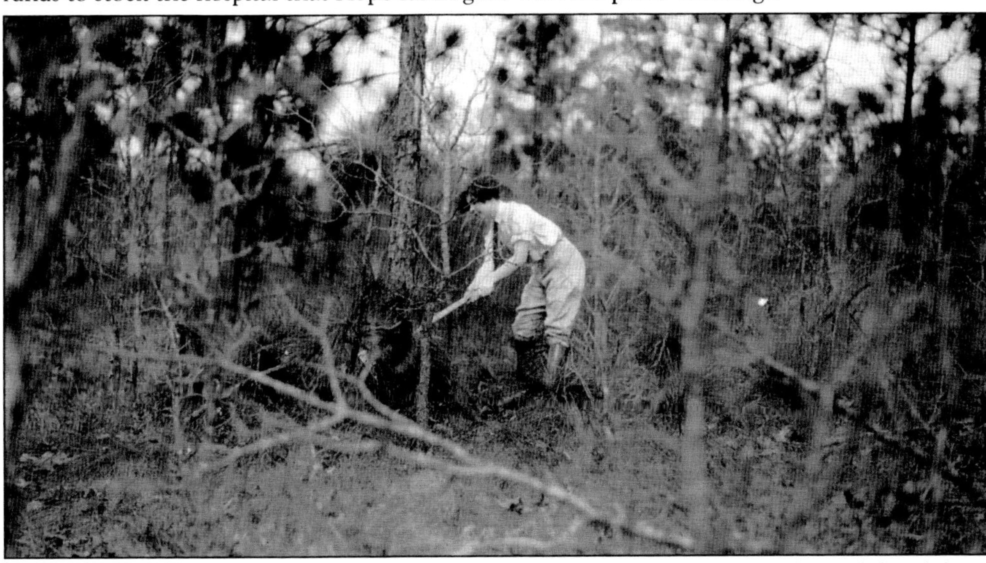

A millionaire work group formed in Aiken, known as the Axe Club. Members of the club are responsible for the many trails in the woods today. They chopped down trees, cleared out vines, and made way for those who followed to enjoy the trails that they envisioned. A modern version of the Axe Club meets at the horse show grounds to prepare it for the Aiken Horse Show. (Brainard.)

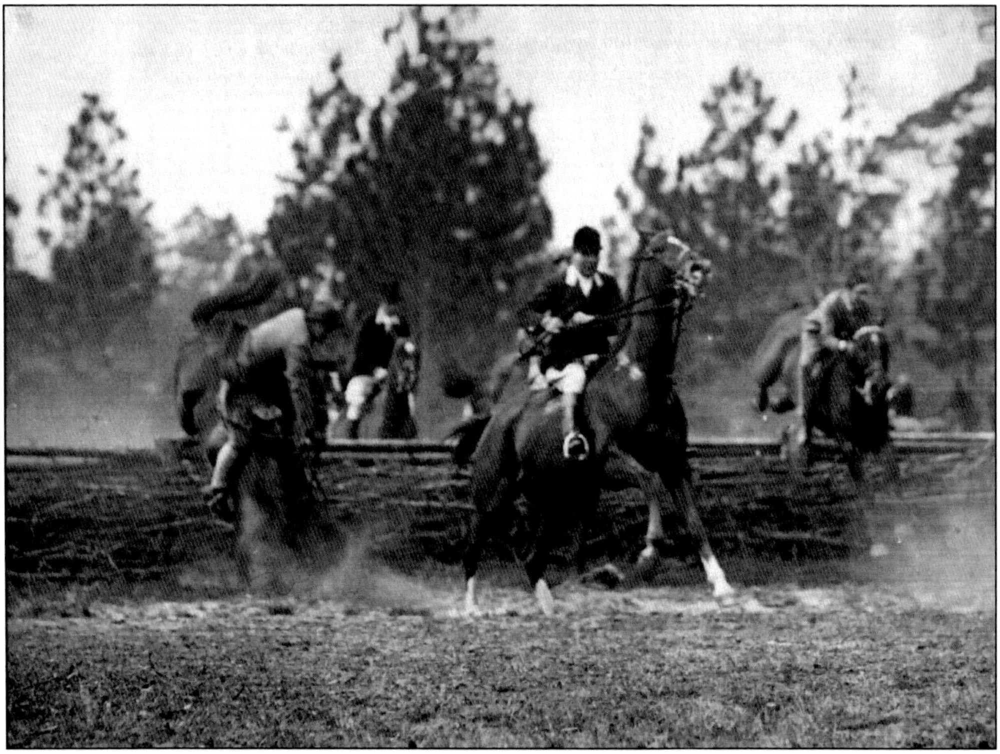

Polo expert and proficient rider Devereaux Millburn takes a spill while Harry Worchester Smith never misses a stride. Neither horse nor rider was injured in this stumble along Juac Hollow. Members of the field were accustomed to riding accidents, and many an Aiken horse lover has gone to the heavenly hunt after a fall in the woods. (Brainard.)

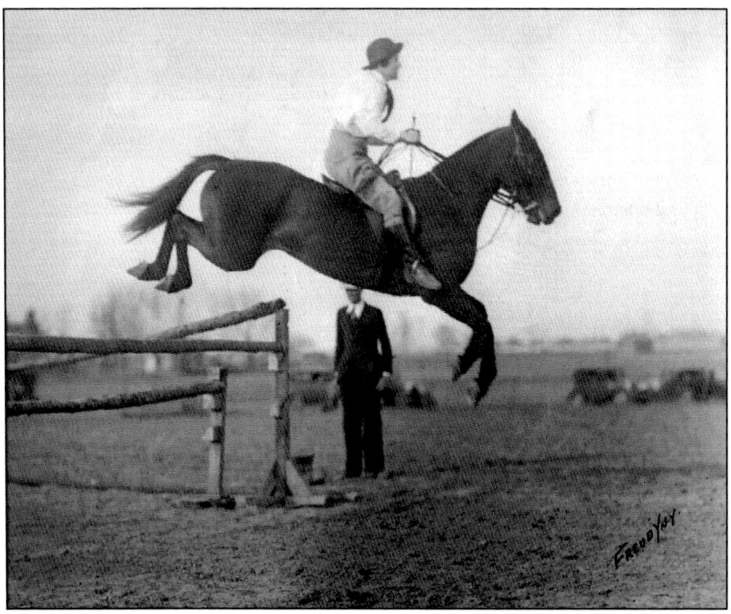

F. Ambrose Clark and Thomas Hitchcock developed new training methods for their racehorses and hunt horses. In some cases, they schooled the horses without riders in shoots laid with pine-brush jumps. Fostering the equines' natural position in air, they believed it prepared the horse for the obstacles when raced at high speed. Here Rita Dolan takes an oxer in classic style. (Brainard.)

Speed is an Aiken theme. Racing horses, buggies, yachts, or speedboats, even racing cars, speed is the thing. Conrad Ruckelshaus (far right) shows off one of his Indianapolis 500 race cars. Aiken's winter visitors were a diverse cross-section of successful businessmen. (Ruckelshaus.)

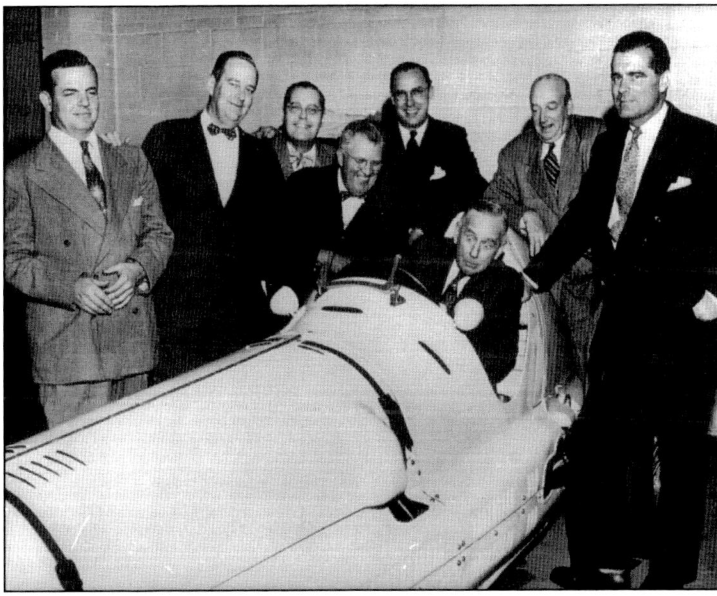

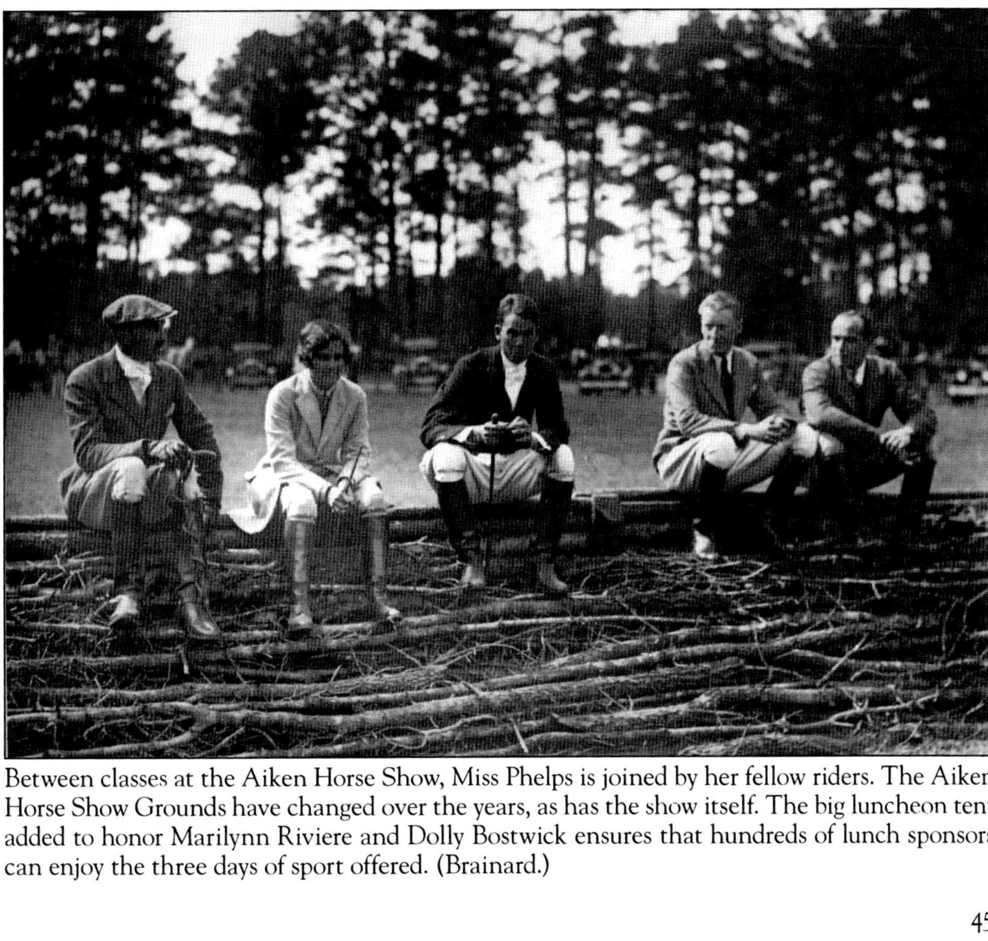

Between classes at the Aiken Horse Show, Miss Phelps is joined by her fellow riders. The Aiken Horse Show Grounds have changed over the years, as has the show itself. The big luncheon tent added to honor Marilynn Riviere and Dolly Bostwick ensures that hundreds of lunch sponsors can enjoy the three days of sport offered. (Brainard.)

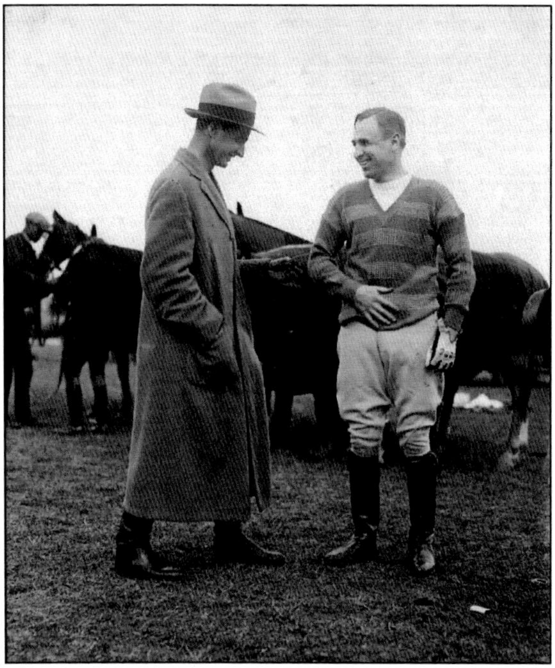

Settling on a wager, Sonny Whitney (left) and Thomas Hitchcock bet on cockfights, horse races, and field trials; wagering was an honorable pursuit between friends and family. The Hitchcock family poker games were a highlight in the Aiken season. Louise Hitchcock once said gambling teaches people to be good winners and losers. (Tower.)

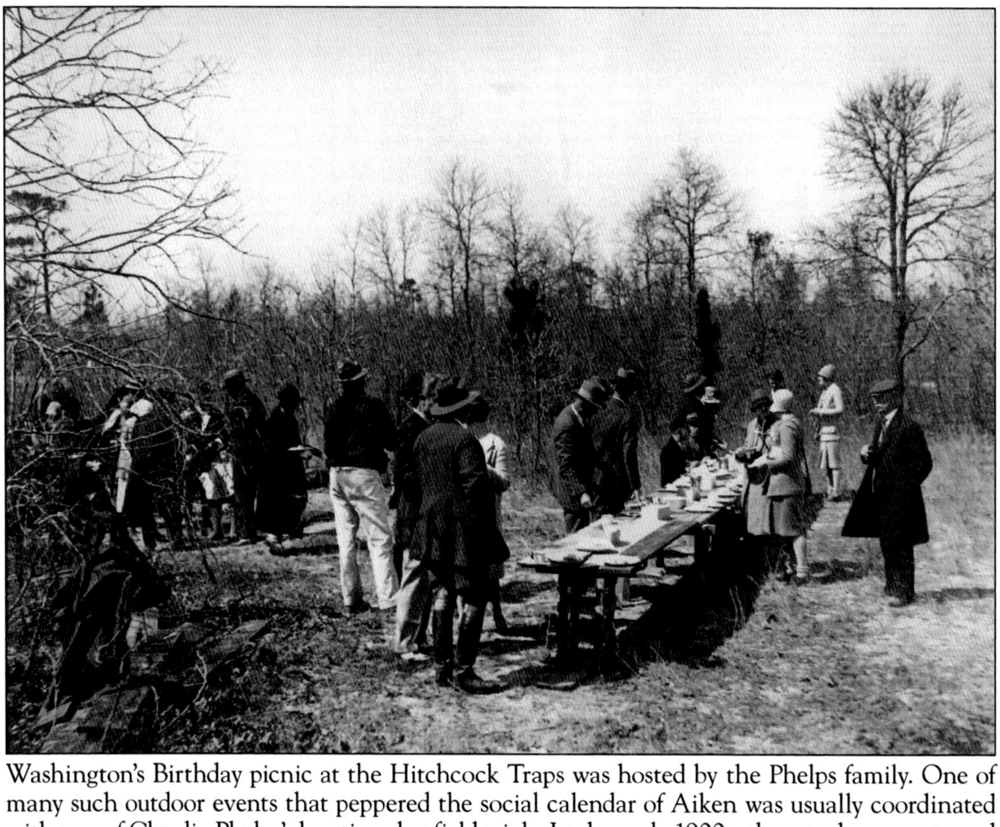

Washington's Birthday picnic at the Hitchcock Traps was hosted by the Phelps family. One of many such outdoor events that peppered the social calendar of Aiken was usually coordinated with one of Claudia Phelps's hunting-dog field trials. In the early 1900s, the woods encompassed over 8,000 acres.

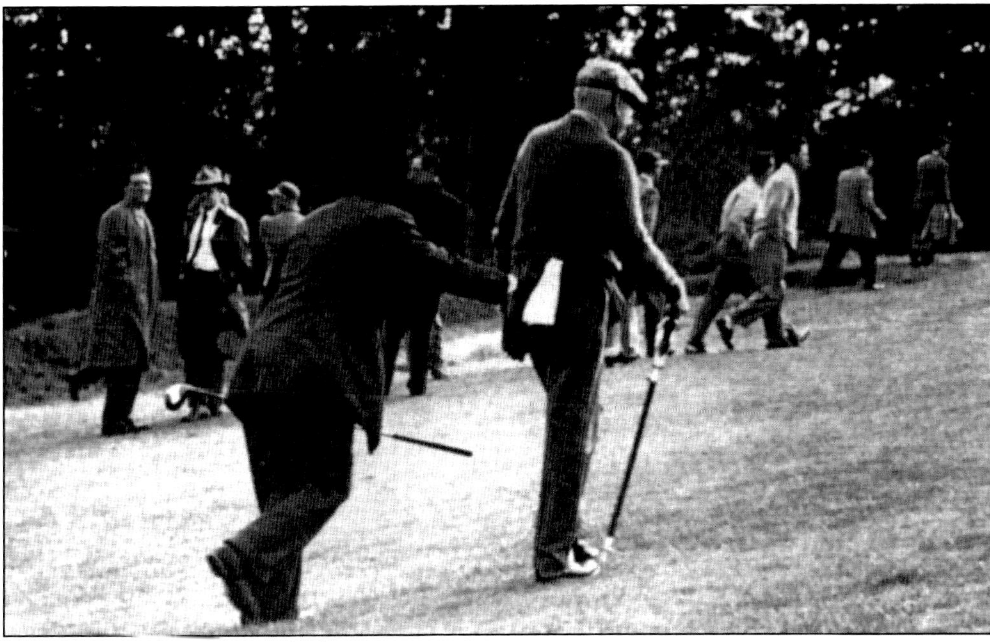

Eugene Grace, at 83, gets a little help walking up to the green during the Palmetto Pro-Am, during which he was teamed with Ben Hogan. Hogan said that Palmetto's third, fourth, and fifth holes are the best three back-to-back par-four holes he ever played. Grace loved the game, and supported golf courses in order for his 250,000-plus employees to play. Fred Astaire once used the putting green at Palmetto to choreograph a dance number in one of his movies.

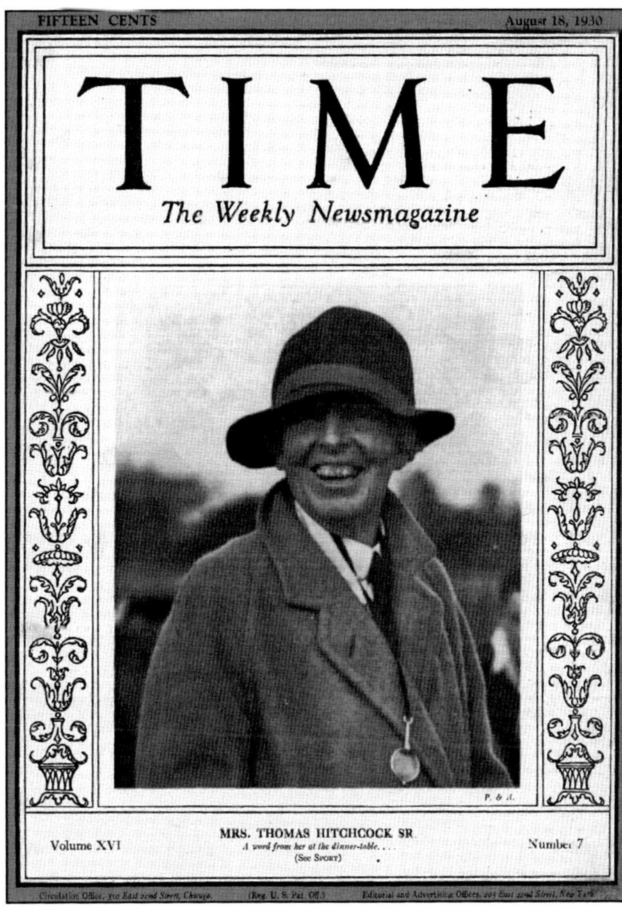

Louise Hitchcock's presence on the cover of this August 18, 1930, issue of *Time* magazine is proof of her respected position within the global sporting community. At the time, associate editor of *Time* John Shaw Billings spent his spare time at his family home Redcliffe in Beech Island. Two decades later, Aiken would be featured on the cover of another of John Shaw Billings's magazines, *Life*.

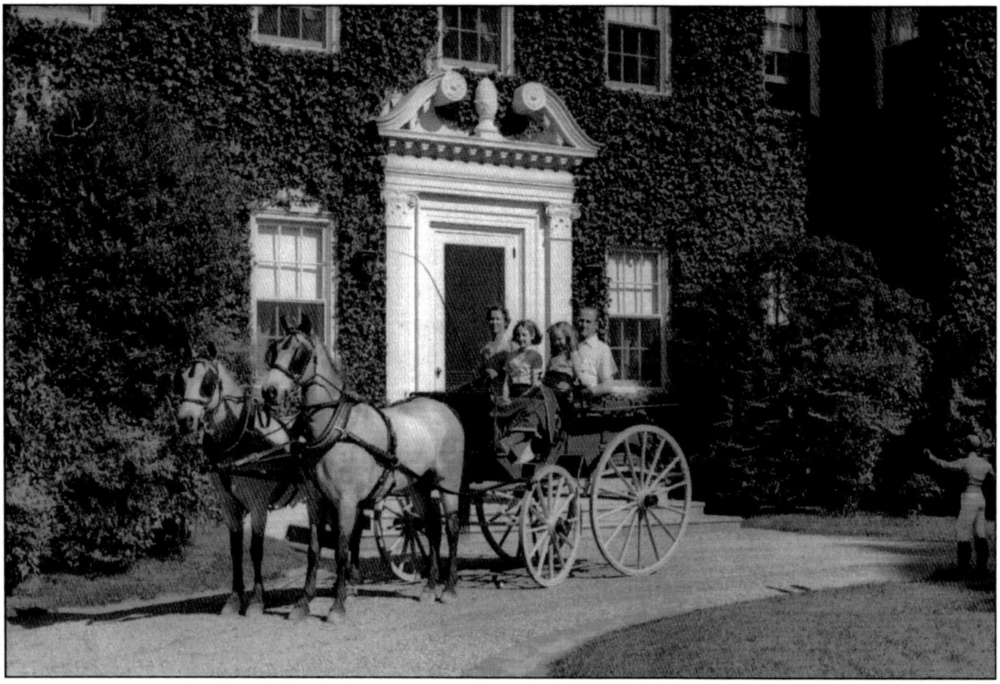

Green Boundary Club, Aiken's private croquet and supper club, was the former home of Francis and William Wood, known affectionately as Aunt Fran and Uncle Bill by many an Aiken child. This carriage could be bound for anywhere, especially with the excited Ruckelshaus and Wood children aboard. (Ruckelshaus.)

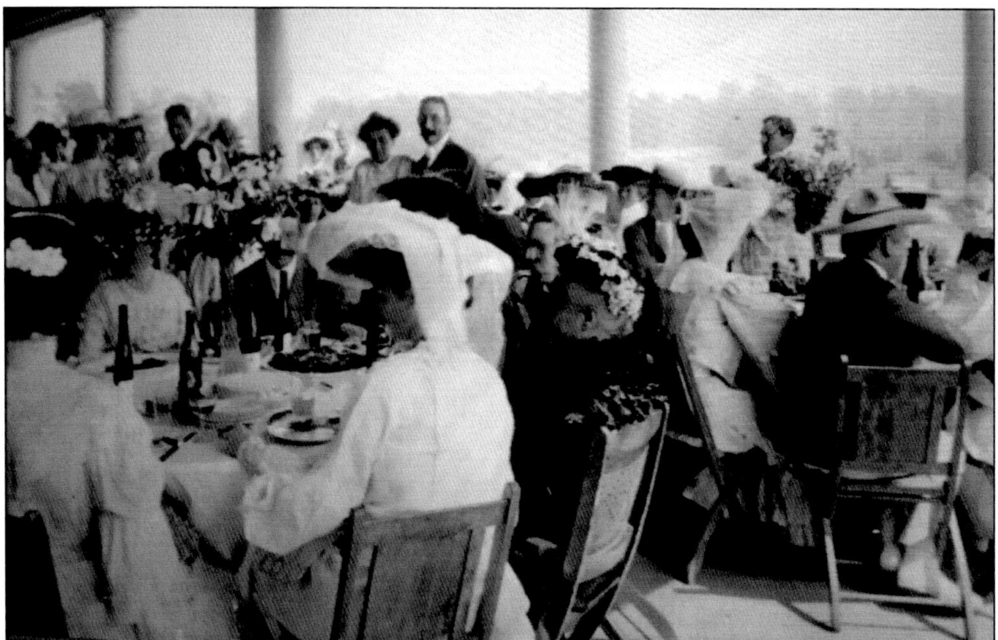

Palmetto Golf Club is reputed to be one of the purest playing courses in the world. Stanford White designed the clubhouse with wide porches and large fireplaces. It is the second-oldest continuously operating golf course in the same location in the United States.

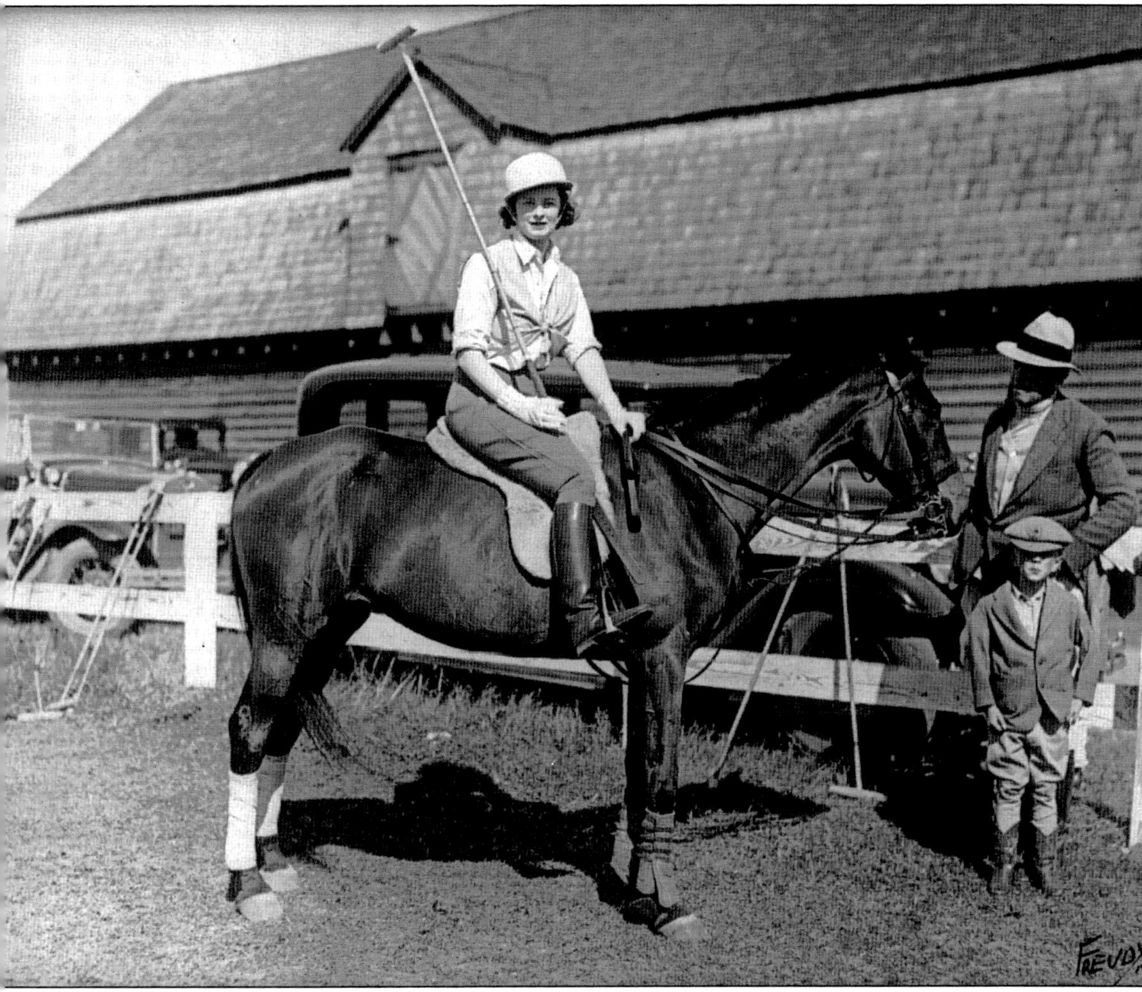

Betty Hassler Ruckelshaus prepares for a chukker of polo. Betty's grandfather had been one of the Aiken Polo Club's first players; her father, an avid player himself, lived at Georgian Court with its indoor tennis court and polo field and had a mechanical horse installed in a pit for practice. Betty inherited the Hassler love of polo and all things sporting. She was a master of foxhounds and champion in equestrian side-saddle as well as devoted historian whose commitment to the preservation of tradition and history helped save George Washington's boyhood home, Ferry Farm, in Virginia. (Ruckelshaus.)

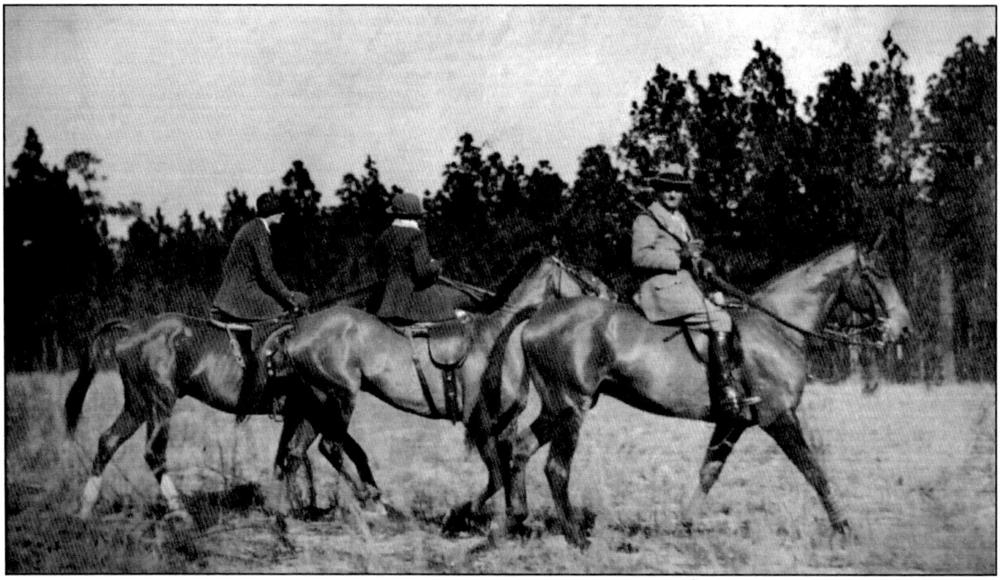

Helen and Austin Niblack are out for a ride in the woods. The Niblacks created a sensation in Chicago when they hosted Prince Edward's visit before his coronation. Later, in Aiken, Wallis Simpson and David Windsor spent time at Dorothy Rogers's home, Rye Patch, where one can see the bricked walls filled in to give privacy to the couple while driving along Whiskey Road. The Niblacks also entertained the couple at Let's Pretend. (Tower.)

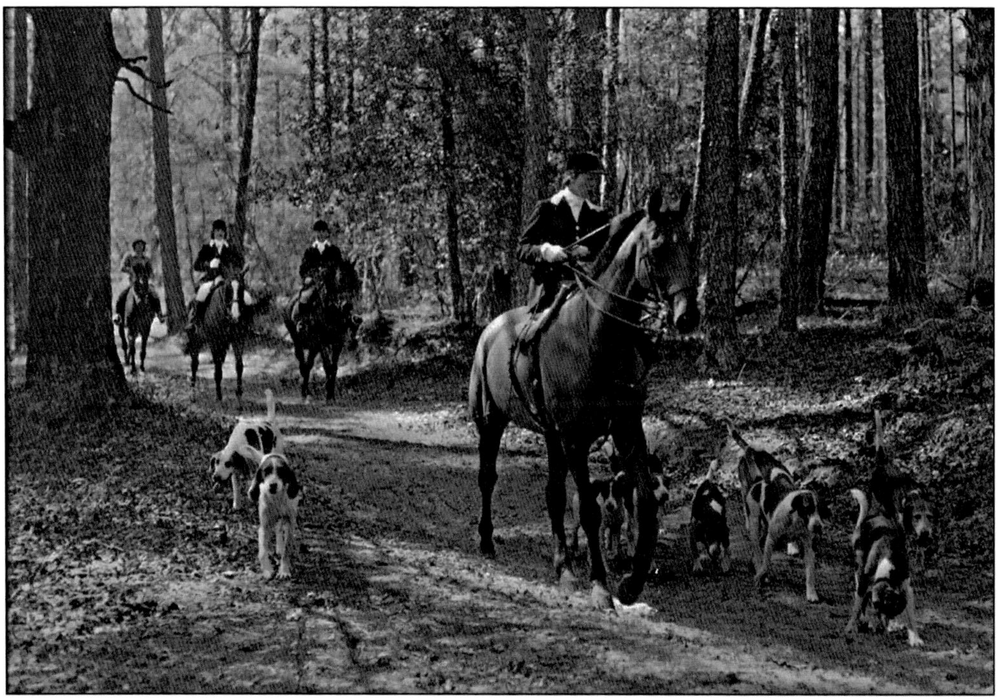

Helen Northrup Knox is pictured here in 1946 with the Aiken Hounds. In E. Somerville's research for her book *The States through Irish Eyes*, she noted the forethought and planning of the generations of families who have preserved the Hitchcock Woods for foxhunting. Today, Helen Northrup Knox's granddaughter Linda Knox McLean is master of fox hounds, or MFH. (McLean.)

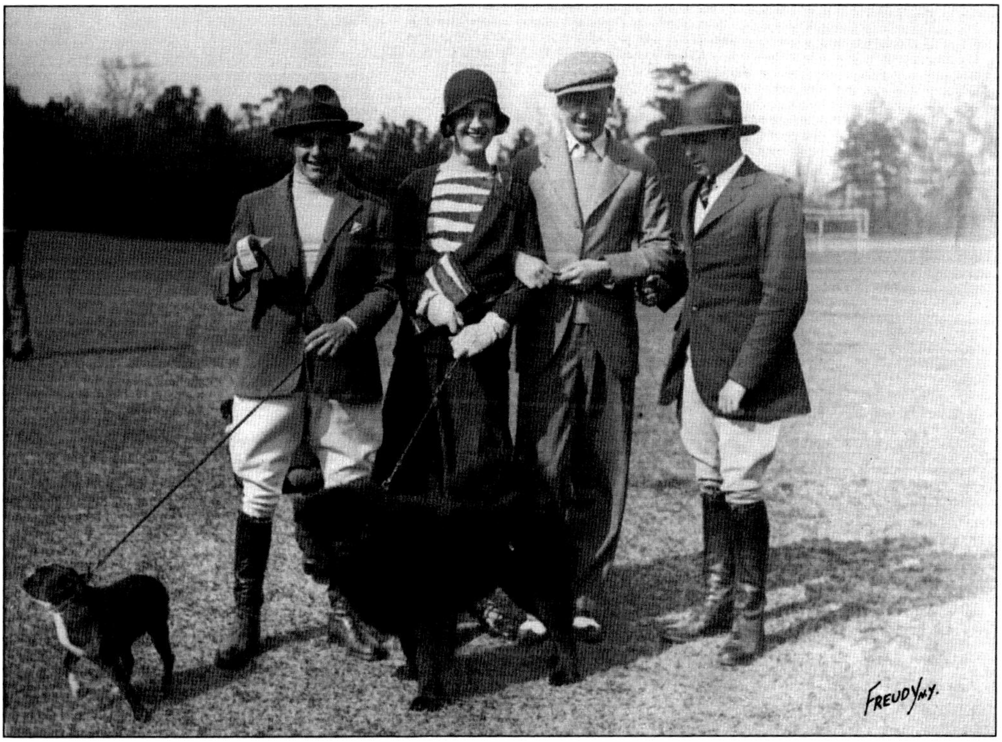

Being seen with one's favorite dog was considered the highest mark of a good breeding. Yeoman farmers in the area like Walker, Weeks, Fulmer, Coward, and Gregorie maintained farm packs, and the Winter Colony brought breeds with national interest such as Claudia Phelps's White West Highland Terriers. Purebreds were coveted then; today, there is great pride in the adoption programs offered through Aiken SPCA and Aiken Friends of the Animal Shelter.

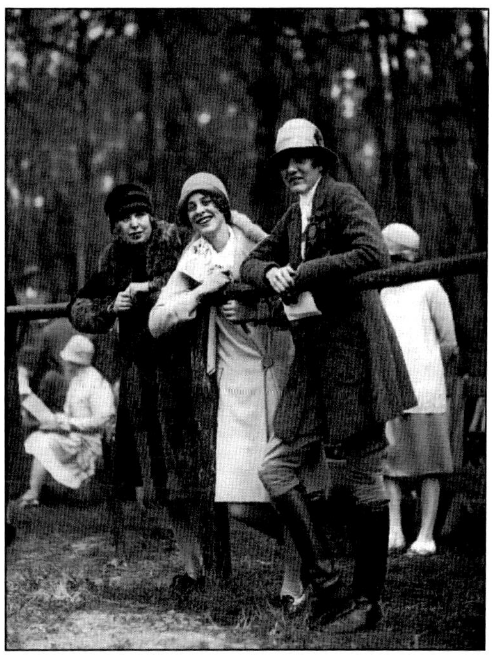

From left to right, Misses Kramer, Phelps, and Dolan are all smiles watching one of Aiken's equestrian sporting events. At the rail, ballroom, and dinner table, the hospitality of slow Southern days and conversation centered on political issues, industrial advancements, or the next great stallion. Aiken was also a key area for the advancement of women's suffrage, fitting given the leading role women have played in all things Aiken. Eulalie Salley funded the Southern suffrage movement, and Martha Schofield was a close friend and political ally of Susan B. Anthony.

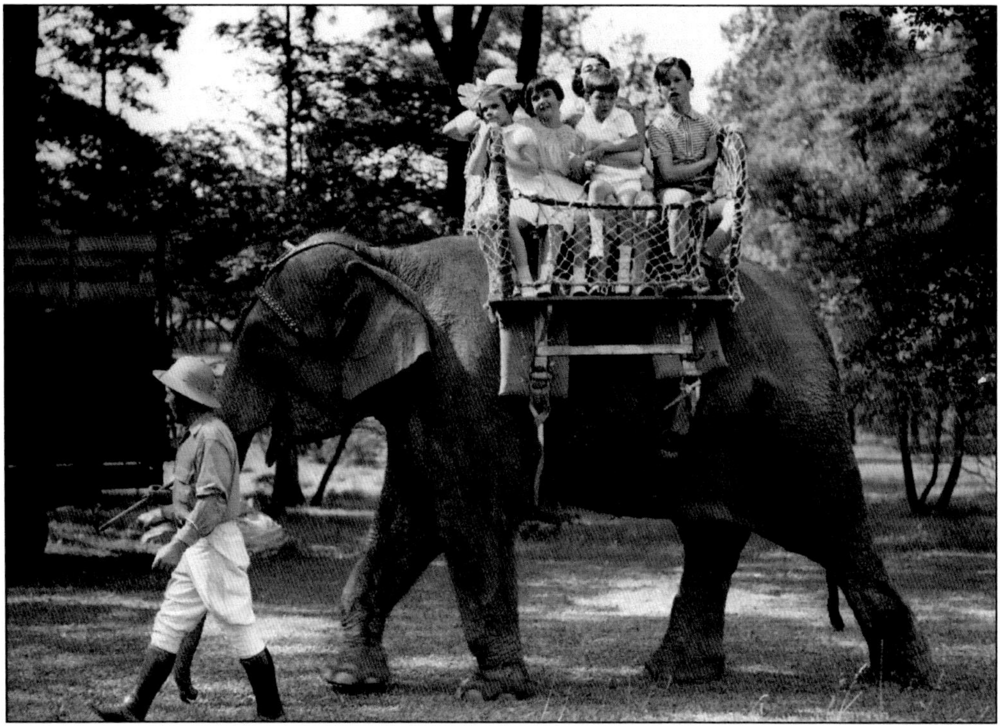

What does a hostess do when planning a party for some of the world's wealthiest guests? Send in the elephants. When the truck delivering this pachyderm to a local Winter Colony estate drove down Whiskey Road, it caused quite a stir. The party guests joked about bringing in a few more and having a race—Aiken style. (Tower.)

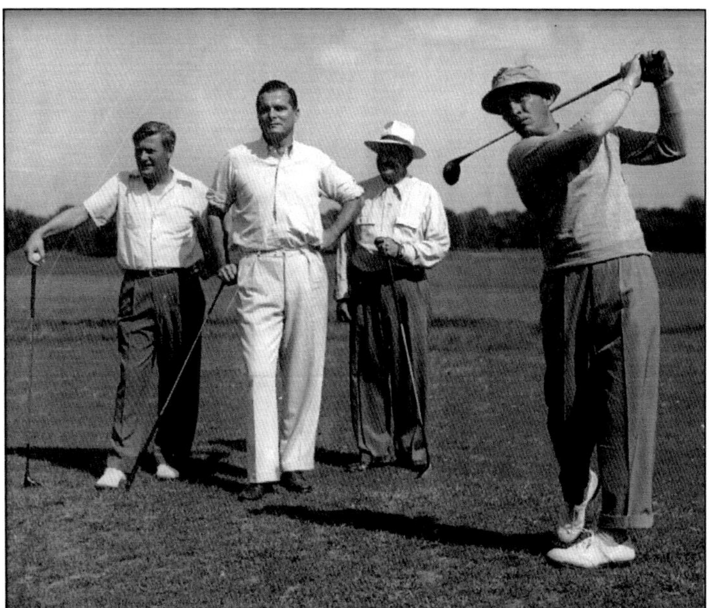

Bing Crosby (pictured playing Palmetto in 1958) and his wife, Kathryn, frequented Aiken, spending time with their close friends Betty and Conrad Ruckelshaus. Bettina, the Ruckelshauses' daughter, recalls being sung to before bed by Crosby. Still connected, the next generation still enjoys time in Aiken. (Ruckelshaus.)

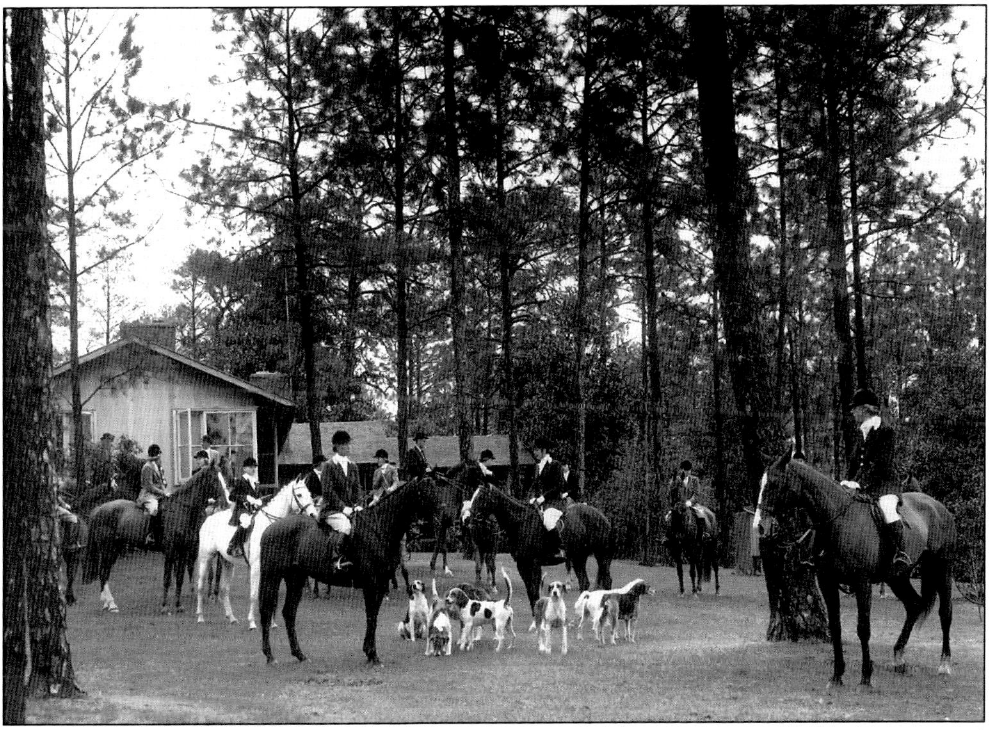

Dolly and Pete Bostwick, both avid foxhunters and he an excellent polo player, supported Aiken Hounds through thick and thin. When horses and humans gather in pursuit of quarry, there is often a tray of port and sherry close at hand; at the very least, a hunt breakfast would follow. (Conger.)

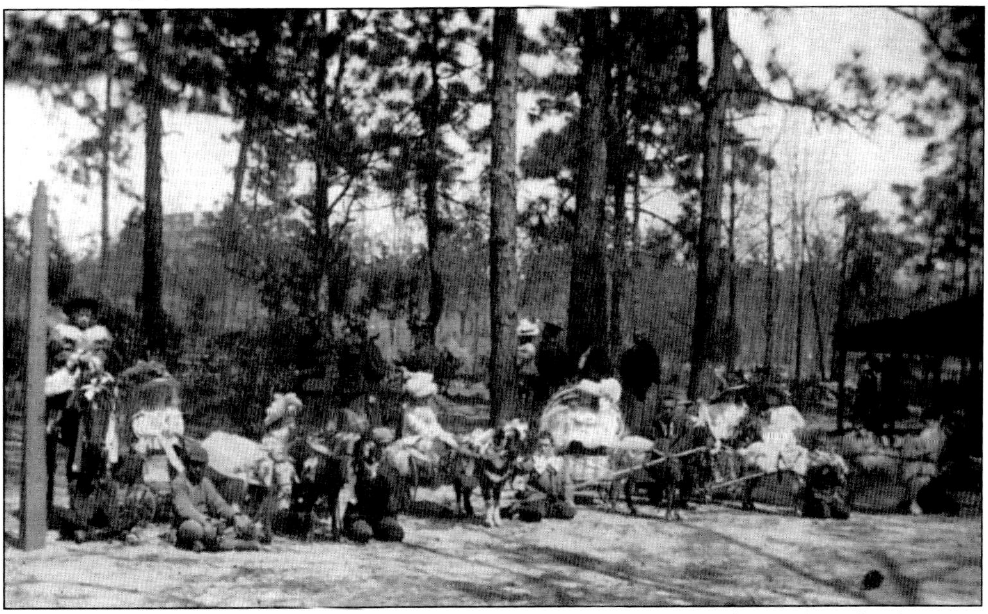

Children gather for the annual Goat Party Picnic with Highland Park Hotel in the distance. Livery stables around town trained goats just for the winter season. In the late 1800s, children could drive the small goat carts through the woods and along the divided parkways.

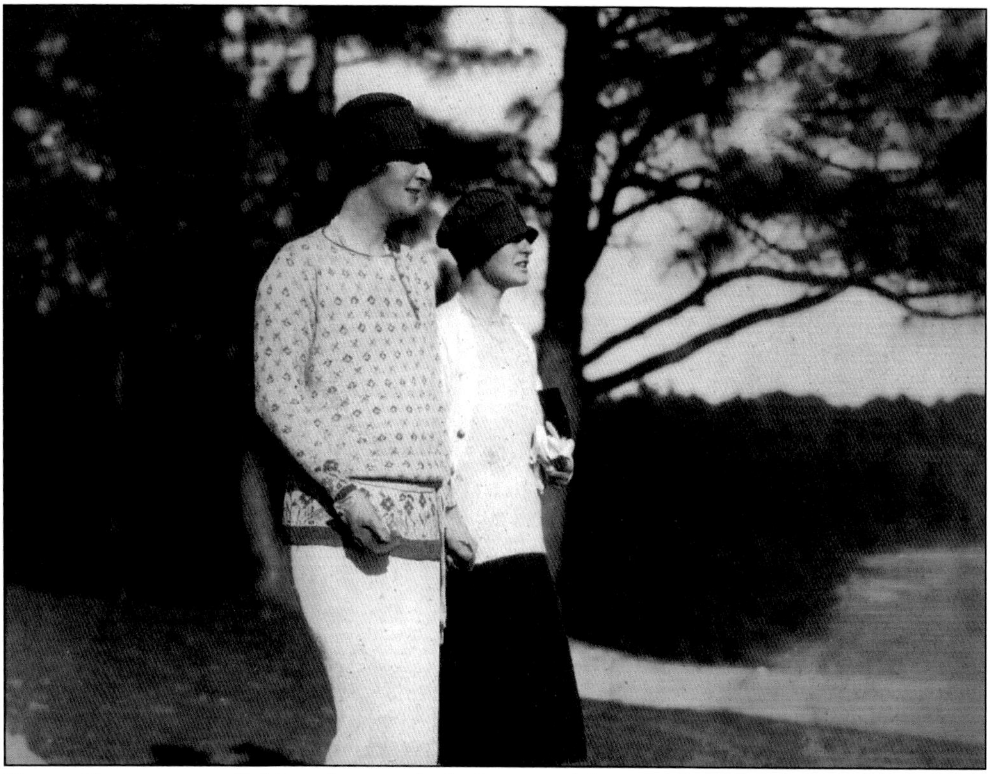

Pictured here are some fashion plates on the links; since Aiken was devoid of the social demands of the big cities, debutantes could showcase their sporting talents. With Palmetto Golf Course as their backdrop, these socialites hit the links dressed to impress. Elizabeth Arden was a frequent visitor to Aiken, as was Edward Bok of *Ladies Home Journal*, so advice was close at hand. (Tower.)

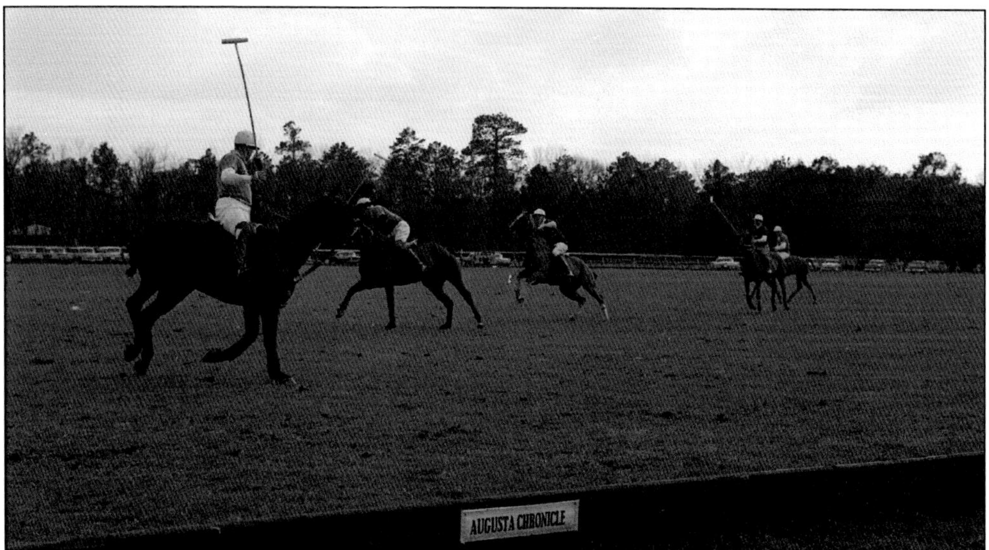

Polo tailgates during games have been and continue to be a social gathering time. Sunday afternoons at Whitney Field feature the mingling of both Southern hospitality and Yankee ingenuity. These lazy afternoons bring people from all walks of life together to enjoy Aiken polo.

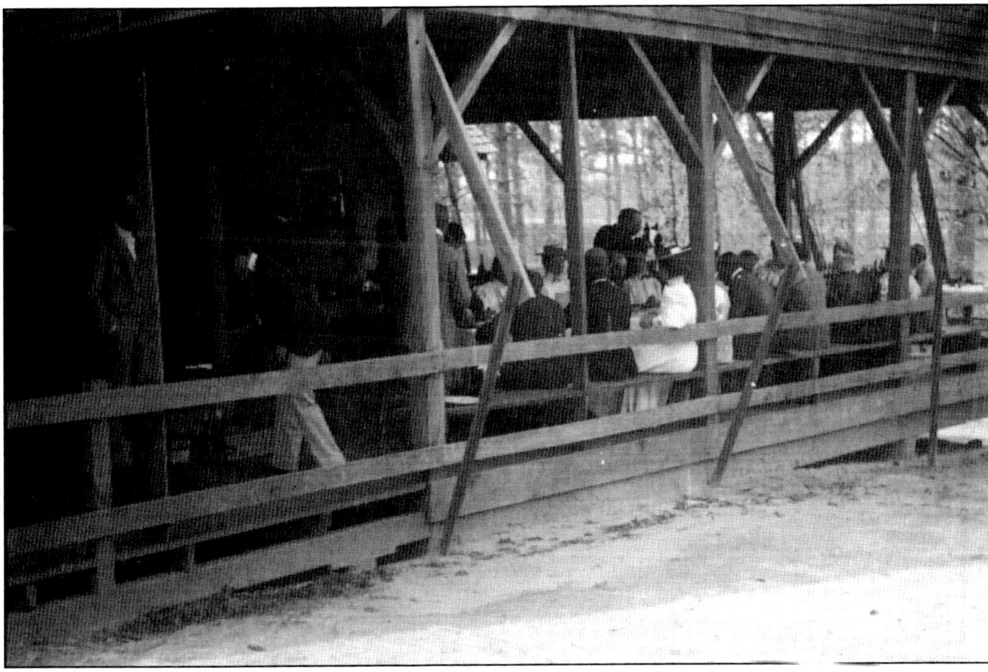

Built in 1874, the Schutzenplotz, a Germanic-style building with indoor range galleries, bowling alleys, and a dancehall, was a gathering place for visitors and residents alike. Offering shooting and bowling, three sports a day without a horse, many non-riders sought refuge from the equine worship that is Aiken. Often mistaken for the Tea Cottage, the covered porches of the Schutzenplotz are recognizable in many photographs of picnics and merriment; however, very few images of the entire building remain. The gardens surrounding the Schutzenplotz were considered by many to be refined and offered a large variety of specimen plantings. The gardens were established by the preeminent botanist of the era, Henry William Ravenel, who lived in Aiken.

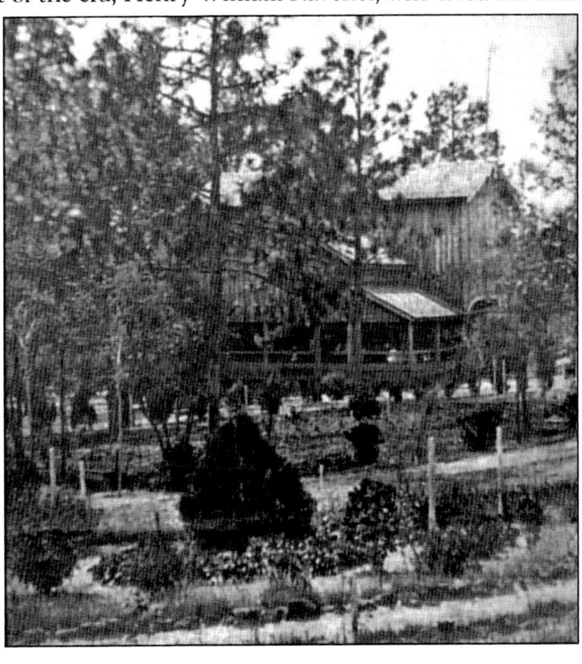

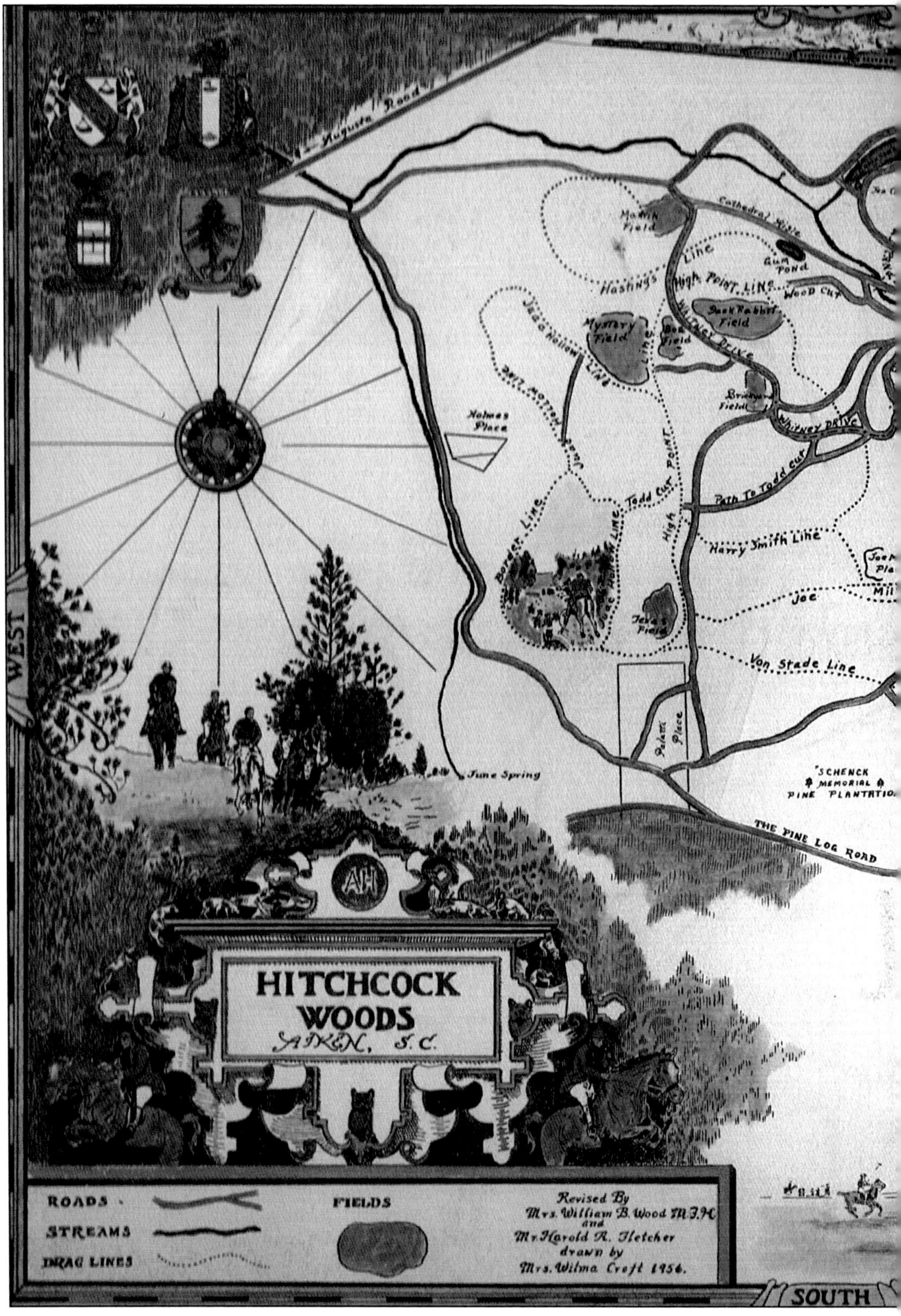

Augusta Road
Cathedral Aisle
Martin Field
Gum Pond
Hastings Line
High Point Line
Wood Cut
Jack Rabbit Field
Mystery Field
Whitney Drive
Holmes Place
Todd Cut
Path To Todd Cut
Harry Smith Line
Border Line
Joe
Von Stade Line
June Spring
Pine Place
SCHENCK MEMORIAL PINE PLANTATIO
THE PINE LOG ROAD
WEST
AH
HITCHCOCK WOODS
AIKEN, S.C.
ROADS
STREAMS
DRAG LINES
FIELDS
Revised By
Mrs. William B. Wood M.F.H.
and
Mr. Harold R. Fletcher
drawn by
Mrs. Wilma Croft 1956.
SOUTH

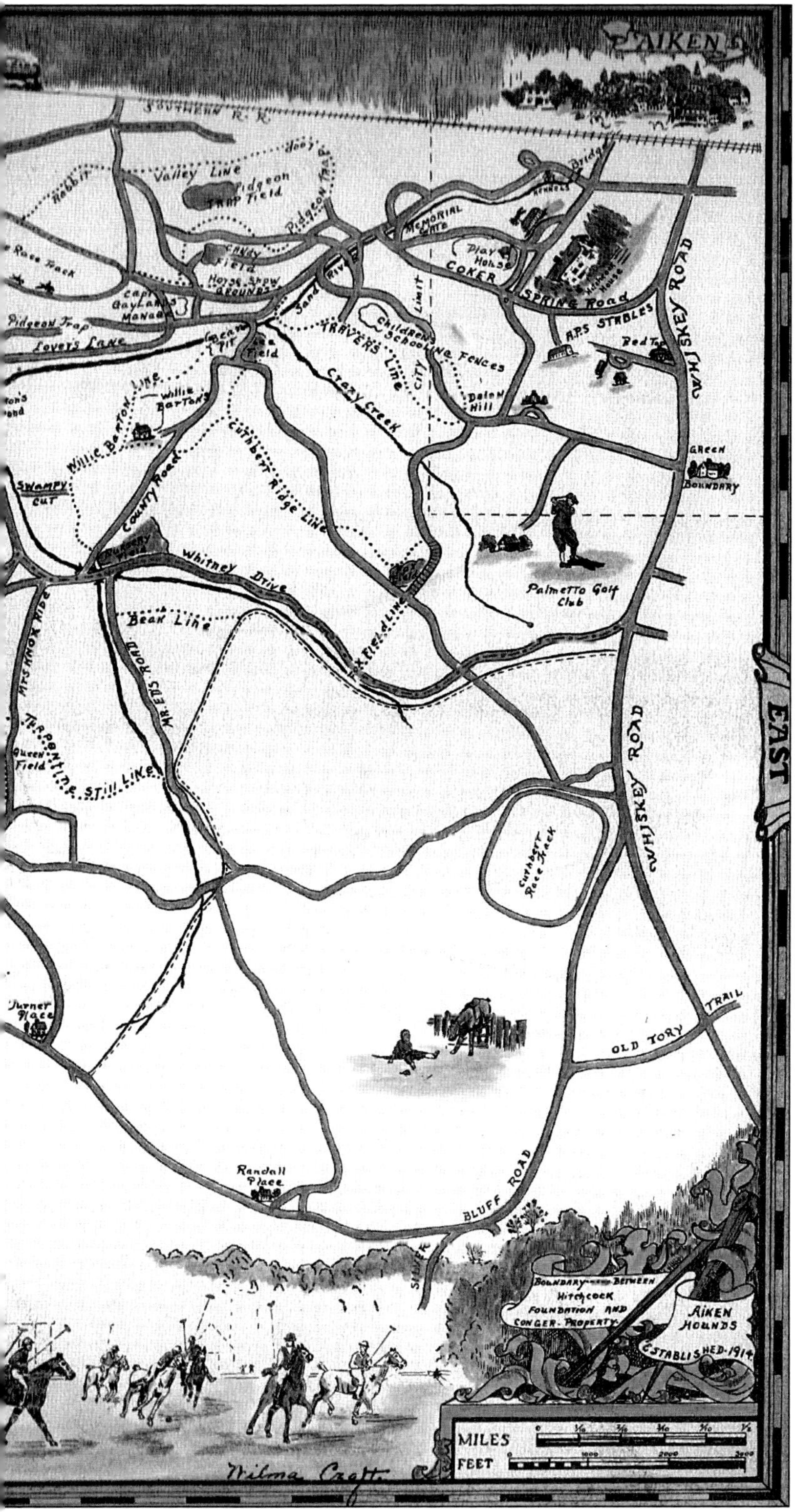

The 1956 Croft map of the Hitchcock Woods shows the Aiken Hounds drag lines, the property barriers, and roads that intertwine and encircle the woods. The sporting playground first of respite-seeking Charlestonians in summer, then the Winter Colony of patients seeking health remedies in the late 1800s, and the home of the swells from 1900 to 1960, Aiken's sporting culture has attracted many wealthy and famous people in the past, and the city's future is shaping up to be filled with similar sporting enthusiasts with compelling life stories to share over a stirrup cup or across a dinner table. (Brainard.)

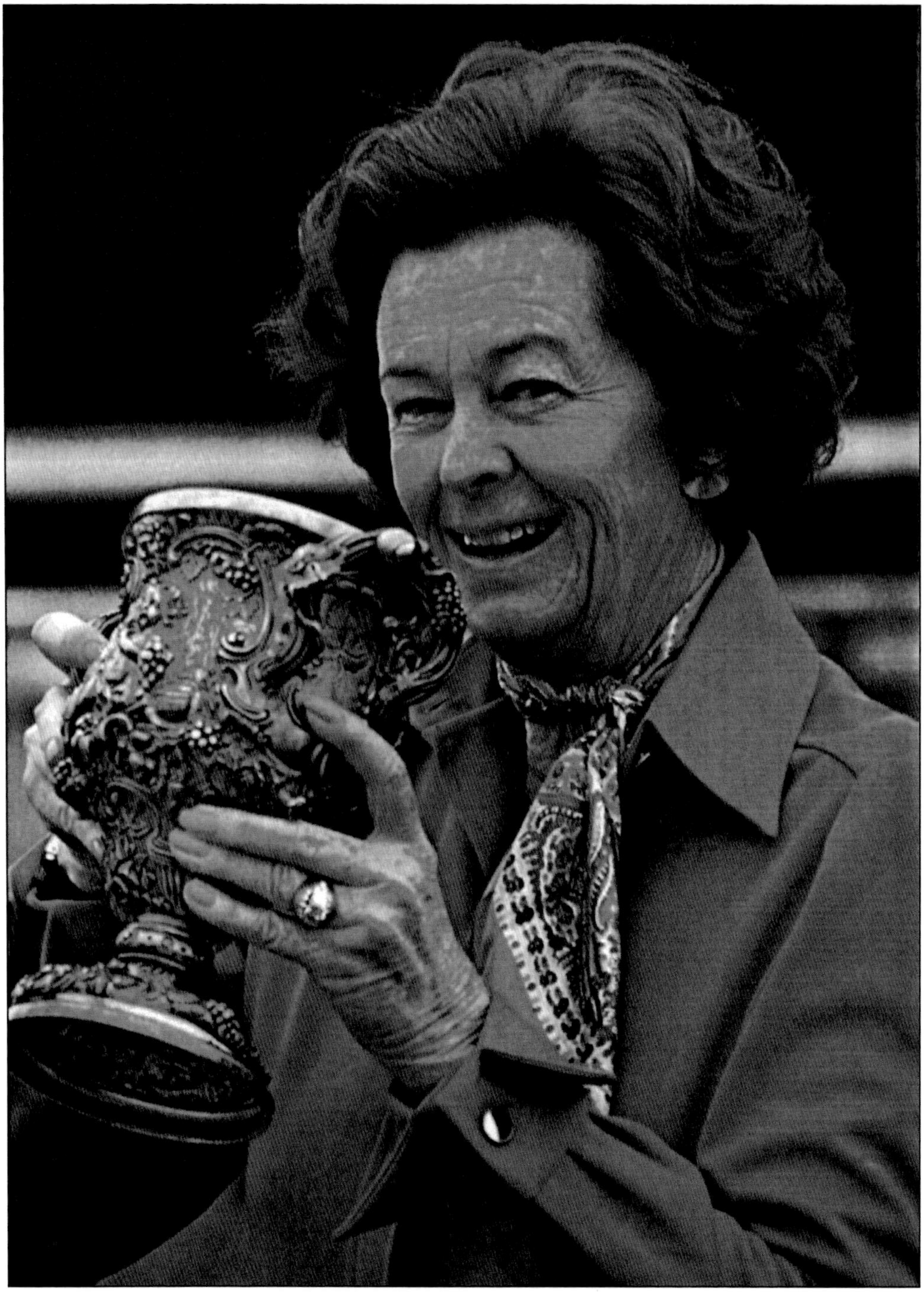

Drinking from the golden chalice, Betty Hassler Ruckelshaus embraced Aiken to its fullest. As a young girl, she played in the gymkhanas and polo matches; later, she was a master of hounds in her beloved Indiana. For several decades, she worked to maintain the tradition of the Aiken Horse Show in Hitchcock Woods. Her legacy will continue as the Aiken Horse Show enters its second century of joyous sport. (Ruckelshaus.)

Four

Sporting when Living was Hard

Wars, Prohibition, Taxes, and Seizure

In Aiken, Allan Pinkerton, a pro-Spain abolitionist, and Lucy Pickens, a pro-Cuba queen of the Confederacy, could dine at the same table with convivial repartee while the rest of the world seemed committed to conflict. South Carolina regiments have fought in every conflict since the Revolution. Aiken lost many native sons at the Alamo (1836), during the Mexican War (1846–1847) and in the Spanish-American War (1898). The state sustained huge losses during the Revolution, Civil War, and both world wars. Aiken also suffered uniquely during Reconstruction (1865–1877) as the only county formed during the federal occupation. Yeoman farmers and freedmen struggled to pay debts from lost crops and make repairs to burned homes. An 1869 article in *Frank Leslie's Illustrated Newspaper* stated, "The Industrial rehabilitation of Southern States is of much importance to the General Welfare of our Nation." Investment, in the guise of resort tourism, is yet another instance where school relationships mingled, creating mutually agreeable outcomes. Doctors prescribing the tonic air of Southern locales to wealthy patients served us well. That same article went on to say, "Perhaps the Healthiest location in the United States is Aiken."

Beyond the losses of war and the failure of Reconstruction was the sting of Prohibition. Southern bootleggers are now famous; yeoman farmers of the South included the freedmen population, and they had found strong commerce in good whiskey. From the cotton gin to sloe gin was a toast of the time, and many stories have been told about late-night runs on Whiskey Road. The next round of conflict in Aiken came when the federal government yet again came into the area and claimed whole towns: 310 square miles were seized for the construction of the Savannah River Site. Houses and businesses were moved from the towns of Ellenton and Dunbarton to new streets in Aiken; it seemed fitting that the streets were Gin, Sherry, and Mimosa. After the initial shock of another federal occupation in Aiken County wore off, locals were glad of new jobs and embraced the influx of new residents. Now, the Savannah River Site is a vital part of the area's socioeconomic landscape.

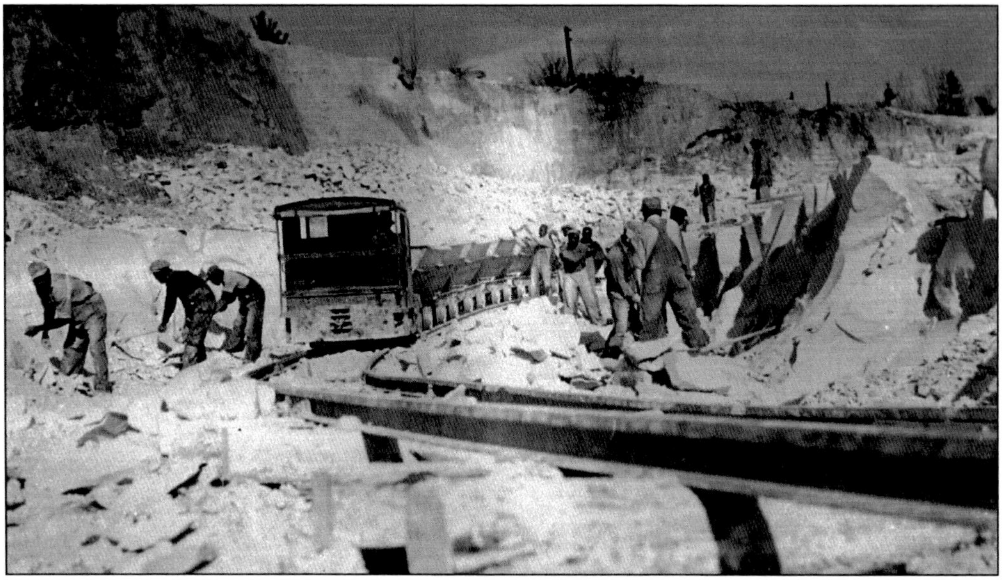

Kaolin and textile manufacturers have been the backbone of Aiken's non-tourist economy. Textile manufacturing had slowed during the Civil War despite its huge success as an industrial complex, and kaolin mining slacked due to the naval maneuvers during the world wars. In 1935, some 500 of the population of 6,000 worked in Aiken's kaolin mines. Kaolin mining is still an active part of the economy. Kaolin is used in products for the paper industry and porcelain manufacturing, like British-owned Wedgewood China, which rates Aiken kaolin as the purest in the world, and for rubber, chalk, and makeup products.

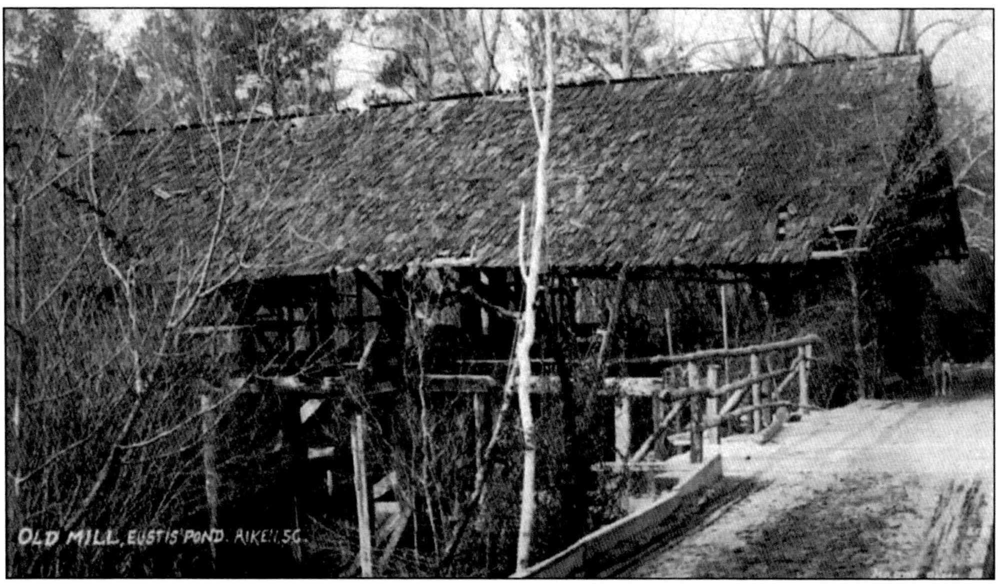

Barton's Mill at Eustis Pond shows the damage by neglect that so many Southern enterprises faced after years of war and great loss. Many of the area farmers saw the need by the 1930s to preserve forests; so much was being recklessly cut since timber was the only income many Southern families had at the time. The original members of the Aiken Soil Conservation District were W.D. Gregorie Jr., W.A. Coward, D.T. Mathis, H. Hahn, and F.W. Atkinson. Their grandchildren are still supporting conservation of Aiken's sporting traditions and farming heritage.

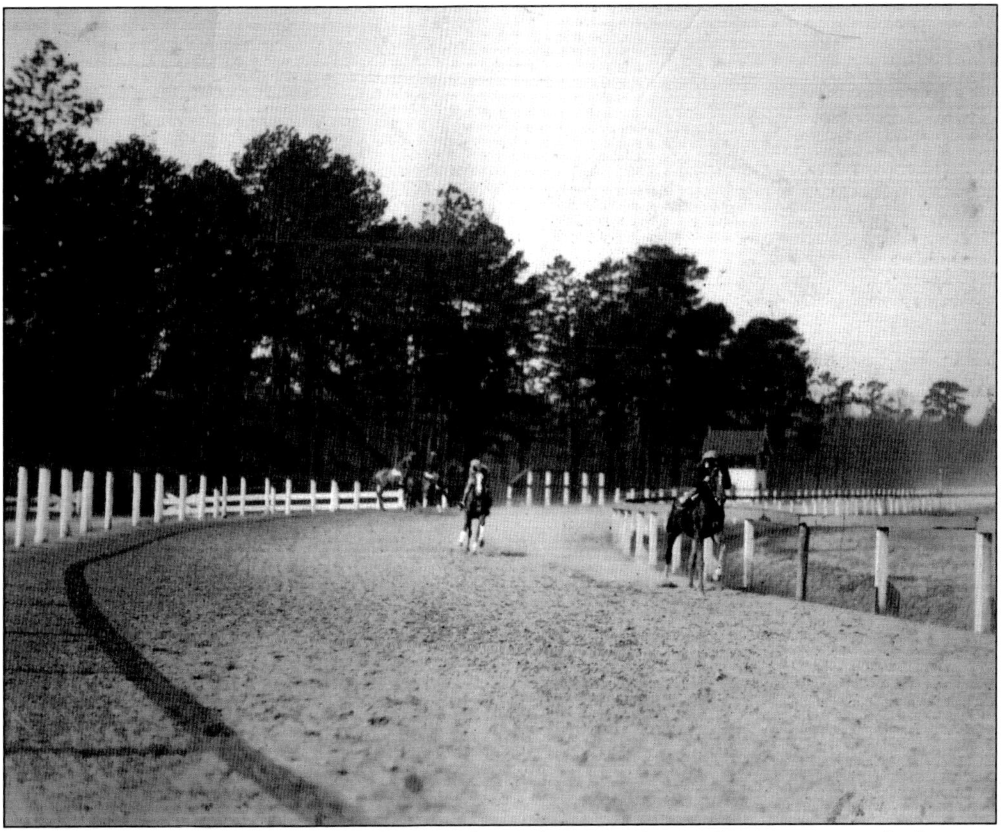

The main training track was finished in 1941 by Fred H. Post, famous horse trainer and salesman. The other training tracks and polo fields built during the Great Depression, and the federal courthouse construction, meant jobs stayed in the area when in other places jobs were hard to find. Even when the tourists went on to other locations, they asked their Aiken staff to travel with them as trusted members of the family. (Tower.)

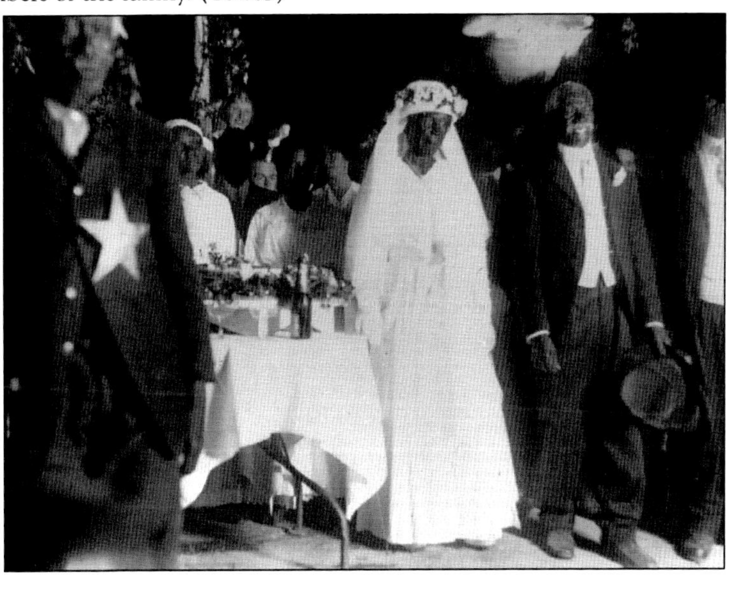

The Joneses never legally married after the war, so the Phelpses helped make it happen. Blending the lives of so many traveling to keep pace with the sporting life of the American royalty was a challenge. When asked about his time with Hitchcock, Pete Greene, America's first African American jockey, said riding those horses was the best thing in life.

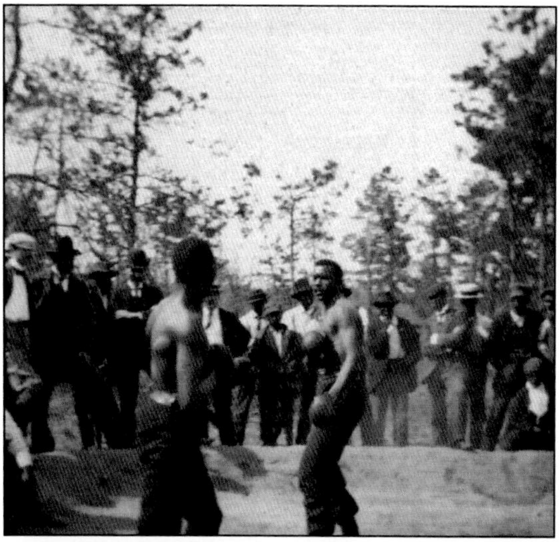

Thomas Hitchcock was a respected pugilist. He taught many men, both white and black, the art and coached them in fitness. Aiken's boxing club in these modern times instills the same concepts of hard work and dedication in young men looking for careers in the sport or just seeking the dedication of a true athlete.

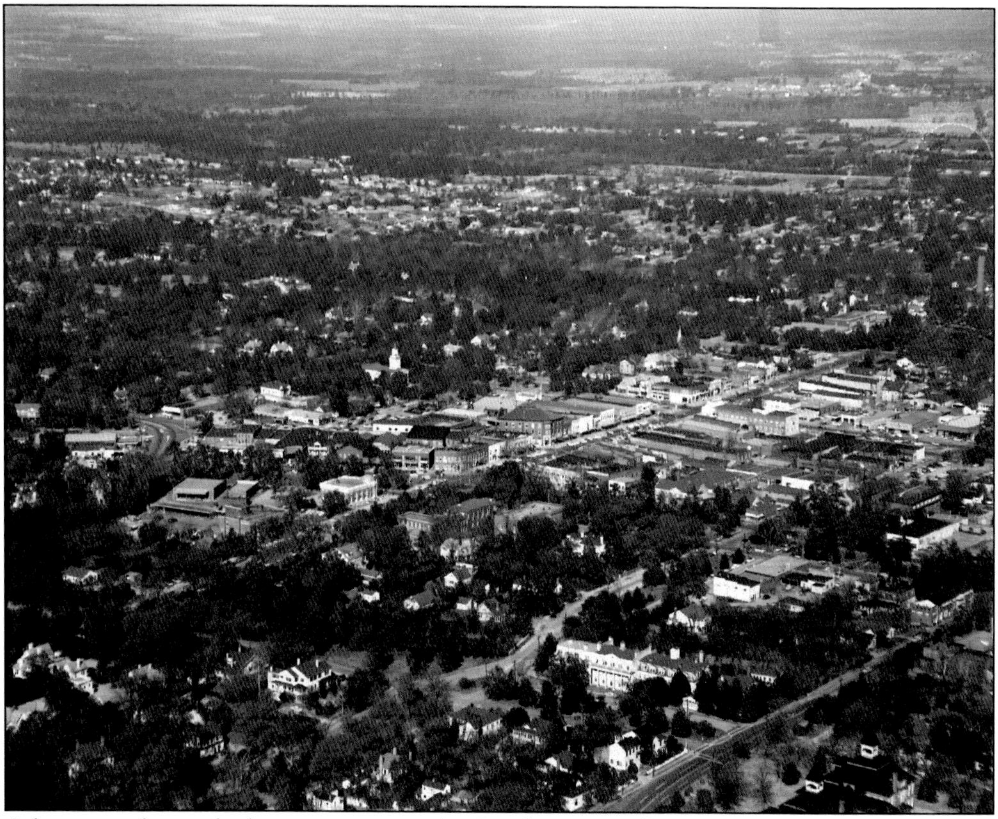

Aiken went from a little resort town in the South to a small metropolis overnight when the Savannah River Site was announced. Temporary housing sprouted up, like Robbins Trailer Village, with its 4,000 units to house workers, while abandoned historic homes were divided into apartments or torn down to make way for new brick ranches. Towns were moved. The fight for property rights against the government's eminent domain brought forth Strom Thurmond. He emerged as an advocate for the little man against the big government. In 1954, Thurmond became the first US senator elected as a write-in candidate. (Lista.)

Rosalie Brown Dolan (pictured), and Hope Goddard Iselin were masters of the mule races in Aiken. During and after World War I, horses were not as readily available, so mule races became a sport both on the flat and over fences. Hope Goddard was an America's Cup sailor, renowned golfer, and game race rider; the mule races were so popular they remained a part of the steeplechase race card until the 1980s.

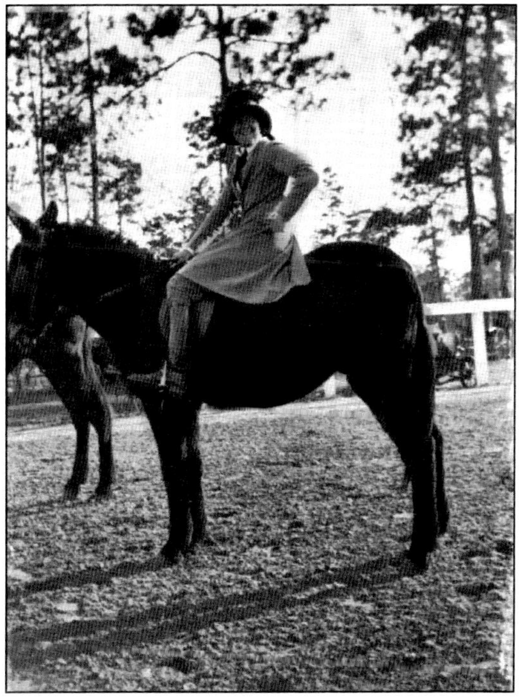

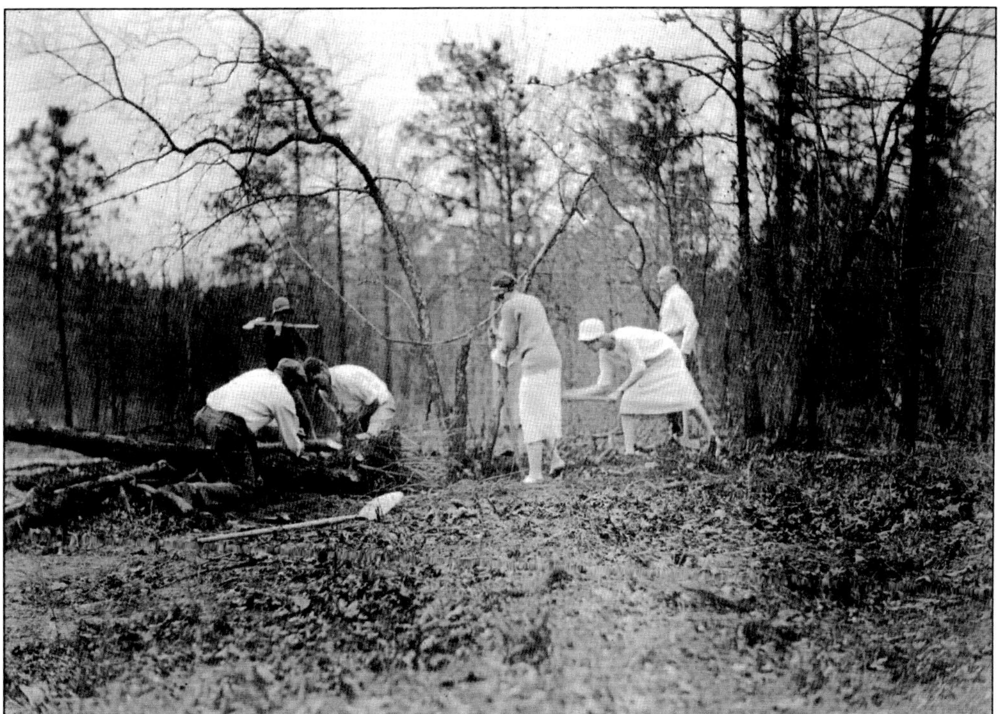

Devereaux Milburn wrote in the centennial program, "The Depression took a toll on Aiken. It even reduced the number of in town Polo fields from 17 to 8." But that did not hinder the enthusiasm for Aiken winters during that time. Clearing areas around the horse show grounds prior to March brought people of all situations together. (Brainard.)

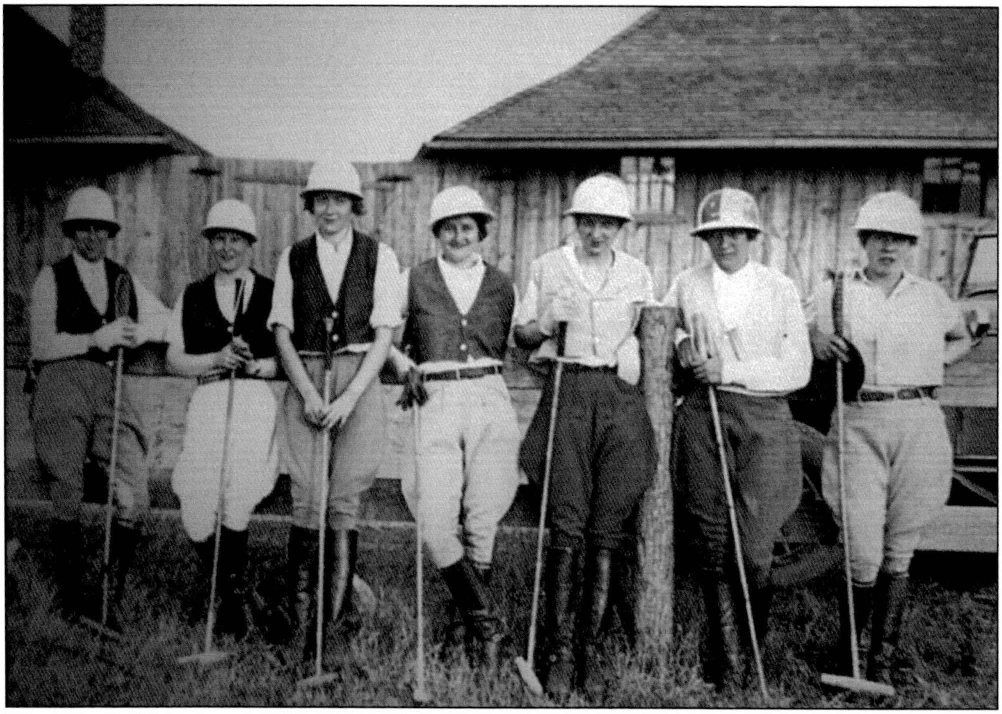

The *New York Times* noted, "In Aiken the women play polo at the same level as the men exhibiting the same prowess and skill." Pictured here from left to right, Molly Crawford, Anne Schley, Frances Post, Louise Richardson, Euna Crawford, Josefa Hoffman, and Margaret Flick played at the handicaps given to their fathers, husbands, and brothers during the world wars in order to keep polo play in Aiken undisturbed. This is why the Whitney Polo Field is the oldest continuously played polo field in the country.

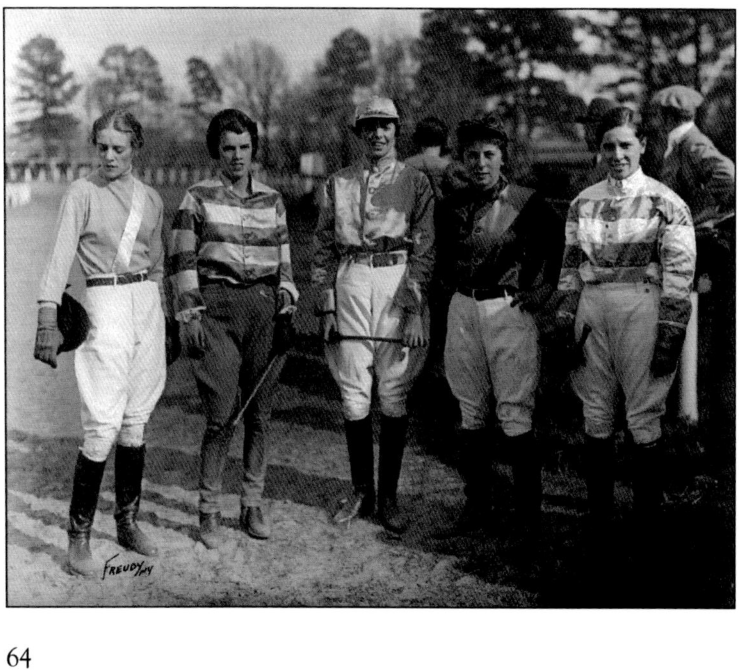

Women also took to the racing silks and rode horses in races when jockeys were at war. Pictured here from left to right are Mrs. Whitney, Balding, Redmond, Olcott, and McKinney, who raced in place of the men. The very popular Diana Cup races were established to showcase the fearless desire for victory that these ladies exhibited when racing. (Brainard.)

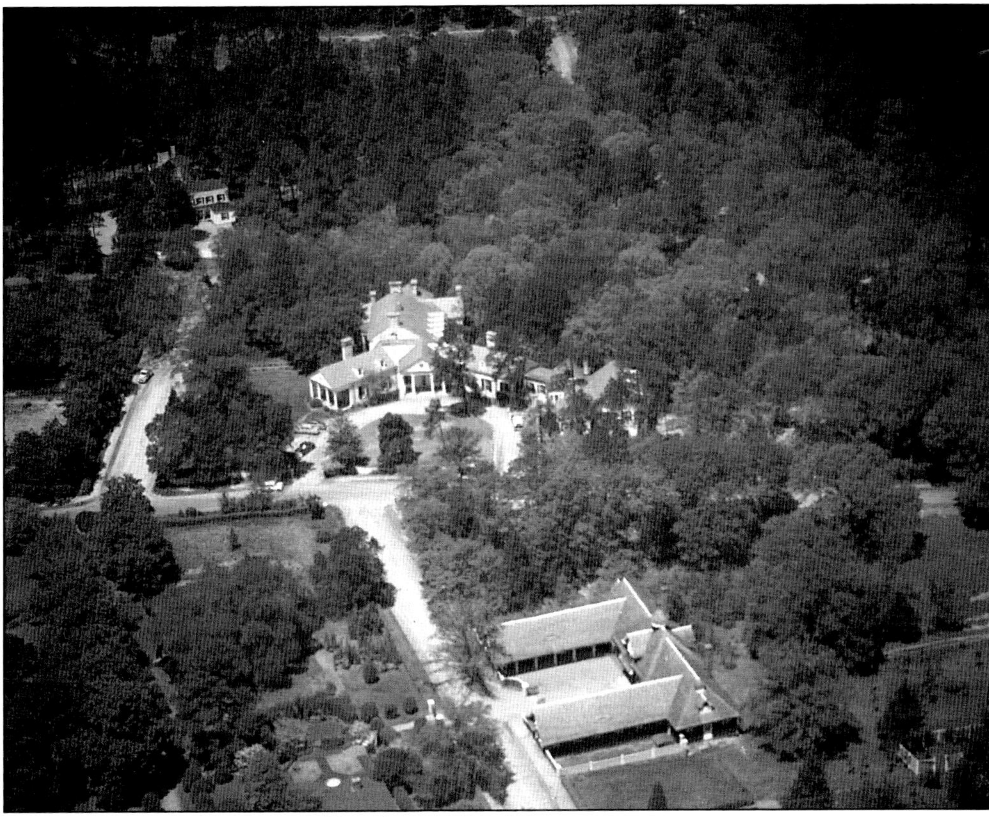

Houses in Aiken have changed hands and purposes many times, a reflection of the hardship the town faced. Either for charitable reasons or because of economic ones, some of the great homes in Aiken have been turned over for public purposes. The Aiken County Museum was originally the Howe Estate. It has also served as the University of South Carolina Aiken campus. The Iselin Estate, Hopeland, and the Rogers estate, Rye Patch, are now public gardens and city entertaining space.

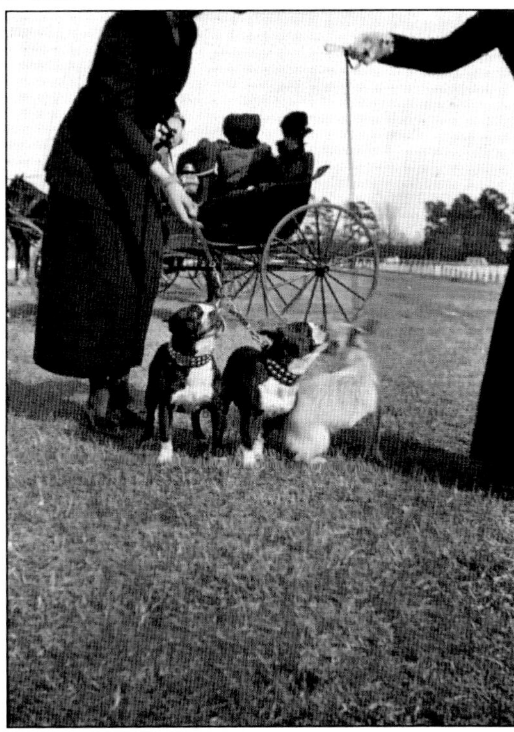

Eleanor Phelps captured her beloved bulldogs on film during an afternoon stroll along the boards of the polo field. Some 125 years later, Aiken devotees follow in the same paw prints of the Phelps canines. The legacy of appreciation for breeds of horses, dogs, birds, and even cats is something Aiken promotes with various animal-rescue groups and the Silver Bluff Audubon Sanctuary.

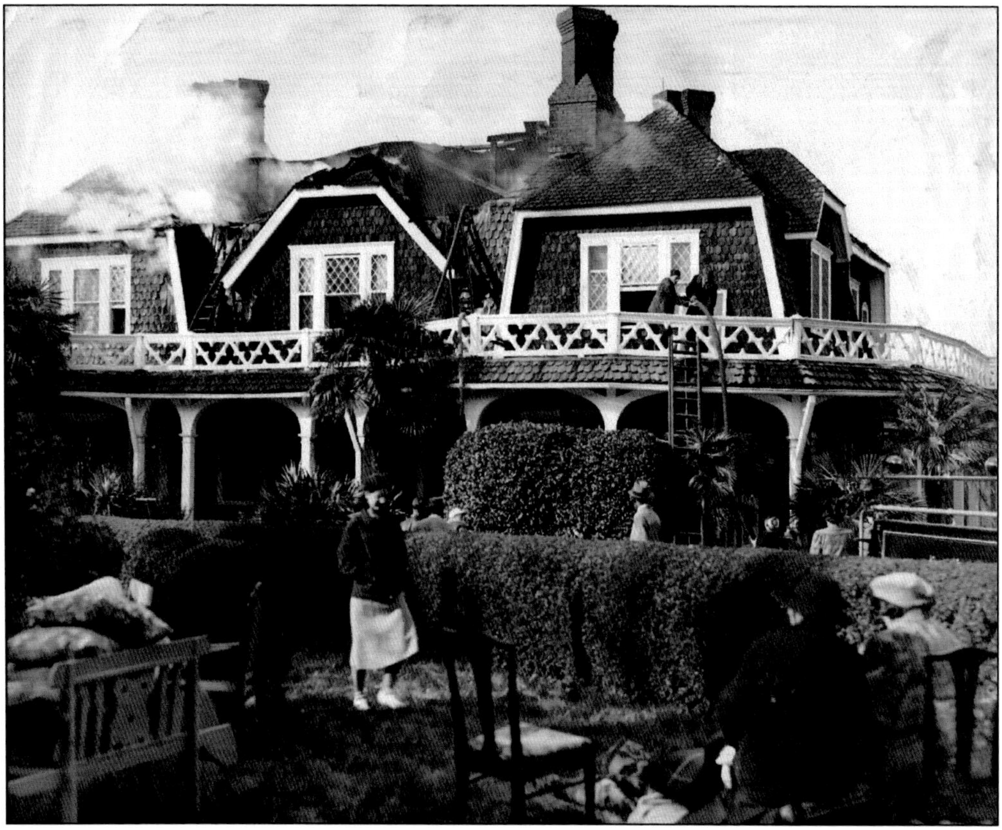

Many treasured architectural buildings both public and private were lost to fires over the years. When Calico Cottage burned, members of the household rescued the grand piano, and someone sat down and played a concert while the neighbors rushed to put out the fire. (Brainard.)

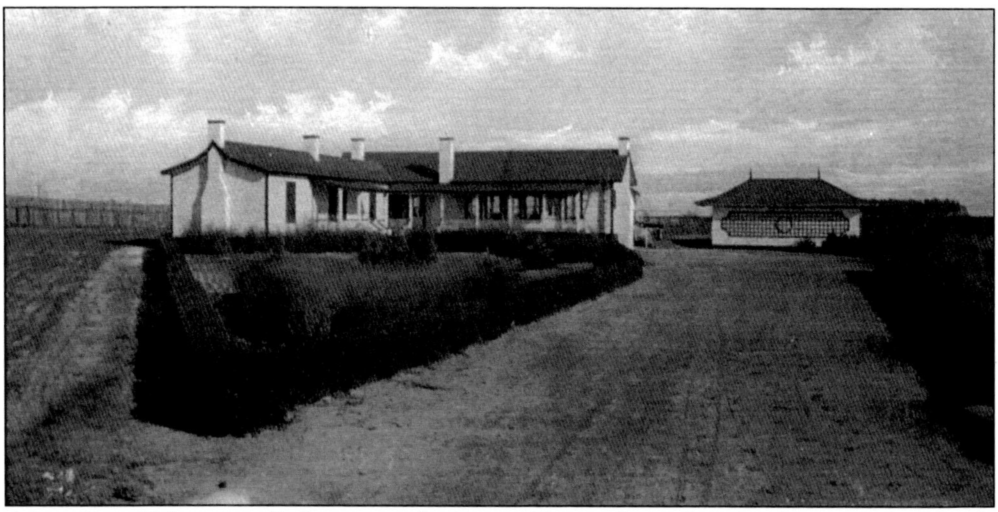

Aiken Gun Club, originally known as the Pigeon Trap, is located at the far east end of South Boundary Avenue. Now a private residence, the gun club is much reduced from its original 15,000 acres. In modern times, several commercial enterprises and manufacturers such as Zeus and Manner Supply can be seen from here in the distance.

Shooting from horseback while in the field is a skill mastered by some. But in times of hardship, squirrel and pigeon was a mainstay in the Southern diet. Celestine Eustis's cookbook *Cooking in Olde Creole Days* has several recipes for rabbit and squirrel ragout.

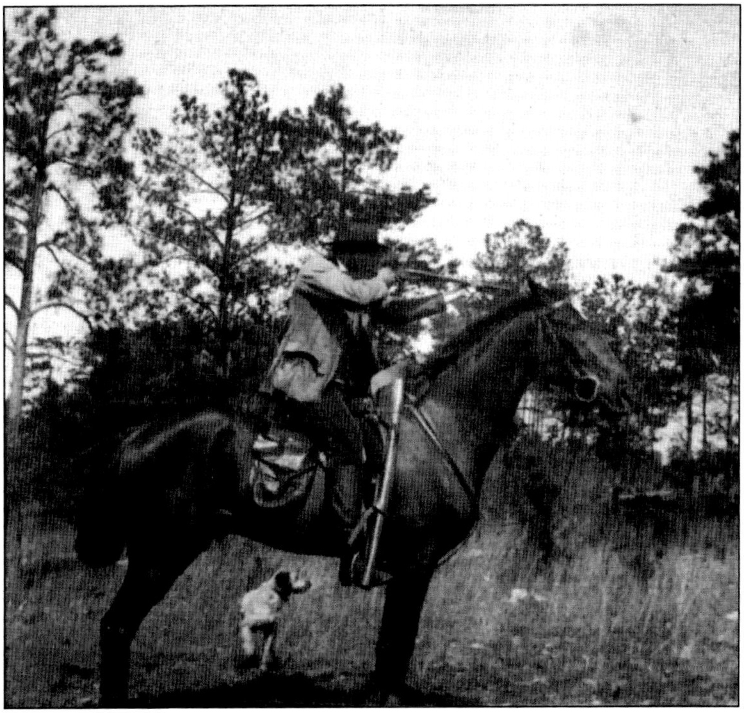

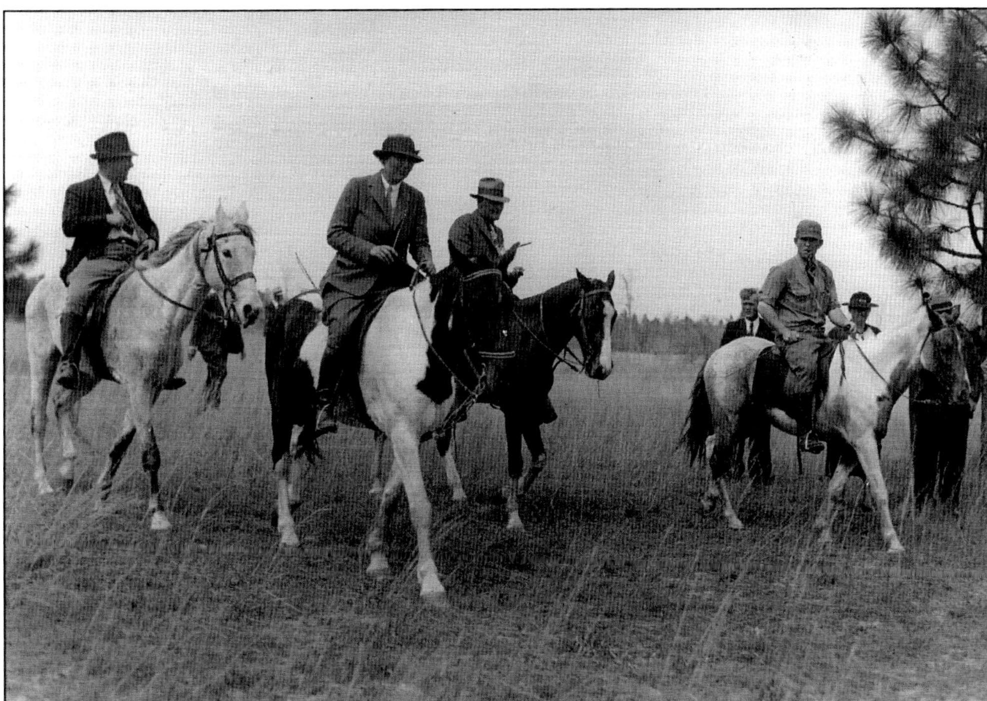

Eleanor Phelps Wilds (center) leads a group into the field for one of the Phelps family sporting trials. Equestrian pursuits in 2008 were determined to be a $74 million industry in Aiken based solely on horse value and entries paid. That legacy would not be possible if it had not been for the families who persevered through hard economic times and the losses suffered during war.

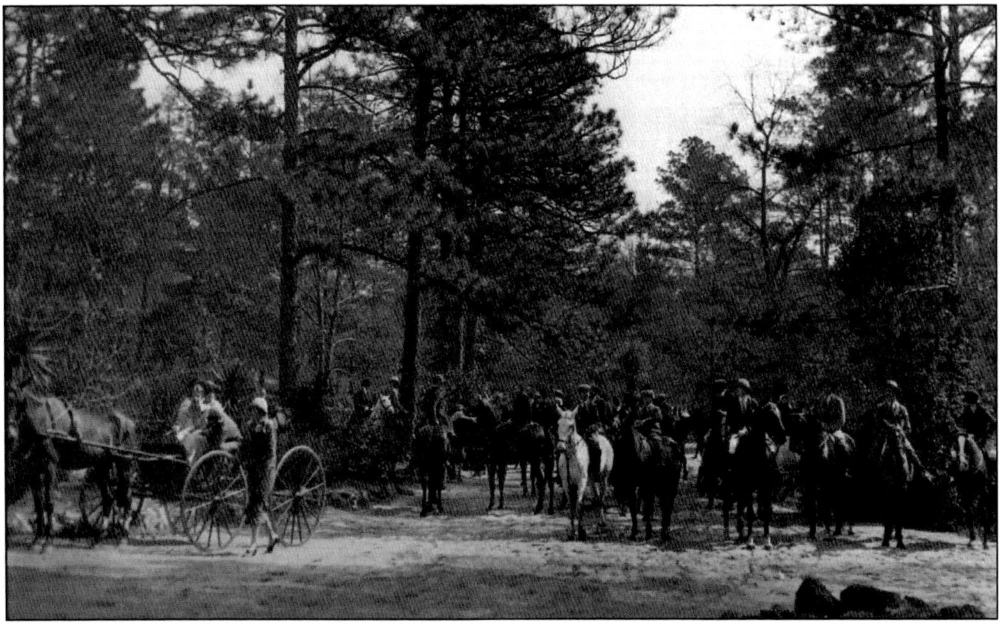

Devereaux Milburn, polo scion, reflected on his times in Aiken during and after World War I, in which he pursued every equine sport available: "The beauty is the horses, they are an essential part of Aiken and that they will continue to be is as certain as anything can be in life, because people who love horses naturally are attracted to Aiken." (Brainard.)

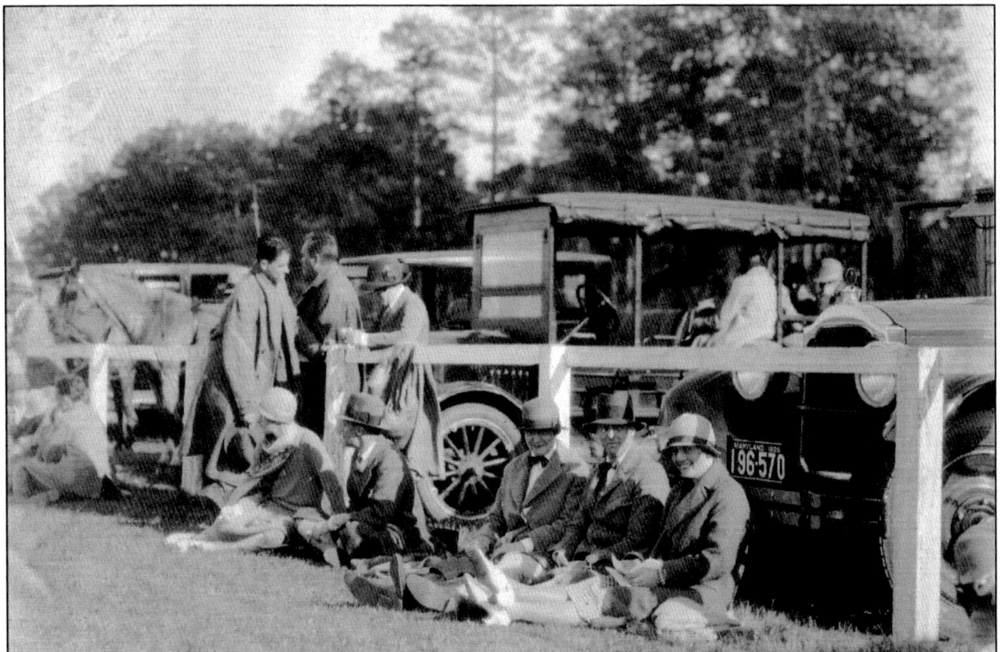

No matter the tragedies and hardships experienced in the world, levity could be found sitting on the grass watching a polo game in Aiken. *Time* magazine noted, "The Bostwicks thought a cure for the Great Depression was 'Polo for the Masses' so they did not charge for parking at either their New York or Aiken games." (Brainard.)

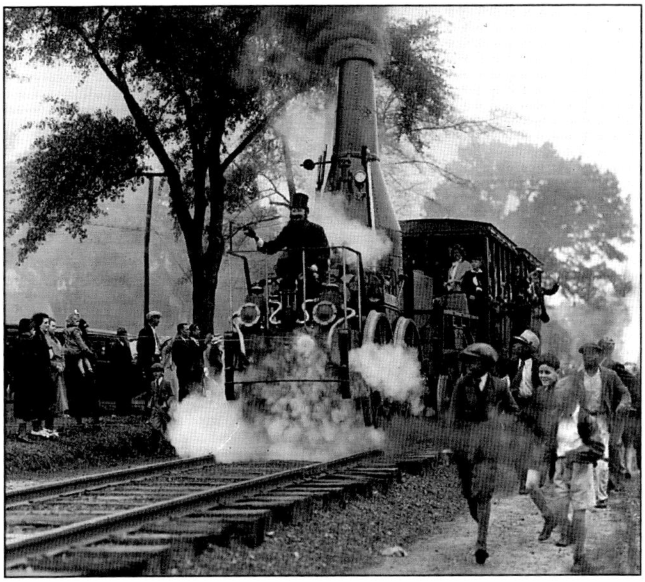

The Best Friend Express was the train line that took passengers from Aiken Depot to Hamburg. The replica of the train seen here in 1957 drew quite a crowd. Festivities centered on bringing the past together with the future. The scientists who worked at SRS and their families brought to Aiken national charitable works that remain a vital part of the community. The American Heart Association and the United Way campaign are examples of Aiken's modern commitment to national causes. (Tower.)

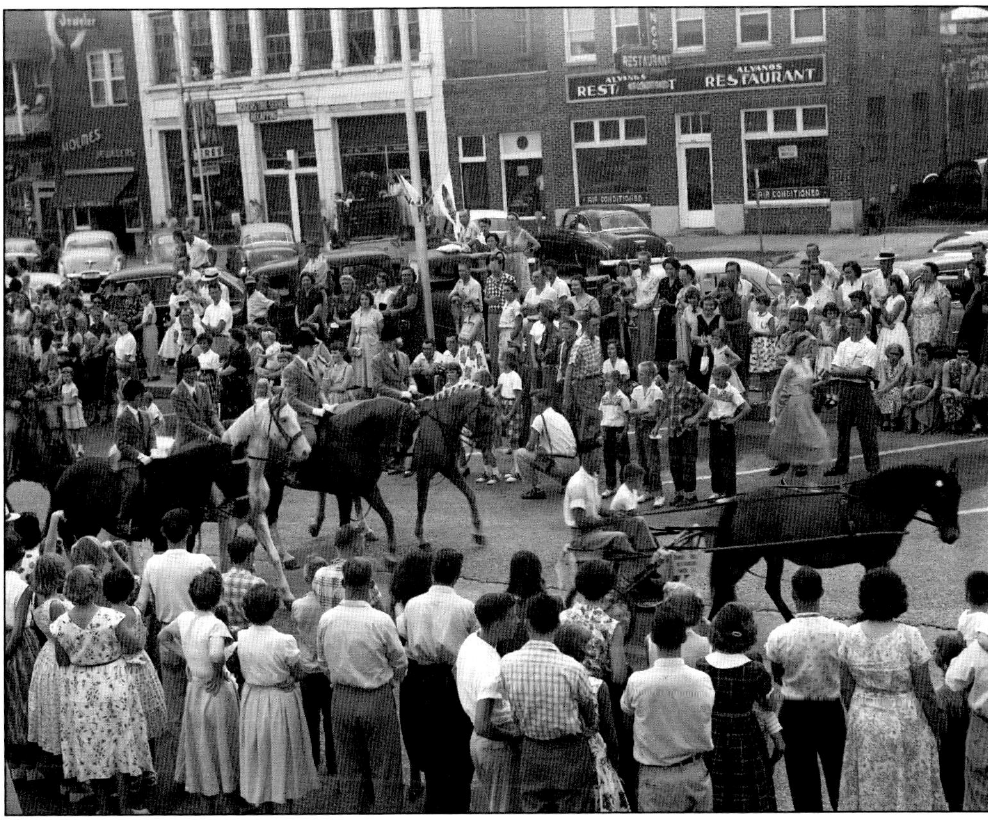

The horse parade brought the community together. By 1957, the division created by the building of the Savannah River Site needed to be quelled, so bridging the gap with a toast to the equine heritage that farmers and foxhunters, Thoroughbred horse racing, and polo, trail riders, barrel racers, and the average cowboy share in Aiken was in order. A travel writer once said: "Where the Horse is King, Aiken is its Shrine."

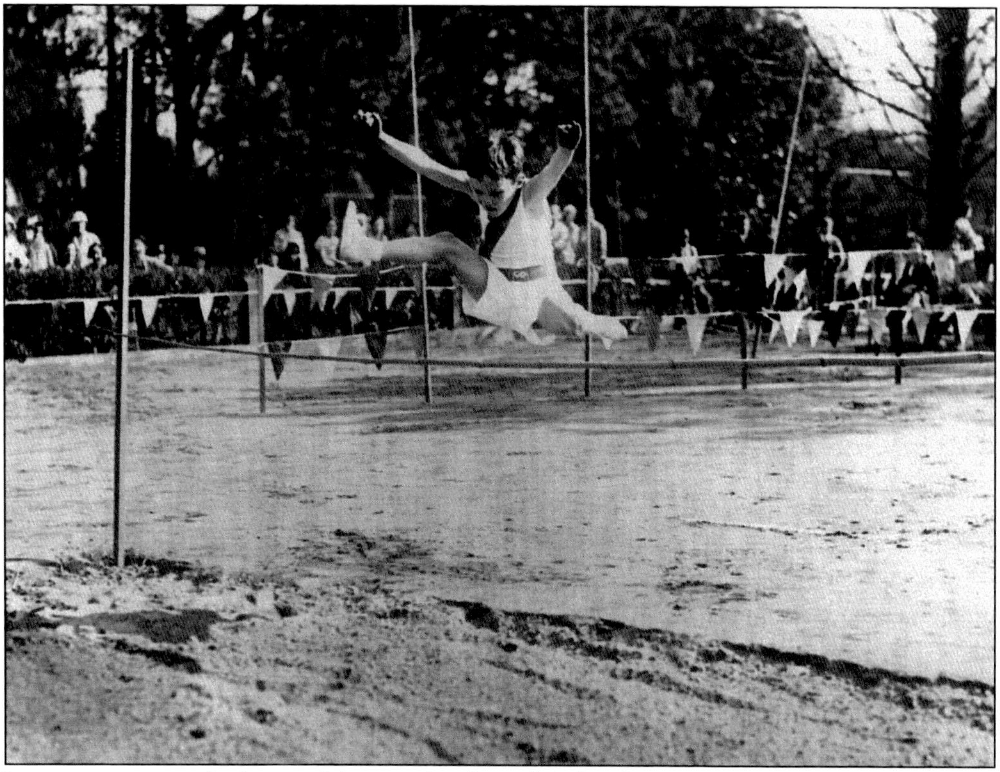

Perseverance is at the heart of the people who call Aiken home. Over the decades, traditions have died away or been absorbed by others. Fermata School, Aiken Day School, and Saint Angela Academy may not exist anymore, and Aiken Prep and Mead Hall may have merged, but the spirit and triumph of those students live on.

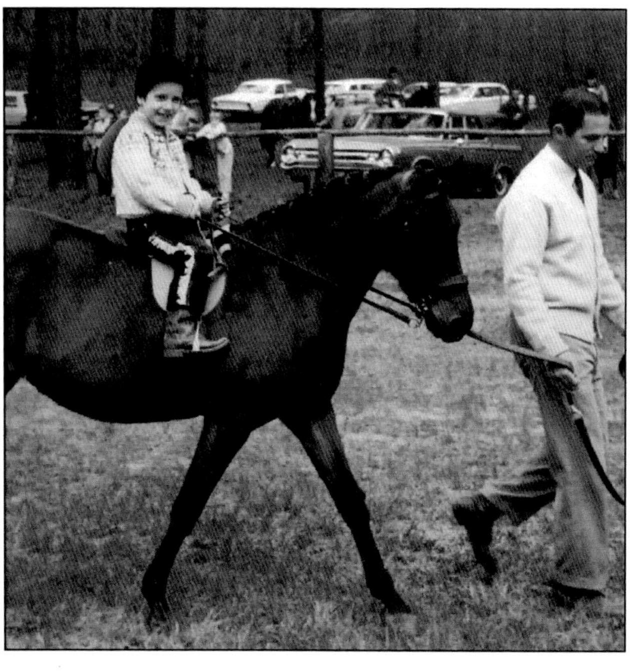

Willard Thompson leads his son Glenn in the lead-line class in 1966. Glenn's pony dropped him eight times this day, and he did not get back on a horse for 30 years. Now Glenn Thompson can be found on his pony with his racehorses schooling on the five-eighths track in front of his Aiken race barn. (Glenn Thompson.)

Frolic Weymouth is in the place to be seen, driving in the carriage parade at Aiken Steeplechase with Gov. Nikki Haley, the first woman of minority descent elected to statewide office. She has been labeled the leader of the new South, and with that comes an understanding of the vitality that innovation and outside investment have brought to the state and Aiken. (Author's collection.)

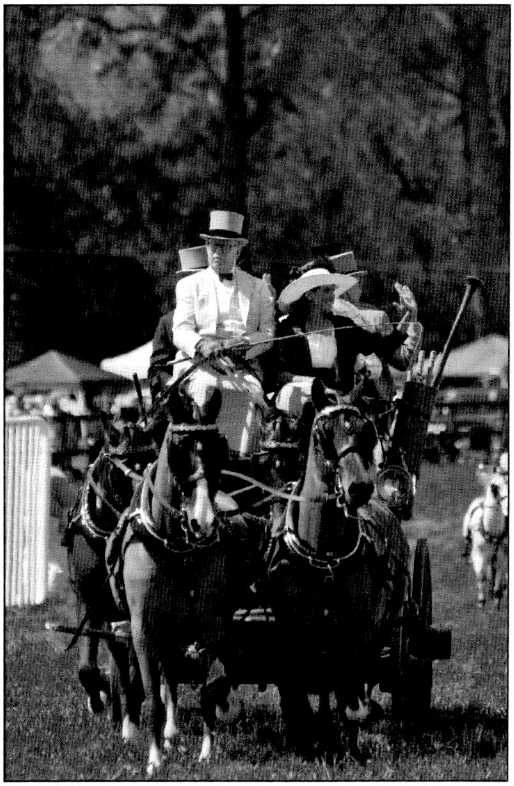

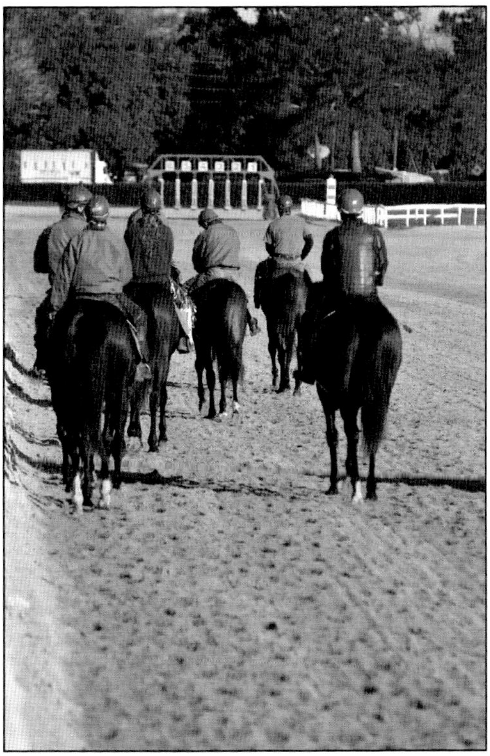

Aiken's draw is not limited to governors or American investment; rulers of nations had interests in Aiken. Sheikh Mohammed bin Rashid Al Maktoum, the ruler of Dubai and prime minister of the United Arab Emirates, and his family have a legacy of fine racehorses and their Darley and Godolphin racing stables sported bright blue when schooling at the training track. (Thompson.)

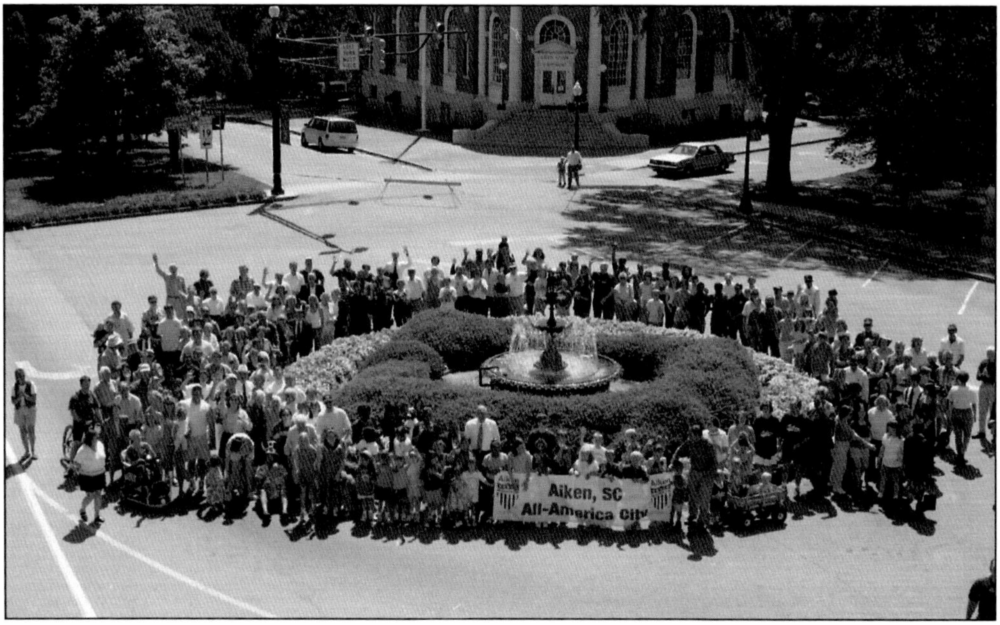

Aiken was named an All-America City in 1997. A great deal of emphasis is placed on the local heritage for rankings such as this, and the citizens were thrilled to be a part of the process. Civic balance has been a priority of public officials since the DuPont announcement and will continue to be going forward.

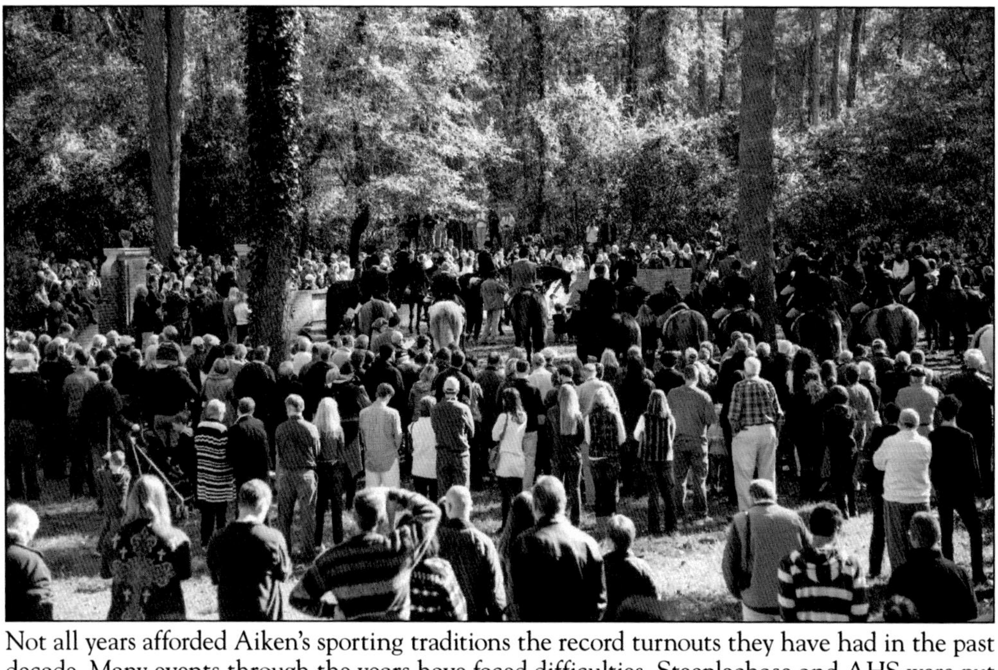

Not all years afforded Aiken's sporting traditions the record turnouts they have had in the past decade. Many events through the years have faced difficulties. Steeplechase and AHS were put on hiatus during World War II. The harness races struggled after the city's ownership, the Trials faced funding issues when the big barns dissolved, and even the blessing has been postponed in the last 100 years. But with Aiken's love of sport and the businesses and volunteers that commit to organizations, traditions rebound and thrive. (Lista's Studio.)

Five

Carrying on Family Traditions

Generations of Horse People, Merchants, and Visitors

Since 1730, the Salley, Toole, Durban, Walker, Coward, Henderson, Kneece, Polier, Williams, Brinkley, Dibble, Price, Cushman, Surasky, and Burckhalter families in the area developed as farmers, merchants, and professionals. Joining their efforts from 1830 to 1880 were the health-resort owners and their affiliated doctors, and from 1880 to 1945, the swells of wealthy American and European aristocrats anchored Aiken life. From 1950 to today, a variety of scientists, engineers, snowbirds, and retirees call Aiken home and so do their children.

A sense of a generational commitment to Aiken sporting traditions have kept them going. In 1995, Linda Knox McLean returned as a fulltime resident to serve as master of Aiken hounds, as her grandmother, great-aunt, and mother did before her. Since 1991, Georgianna Conger Wolcott works as a fulltime volunteer for the Aiken Steeplechase Association in honor of her father, Ford, and his dedication to that sport's continuation in Aiken. The Coward brothers are involved in many of Aiken's sporting concerns, while Alice Knowles, Dolly Bostwick, and Glenn Thompson are at the Aiken Training Track with their Thoroughbreds running the same turns as their parents' and grandparents' horses.

Into the future, Grace Ellis, Alan and Patricia Corey's granddaughter, plays polo with the Kneece children, and Arden Wildesin is building her sporting resume as her parents help to protect the pine forests from being forever lost. The Toole-Miller equine force is apparent at the Aiken Horse Show and with Aiken Hounds. Camden Riviere, a champion court tennis player, is the product of several generations who fostered sporting talent. Kevin Kisner's daughter has already been given a golf club, so the next generation will be ready to tee off at Palmetto.

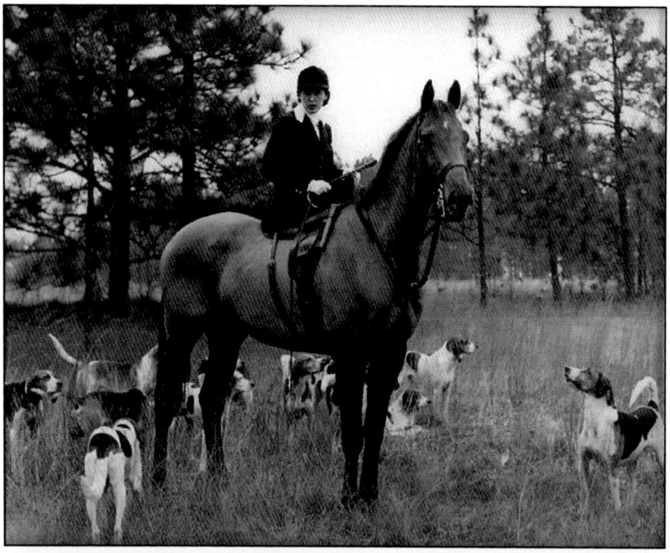

Linda Knox McLean, Julian Peabody, and Stephany Hitchcock have promoted the sporting life their parents and grandparents worked hard to protect. The Hitchcock Woods Foundation sponsors an annual essay contest, the Celestine Eustis Prize, to foster that same spirit in the next generation. Helen Knox, pictured here, passed on her Aiken convictions to her descendants. (McLean.)

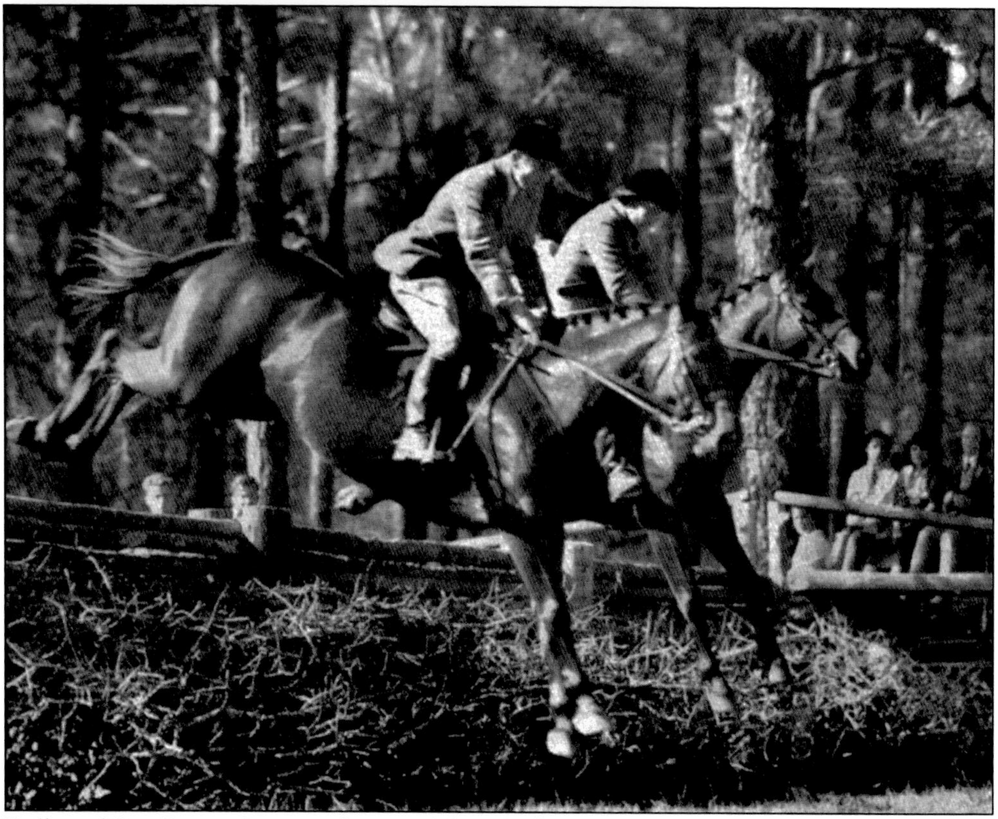

Dolly and Pete Bostwick were a force in Aiken. Dolly von Stade Bostwick served as a master of Aiken hounds for over 25 years. Pete, a world-renowned polo player and racehorse trainer, passed on those passions to his polo-playing son Charlie and his racehorse-training daughter Dolly. The Bostwick grandchildren have participated in the family and costume classes at the Aiken Horse Show, and granddaughter Tara Gail has had much success on the national horse-show circuit. (Ruckelshaus.)

The Aiken Horse Show (AHS) has long been the scene of the passing of the proverbial baton; as a young girl, Linda Knox McLean watches the show ring with her grandmother Helen Northrup Knox. The Knox family legacy in Aiken goes beyond horses into golf and court tennis. Linda and her brother Norty live on through their children and their grandchildren, who represent the fifth generation of Knoxes to ride to hounds or strike a ball in Aiken. (McLean.)

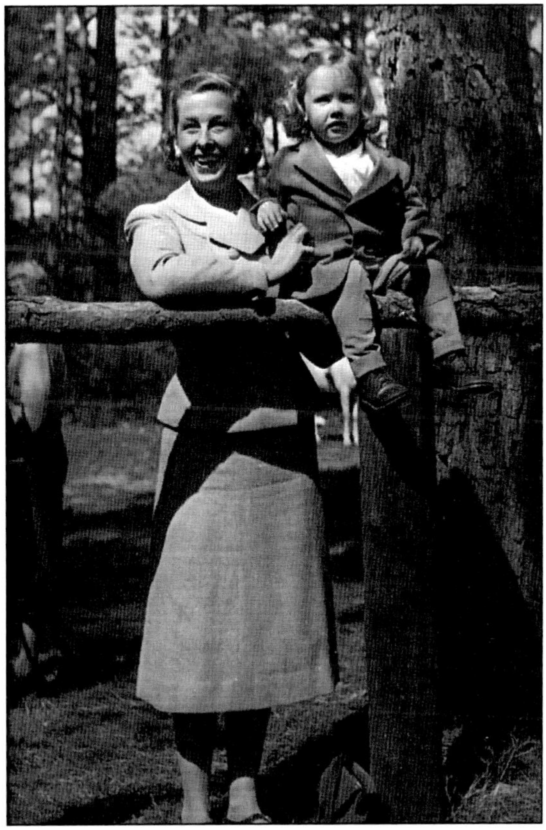

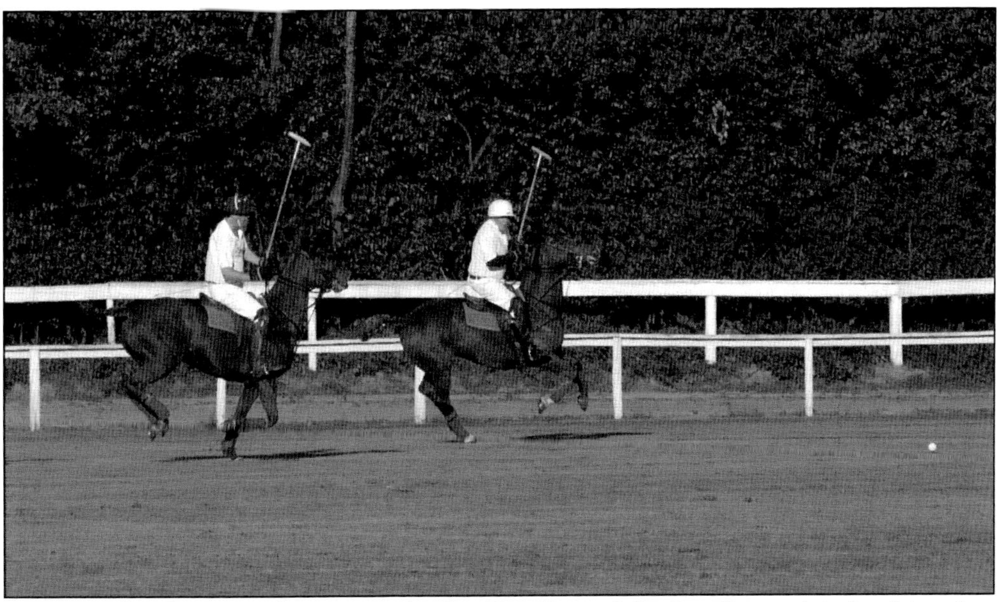

In 2015, Aiken lost one of its scions of polo, Alan Corey. Like Pete Bostwick before him, they both died at 73 playing polo. Going out with one's boots on is a great reward for a life spent in the saddle. Pictured here are Geoff Ellis (left) and Alan Corey, father and stepson teammates chasing down the line of the ball. (Author's collection.)

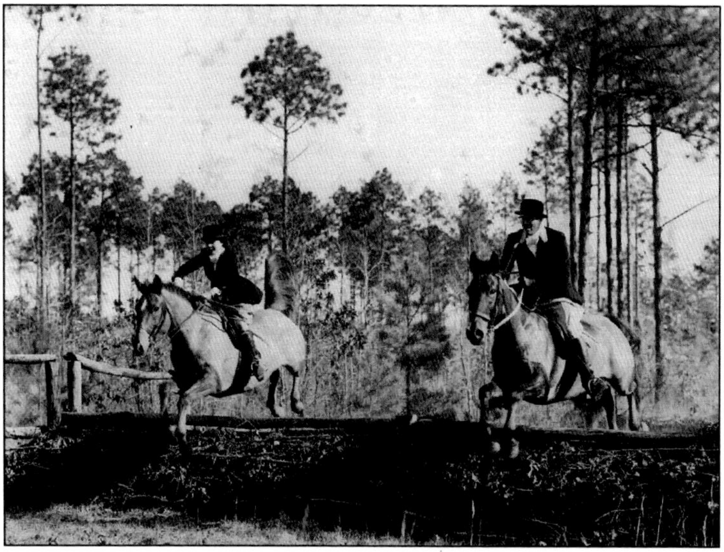

Over the fences at Cathedral Aisle, Courtney Conger (left) and Ford Conger are in perfect sync. The Congers' granddaughter Caroline Wolcott was the junior whip with Aiken Hounds in 2013. Daughter Georgianna and her brother Alan are both very involved in the Aiken Steeplechase, and grandson Ford has taken a keen interest in the sport of horse racing. (Conger.)

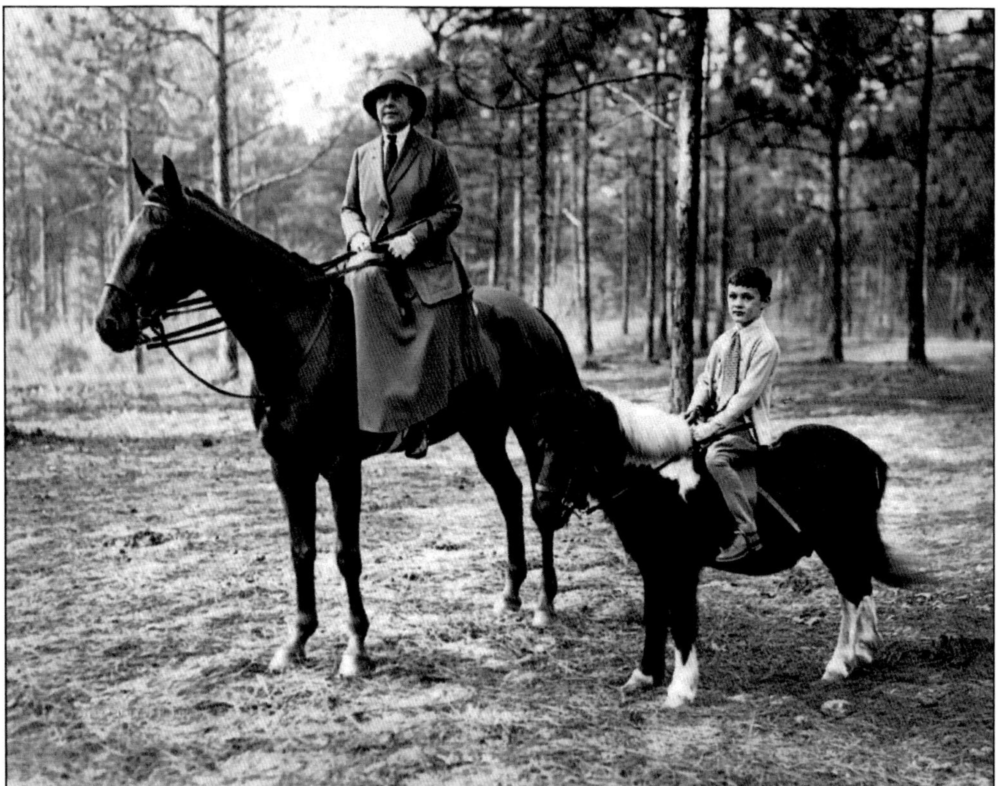

Rita Dolan and the Toland and Sellar grandchildren have long been associated with AHS and Aiken Hounds. Rosalie Sellar Brainard passed away during hunting season in 2014. It is through her husband, Peter's, memorial legacy that many of the Dolan Sellar family photographs appear in this book for the first time in print. (Brainard.)

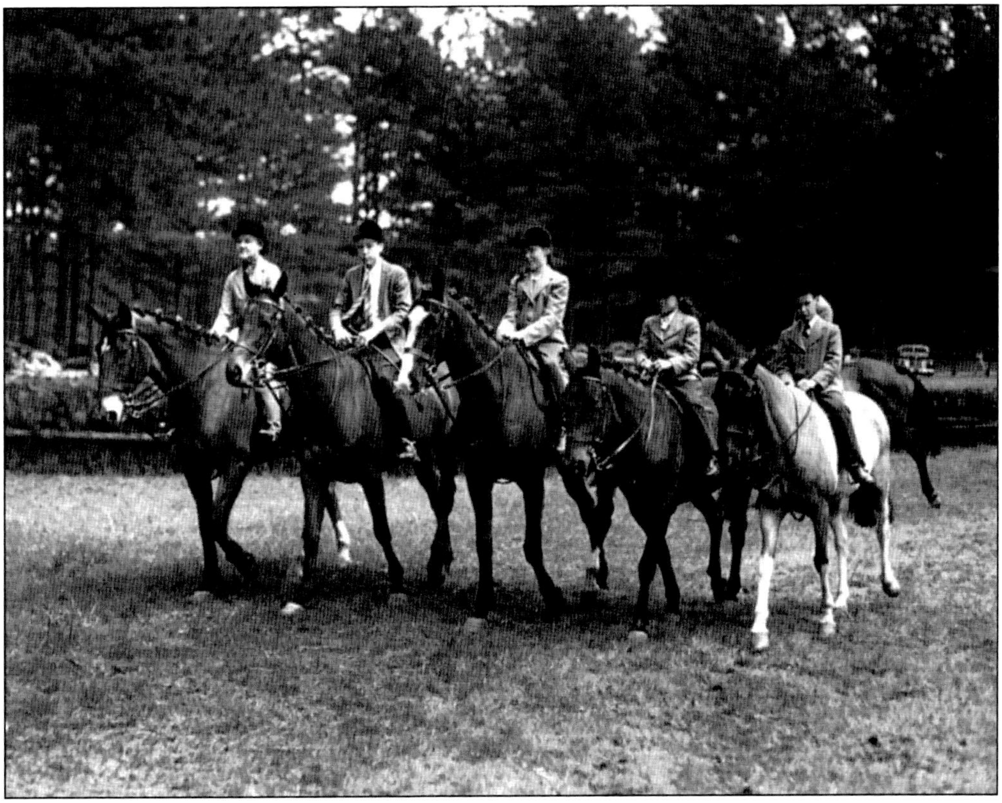

The family class at AHS was a veritable who's who of Aiken's past and future. The Dolan family, pictured here, showcases festive braiding and matching turnout. Judged on skill and coordination, the family class is a coveted prize and grows more competitive each year. (Brainard.)

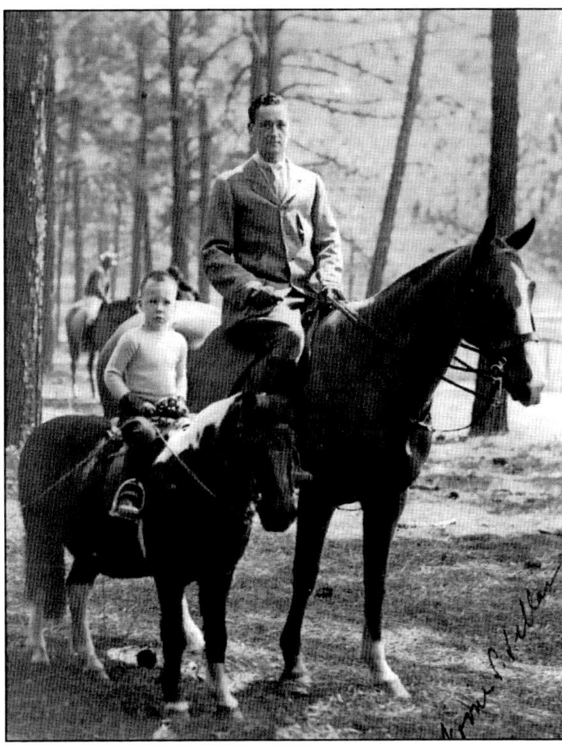

Father and son Norrie Sellar and Junior take to the woods for a casual ride. From their stables on Berrie Road at Calico Cottage, the Sellars could reach Travers Line and Captain Gaylard's fences with ease. (Brainard)

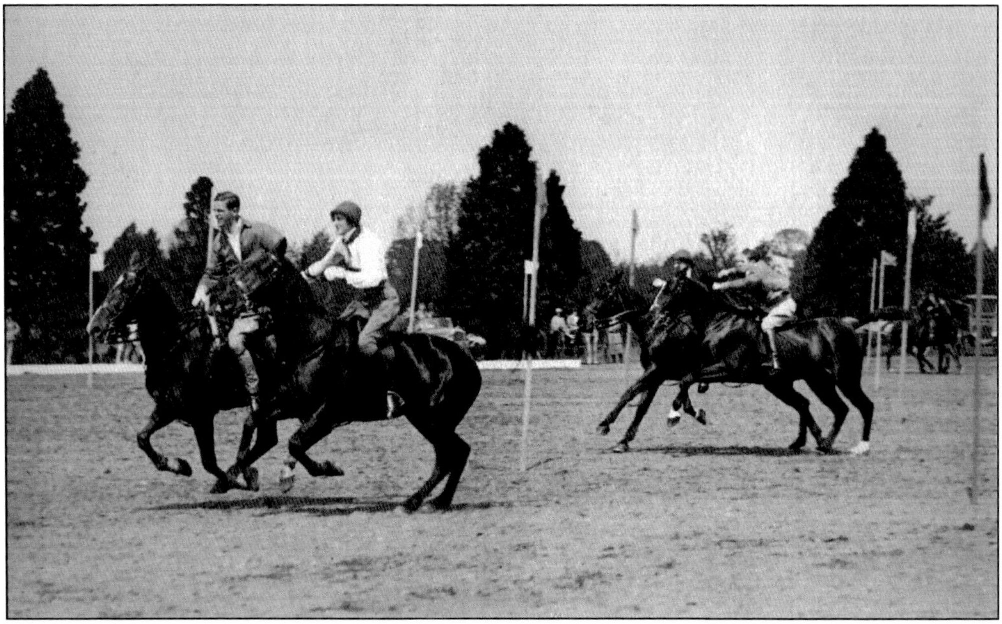

This gymkhana shows mom and dad teaching son and daughter how to handle their horses. Alix Dolan Toland spent much of her time in the woods foxhunting, riding, racing, playing polo, and just having fun getting through the flags.

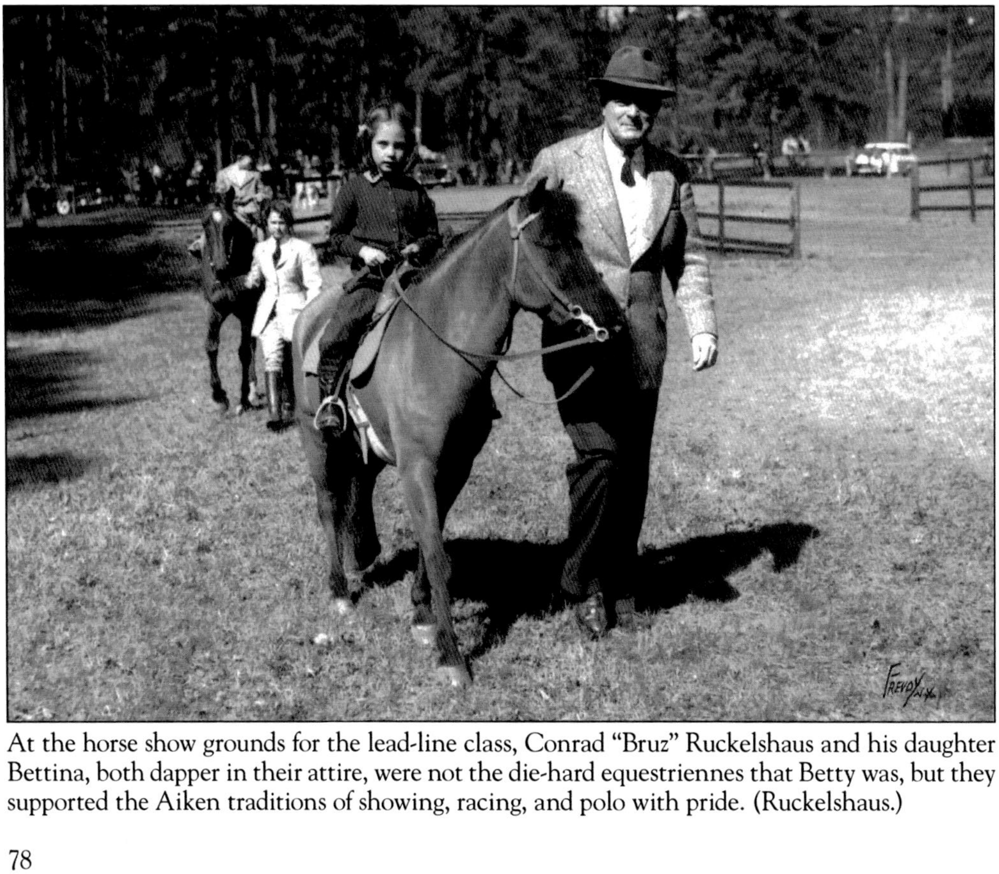

At the horse show grounds for the lead-line class, Conrad "Bruz" Ruckelshaus and his daughter Bettina, both dapper in their attire, were not the die-hard equestriennes that Betty was, but they supported the Aiken traditions of showing, racing, and polo with pride. (Ruckelshaus.)

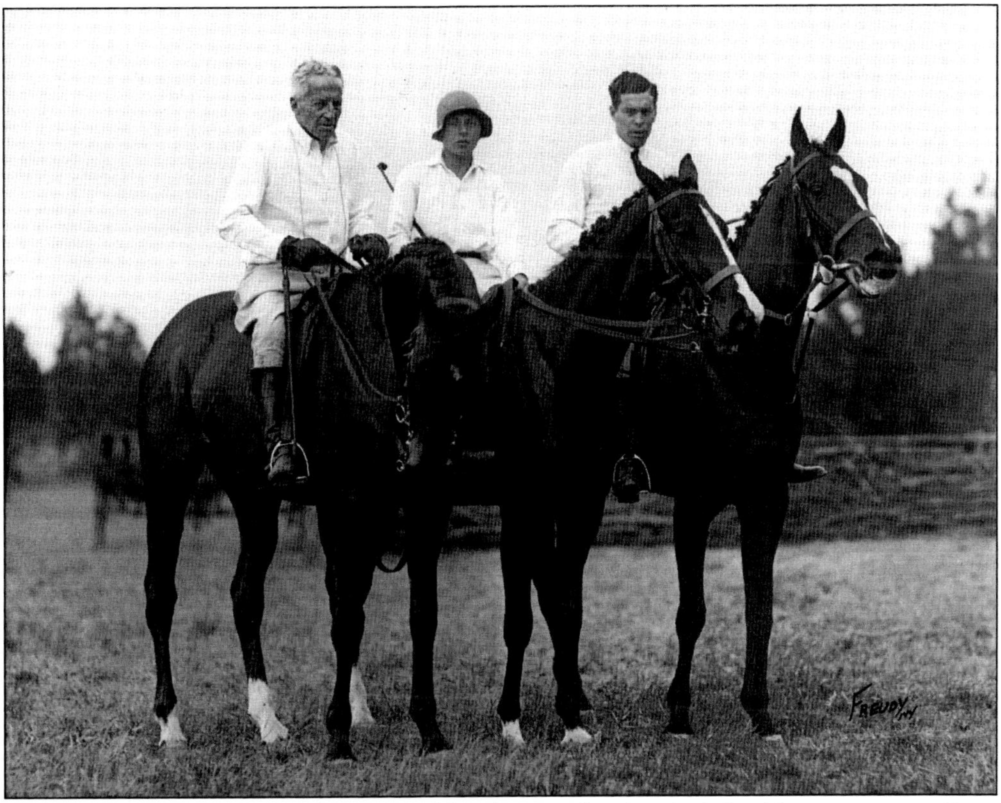

Hunter trials and hunter paces have joined families together for a little healthy competition. From left to right, Harry Worcester Smith, Jean Olcott, and Crompton Smith prepare for the Aiken hunter trials in the 1930s. From a different collection of photographs, the same trio is seen again below. During the middle of the race, the three take an Aiken at top speed. However, in this year, they only finished in second place.

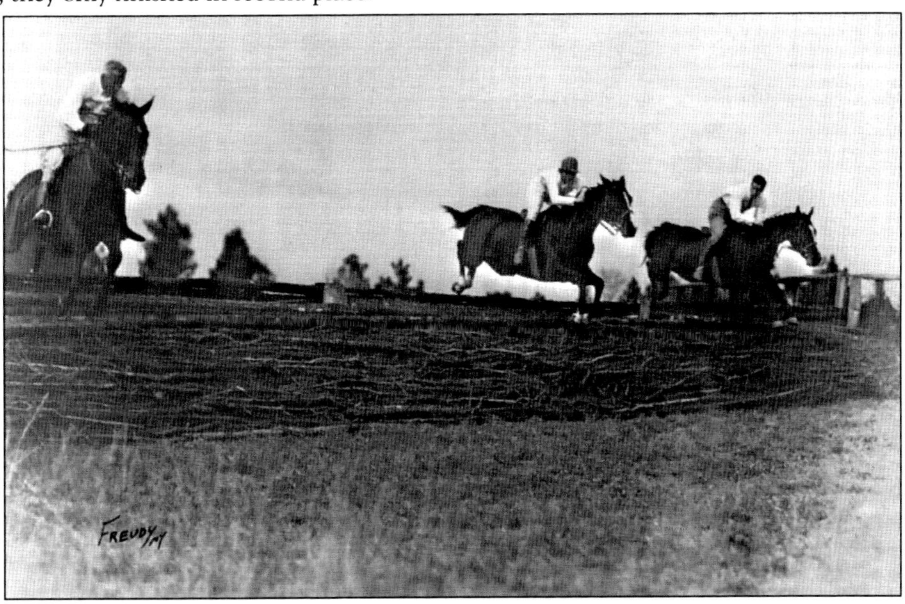

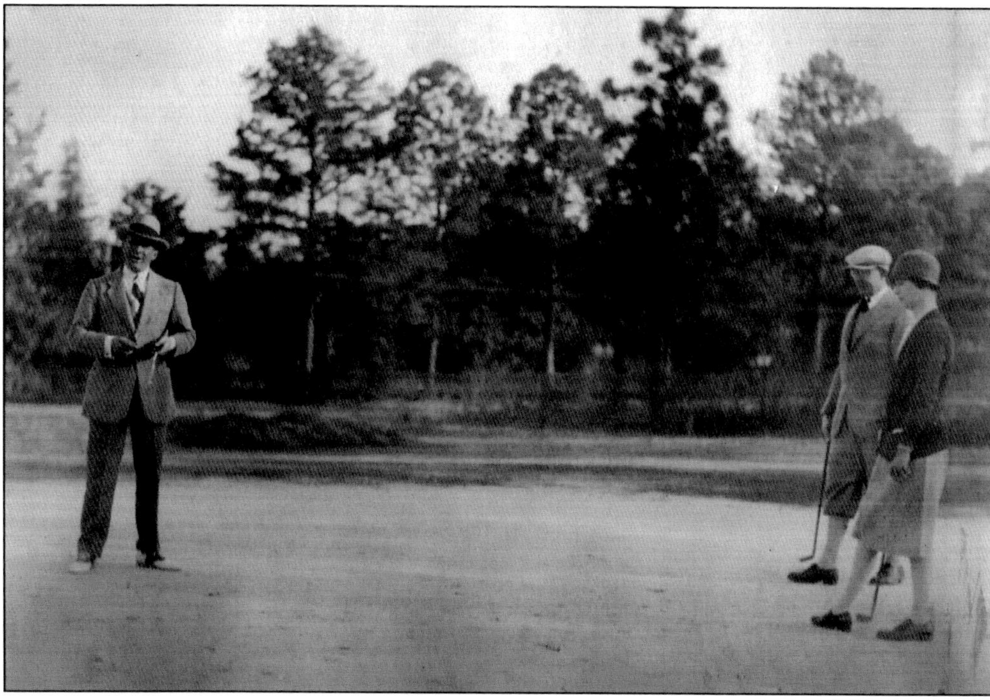

Harry Payne Whitney and the Spauldings enjoy a bit of putting before supper. When one thinks of sporting in Aiken, golf and horses come to mind, but many of Aiken's swells were sailors. From naval commands such as W.C. Whitney's service as secretary of the navy to Hope Goddard Iselin's America's Cup races, land-locked Aiken attracted sea legs and horse legs alike. (Tower.)

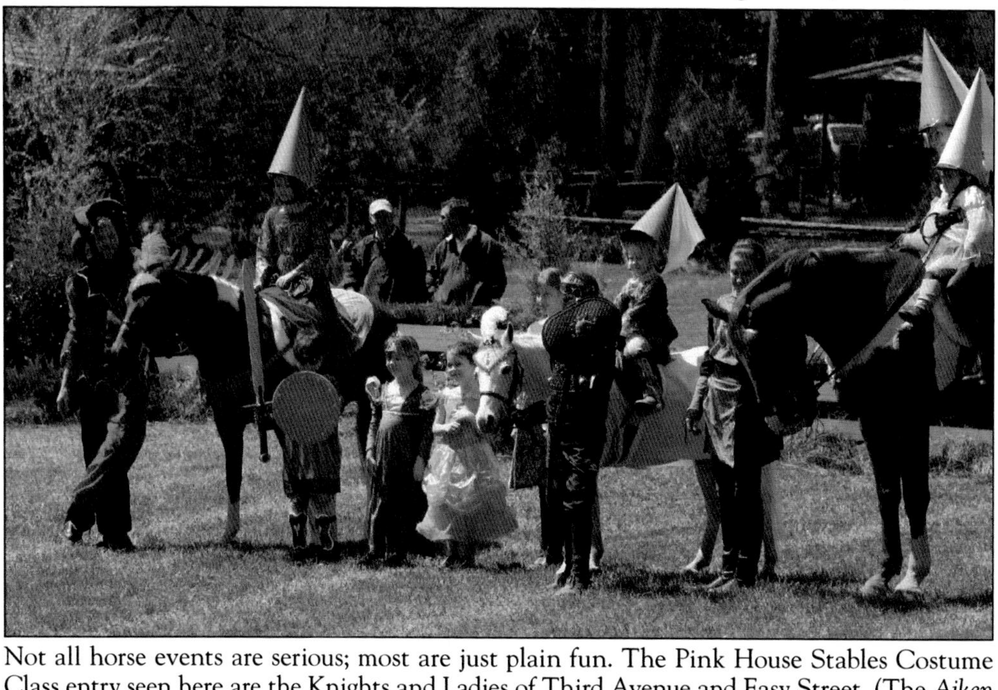

Not all horse events are serious; most are just plain fun. The Pink House Stables Costume Class entry seen here are the Knights and Ladies of Third Avenue and Easy Street. (The *Aiken Standard*.)

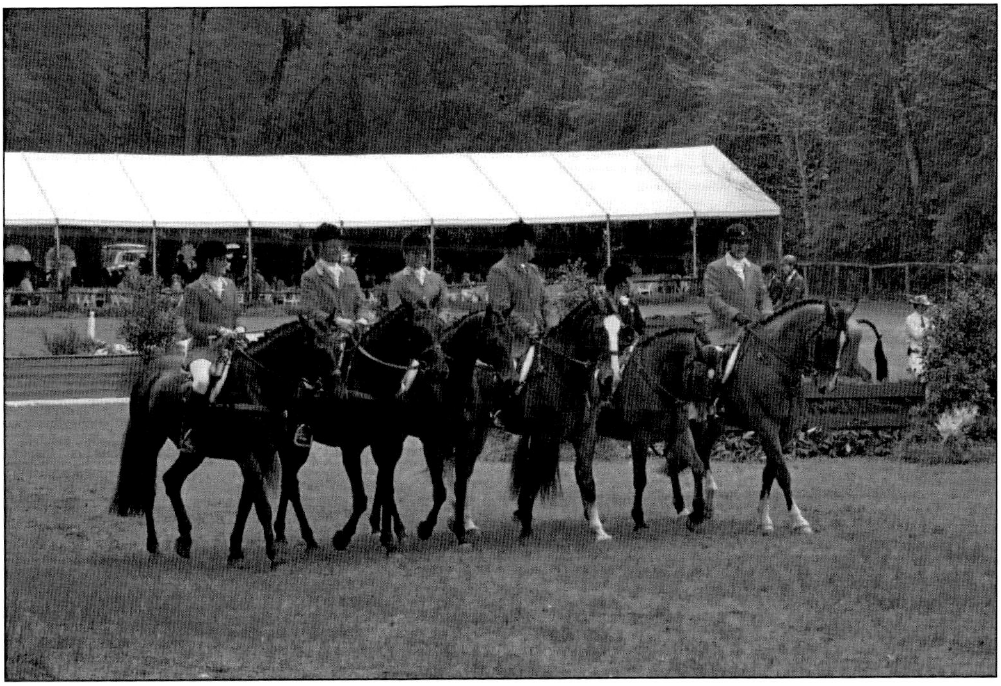

In Aiken, families are made up of generations, stepchildren, half-siblings, in-laws, first and second cousins, and even those close friends dubbed aunt and uncle. Pictured above are, from left to right, Nancy Wilson, Epp Wilson, Wendi Wilson Gunnell, Nelson Gunnell, Thomas Gunnell, and Mark Thompson. This extended family represented more than 14 foxhunts, each adult wearing their scarlet coat and hunt colors from their home hunt. The well-matched team and their military precision took home the blue ribbon in 2013. To the right is Skipper Perry as he prepares for the mule race, while Ash Milner steadies the mount. Friends and family come together to keep traditions alive as much for the fun as for the competition. (Above, HWF; right, Teddy Milner.)

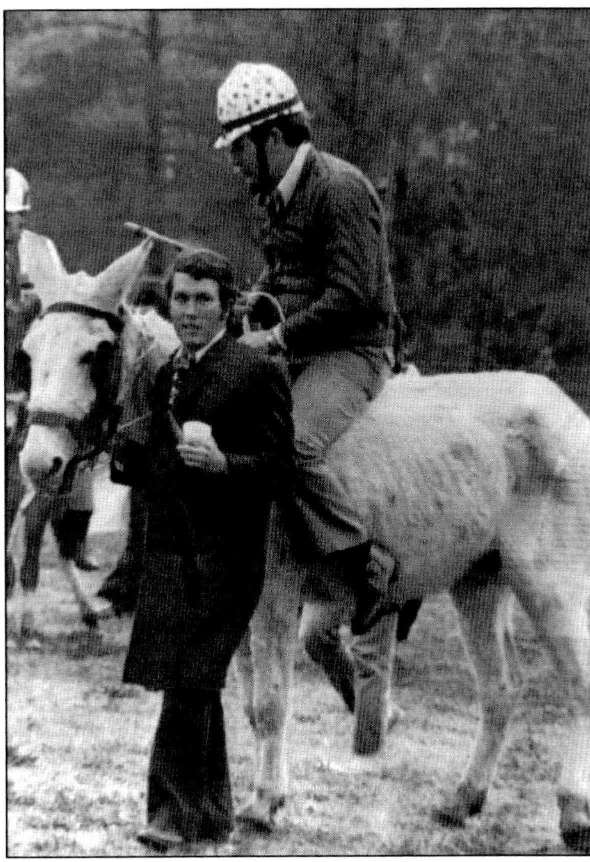

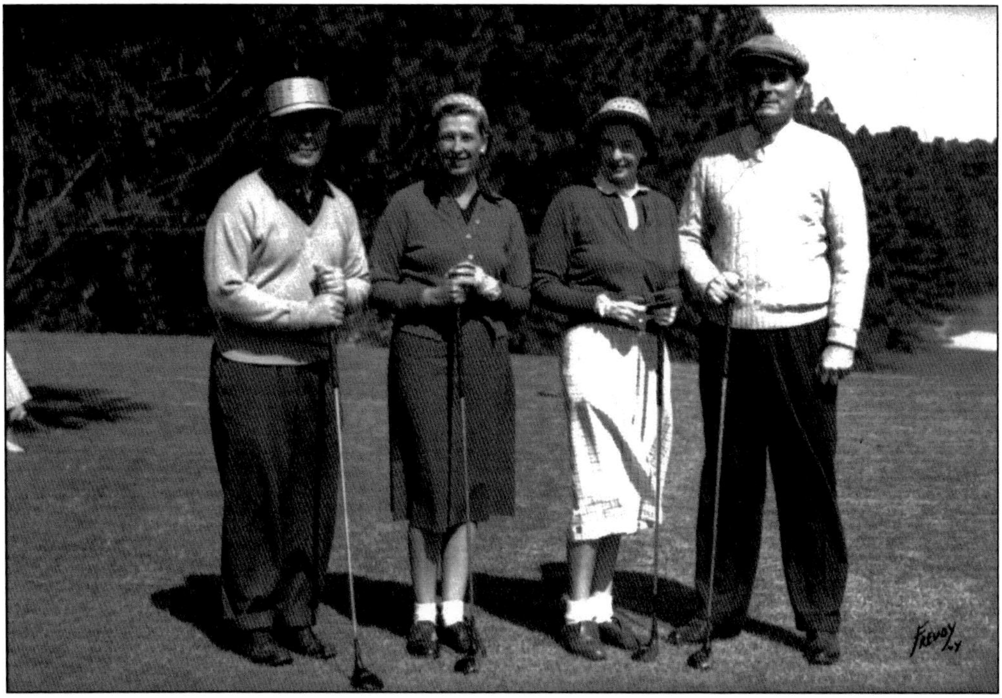

Ladies playing golf in Aiken from their own tees have been a part of golf vernacular for 100 years. Passing on the legacy of sport from mother to daughter is something that Aiken is also known for, whether it is foxhunting, polo, or golf. From left to right, Seymour Knox, Helen Knox, Betty Ruckelshaus, and Bruz Ruckelshaus set out to play golf at Palmetto. Mothers also passed on to their daughters a love, almost competitive, of entertaining. Dorothy Roger's Easter party was a highly anticipated event for the children of the swells. The egg hunt in itself became a sporting contest of sorts. (Both, Ruckelshaus.)

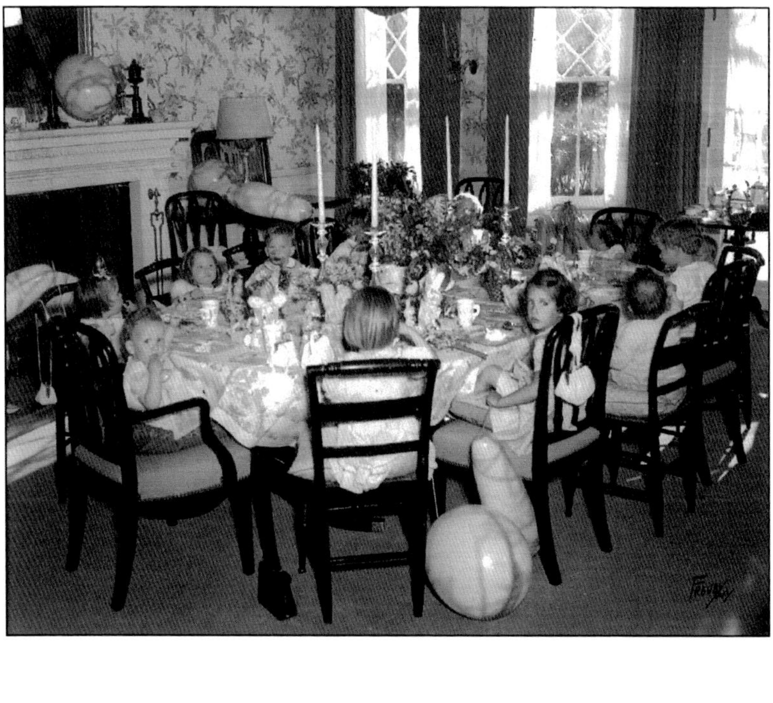

Canadian families have been a part of Aiken's tourist economy for centuries. The Burns family, from Toronto, have been avid sporting enthusiasts in Aiken for three generations. Here the Burns ladies ride while patriarch Latham and father, Fred, mix Pink House Punch. Paddy Ann and the girls have been at the center of many of the important civic events that make Aiken so special all year round. When he flipped the switch on the lights for the last time in 2015, Latham's passing marked a sad day for Aiken's horse community. (Bossard.)

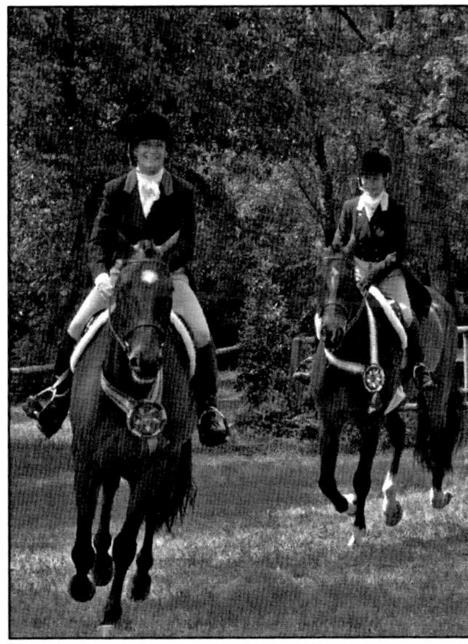

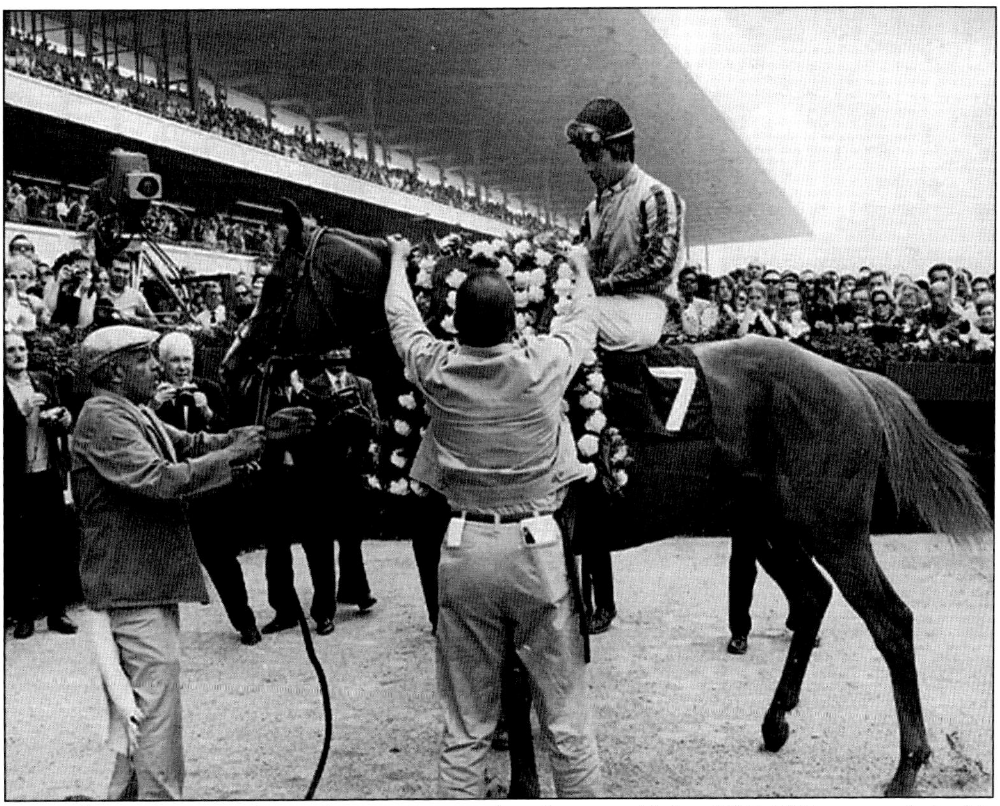

Joan Whitney Payson inherited a great fortune from her grandfather W.C. Whitney, and also his love of sport. The first woman to outright purchase a major-league franchise in North America, her Miracle Mets won the World Series in 1969. When a *New York Times* reporter asked her if this was the biggest "upset" in sports history, she said "No, when my Stage Door Johnny won the Belmont last year, that was the greatest upset in sports history, this is a close second." (Aiken Thoroughbred Racing Hall of Fame.)

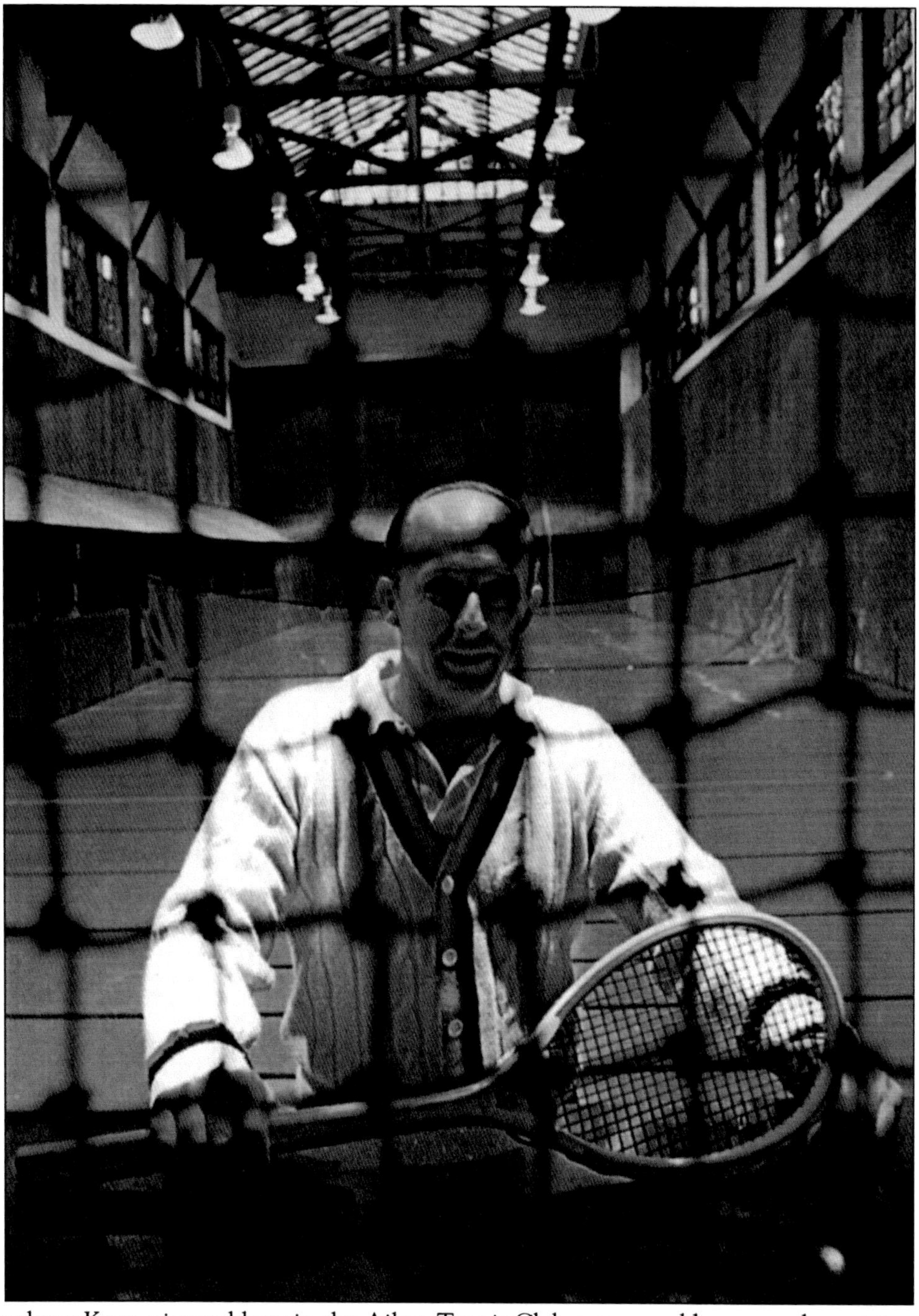

Northrup Knox, pictured here in the Aiken Tennis Club, was a world-renowned court tennis player. He learned court tennis in Aiken while attending Aiken Prep School and became world champion from 1959 to 1969, retiring undefeated. Both of the succeeding champions were the brothers Bostwick, Pete and Jimmy, with whom he played regularly. Court tennis is referred to as a game combining the strategy of chess, the hand-eye coordination of lawn tennis, and the endurance and acuity of polo. It is no surprise that court tennis is still a popular sport in Aiken. There are only 11 other courts in America, and 43 in the world. (Ruckelshaus.)

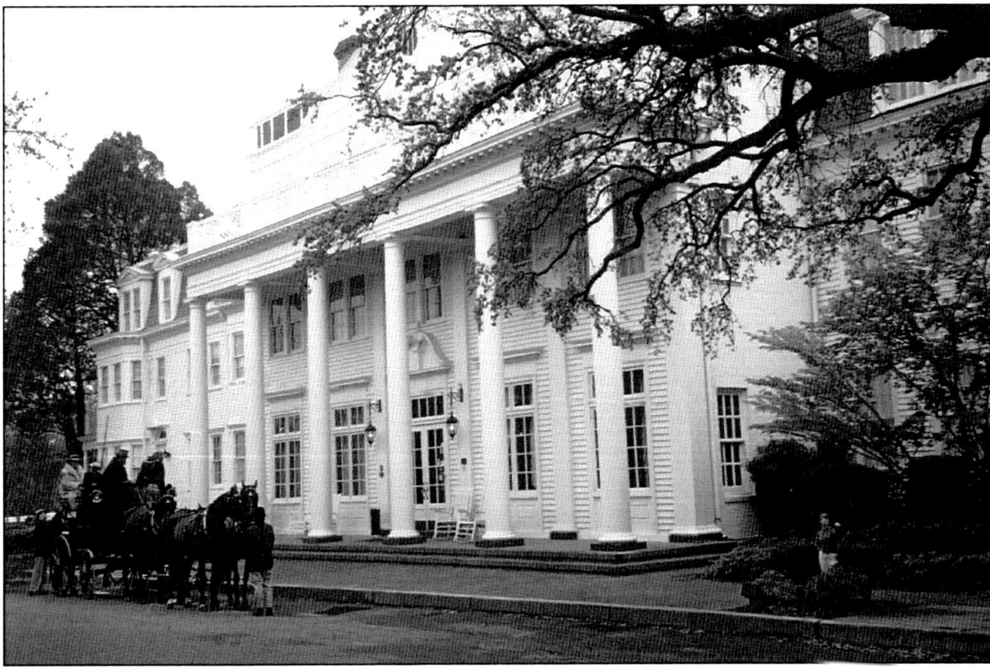

The streets and 15 miles of parkways within the city of Aiken are laid out to make driving carriages easier and walking a pleasure. Hotels and inns were built to accommodate the increase in population. Today, the Willcox (pictured) has become Aiken's living room and is a remaining example of why Aiken was such an attractive tourist destination. The most recent purchase of the Willcox by the Ellis family formally connected Canada and America under the banner of hospitality by literally flying the flag of both countries out front. (The *Aiken Standard*.)

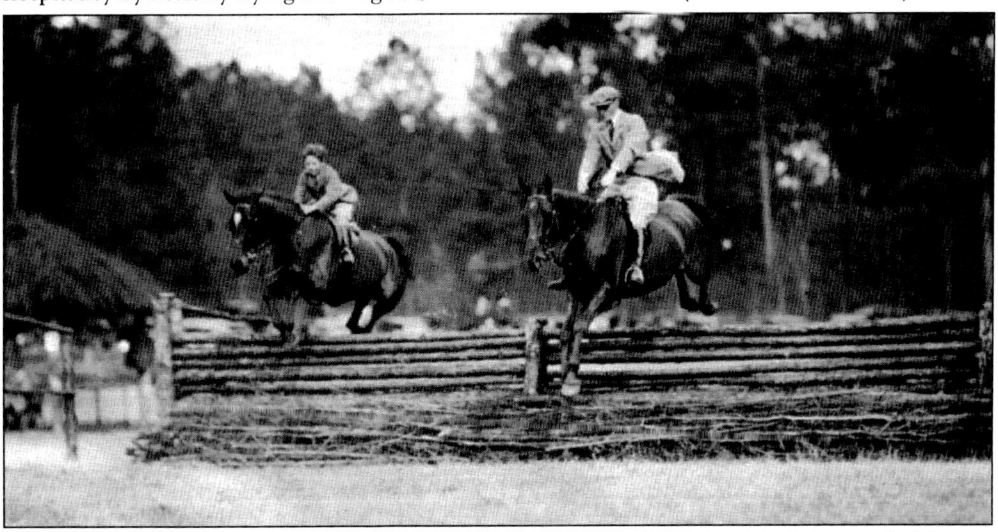

G.H. "Pete" Bostwick and his older brother Albert Jr., pictured jumping an Aiken at AHS, were members of a true American sporting family. The Bostwick family through the years has been a sustaining force in the horse world and beyond: Lillian Stokes Bostwick Phipps with eight American Grand National Winners, Dunbar with his winning Standardbreds, Albert and his Preakness winner, Pete with polo and Racing Hall of Fame induction, and Dorothy, the first woman to be issued a helicopter license. (Aiken Thoroughbred Racing Hall of Fame.)

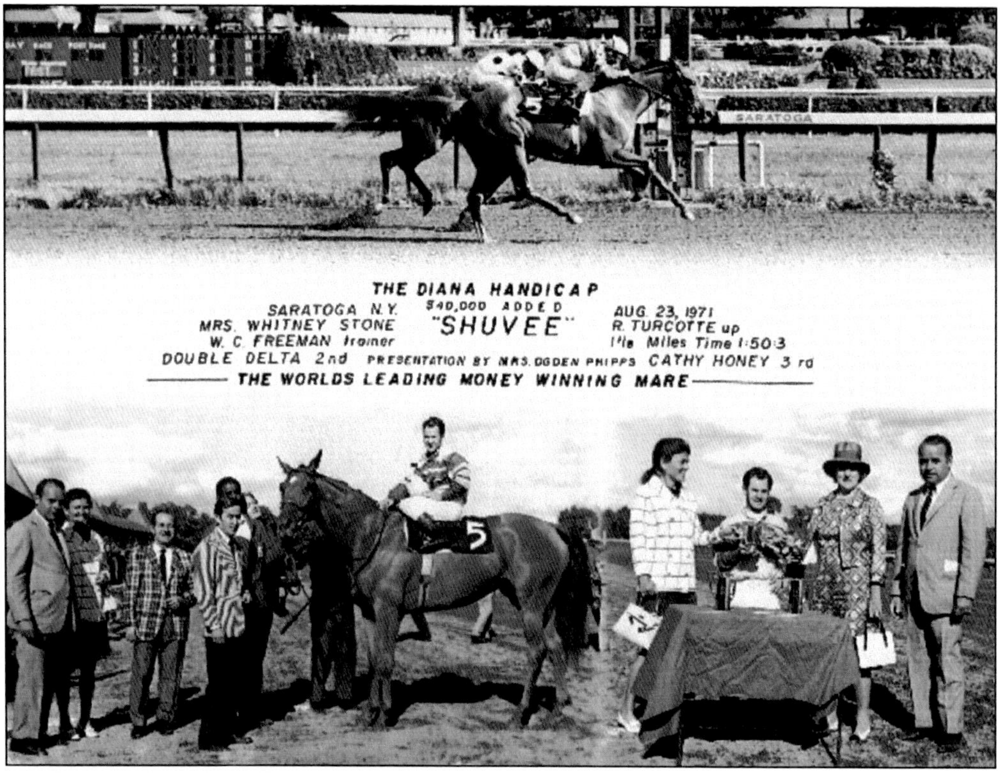

Iris Winthrop Freeman and her husband, Willard C. "Mike" Freeman, have remained committed to the Aiken Training Track and Hitchcock Woods Foundation since their early days. Fitting that Mike Freeman, an Aiken trainer, should have the top money-winning mare Shuvee win the Belmont Park Diana Cup in 1971. Aiken lost a great trainer when Mike passed away, but his legacy continues in the works Iris does for so many worthy causes within the community. (Aiken Thoroughbred Racing Hall of Fame.)

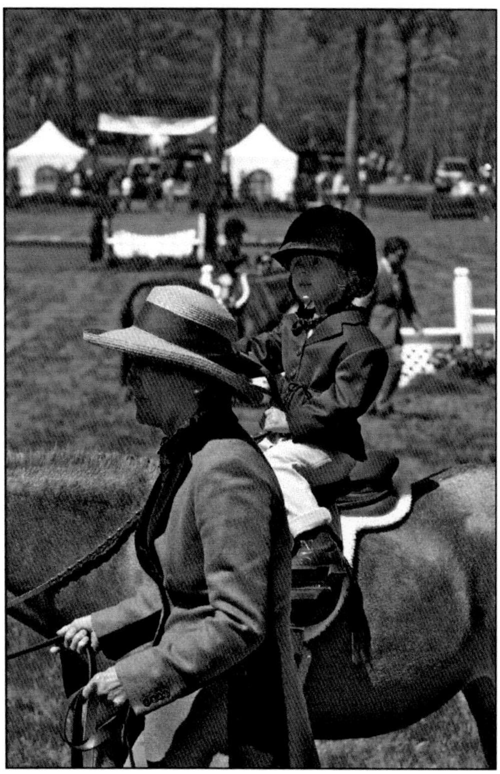

Even the British love Aiken. Gail Balding King has exposed many foreigners to Aiken as an unofficial equine ambassador. Aiken continues to attract people from Germany, France, Australia, Japan, Canada, Argentina, and Brazil for work and play. King's sense of place and her dedication to preservation has her children and grandchildren returning home to Aiken as well. (Bossard.)

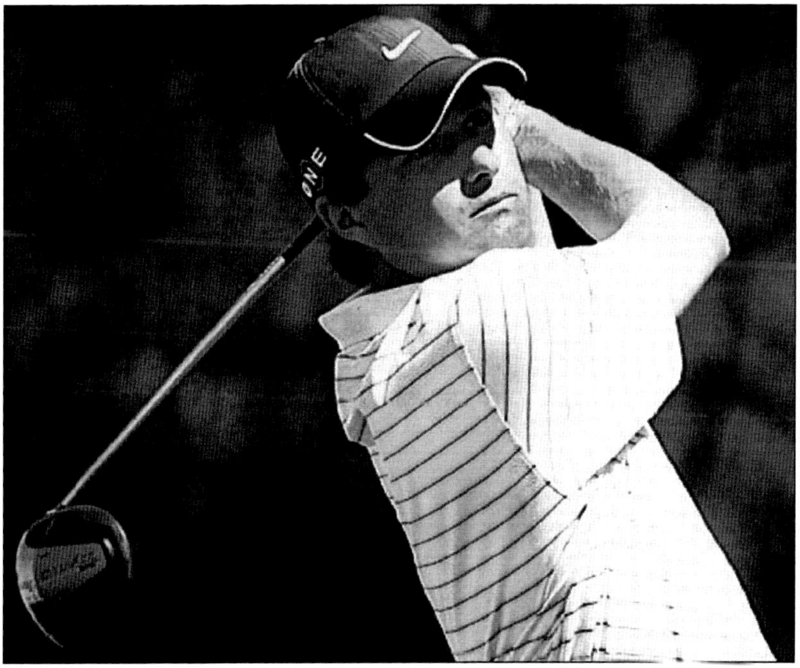

Kevin Kisner is swinging his way onto the world golf scene. In 2014, Kisner made headlines for inviting his dad, Steve Kisner, an Aiken home builder, onto the Pinehurst links to caddy for him in his first US Open. Kisner's game took off, earning him accolades as he climbs the world rankings. (The *Aiken Standard*.)

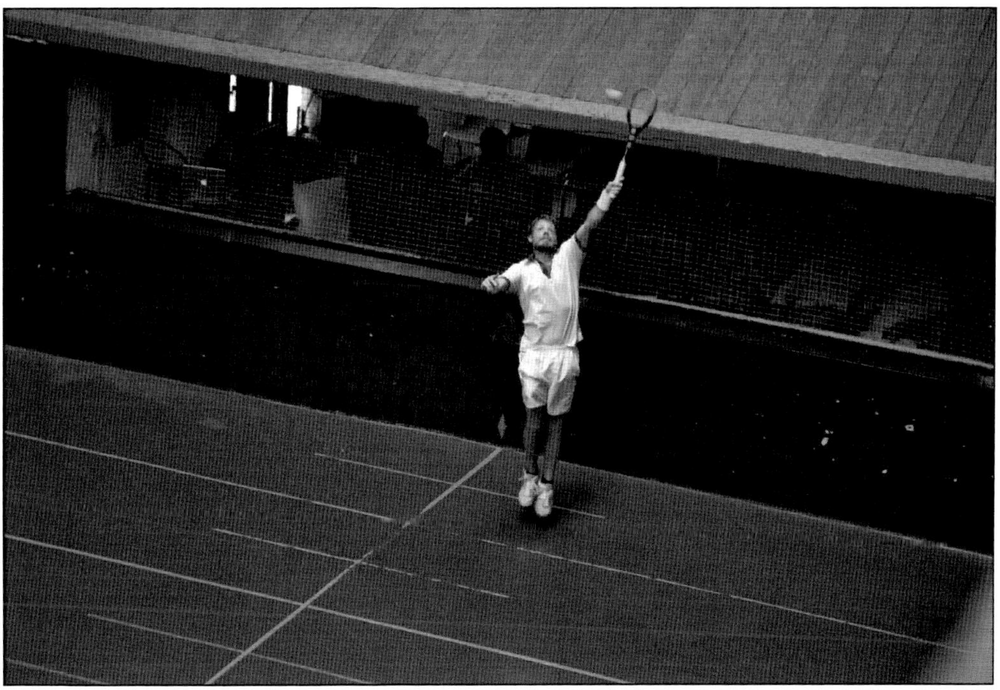

The next generations of sporting superstars have taken their place in national and world championships. Camden Scott Riviere is the national champion and soon to be world champion in court, or real, tennis. Riviere is carrying on the tradition of tennis sport for which Aiken is known. (Riviere.)

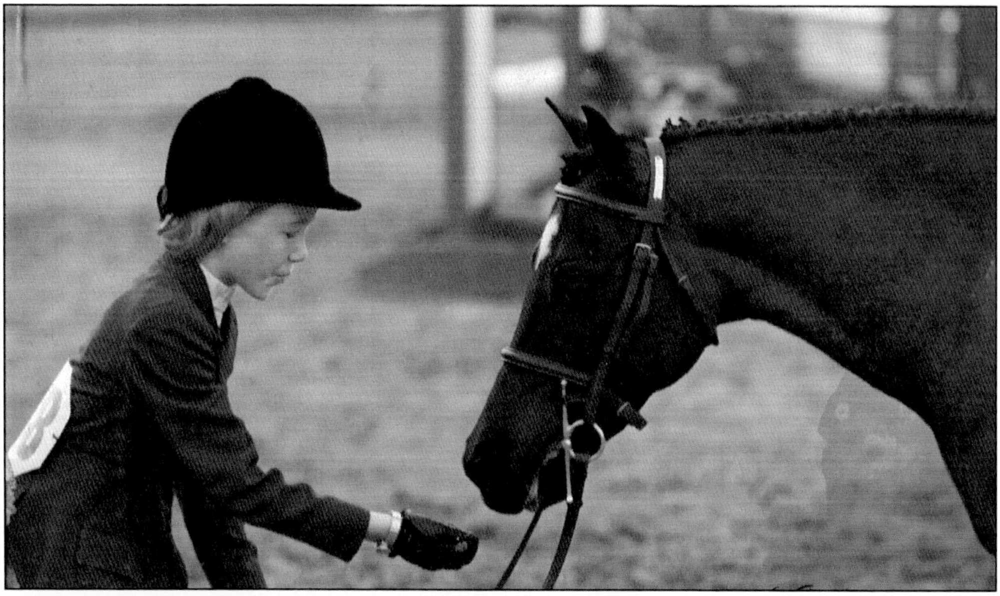

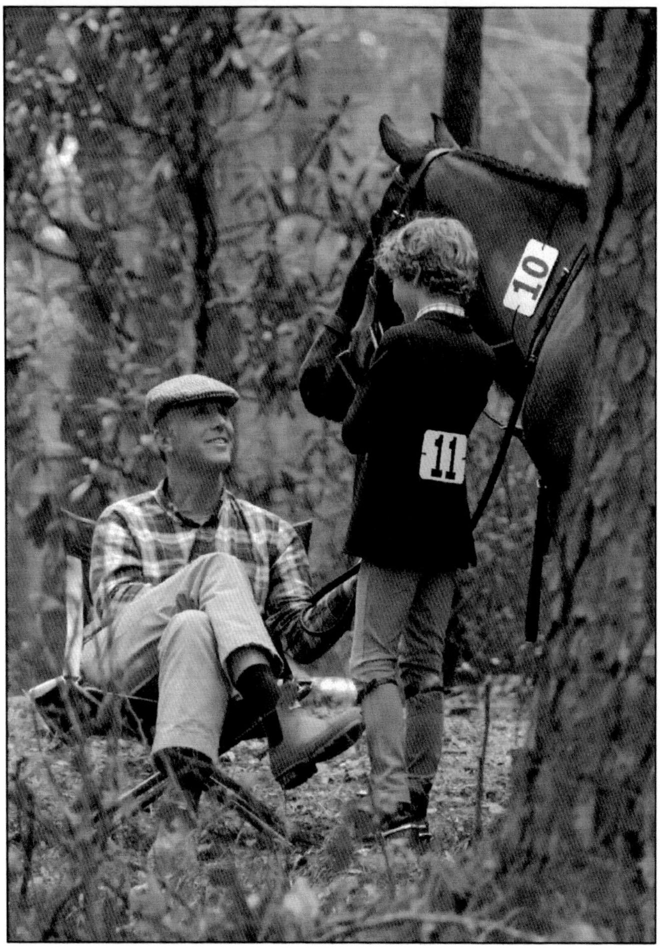

Many champions have been made in Aiken, and through the years, national and world champions have called Aiken home. Junior champion small pony hunter of America in 1984 Farnley Love Child and rider Tearson were the pride of her mother, Sandra Stokes Thomas. These two ladies have long been supporters of all things Aiken. (Thomas.)

Horse people are drawn to Aiken, and the Fenwick family is synonymous with horse sports. Daisy and Tommy Fenwick, pictured here with his father, are the fifth generation of riders from the Maryland family that comes to Aiken to support the Aiken Horse Show or Aiken Steeplechase. (Bridges.)

Linda Knox McLean has been coaching her granddaughter Isabel Schmon in the art of riding. Fostering the next generation of sporting and heritage leaders for Aiken is a fun business for this grandmother who preserves the Knox family traditions in both the United States and Canada. (McLean.)

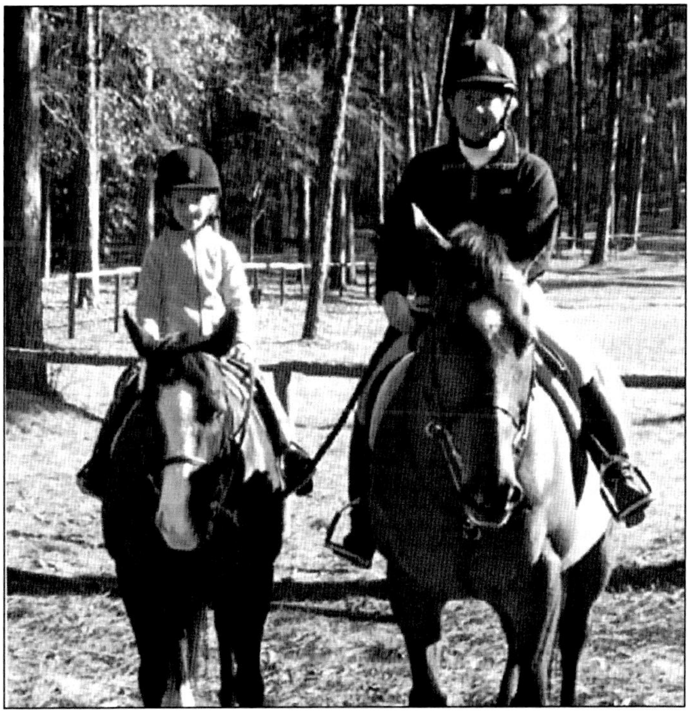

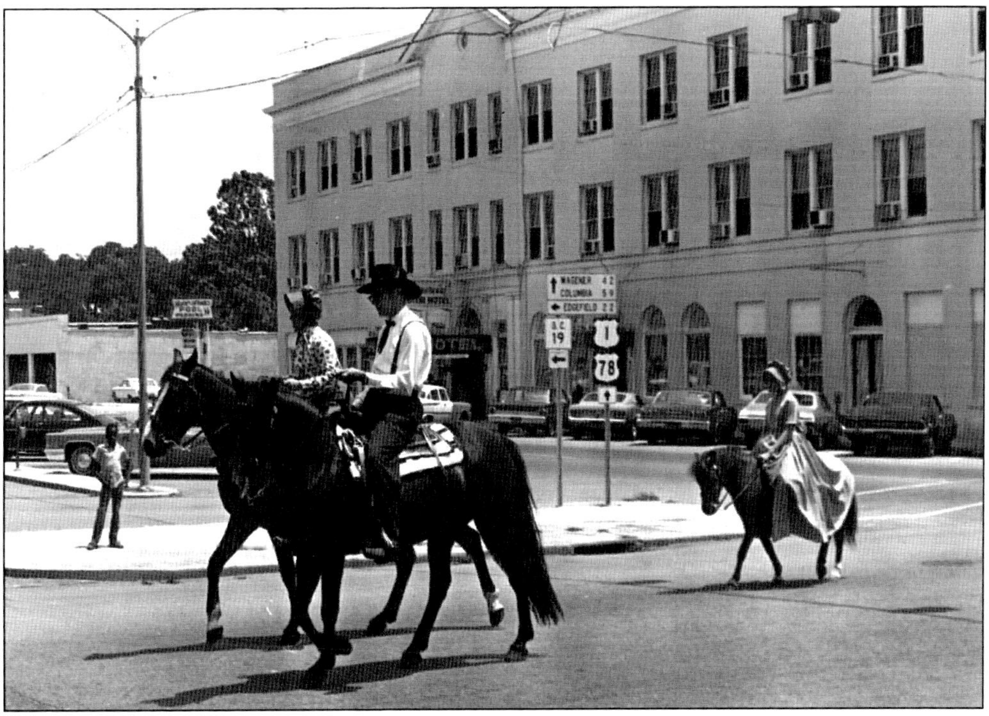

The Commercial Hotel, now Hotel Aiken, has remained a cornerstone of Aiken's thriving downtown scene. The legacy of family-owned and operated businesses has kept shoppers and diners returning. Over the decades, the businesses, names, and owners change, but the strength of family and small businesses remains. (Lista.)

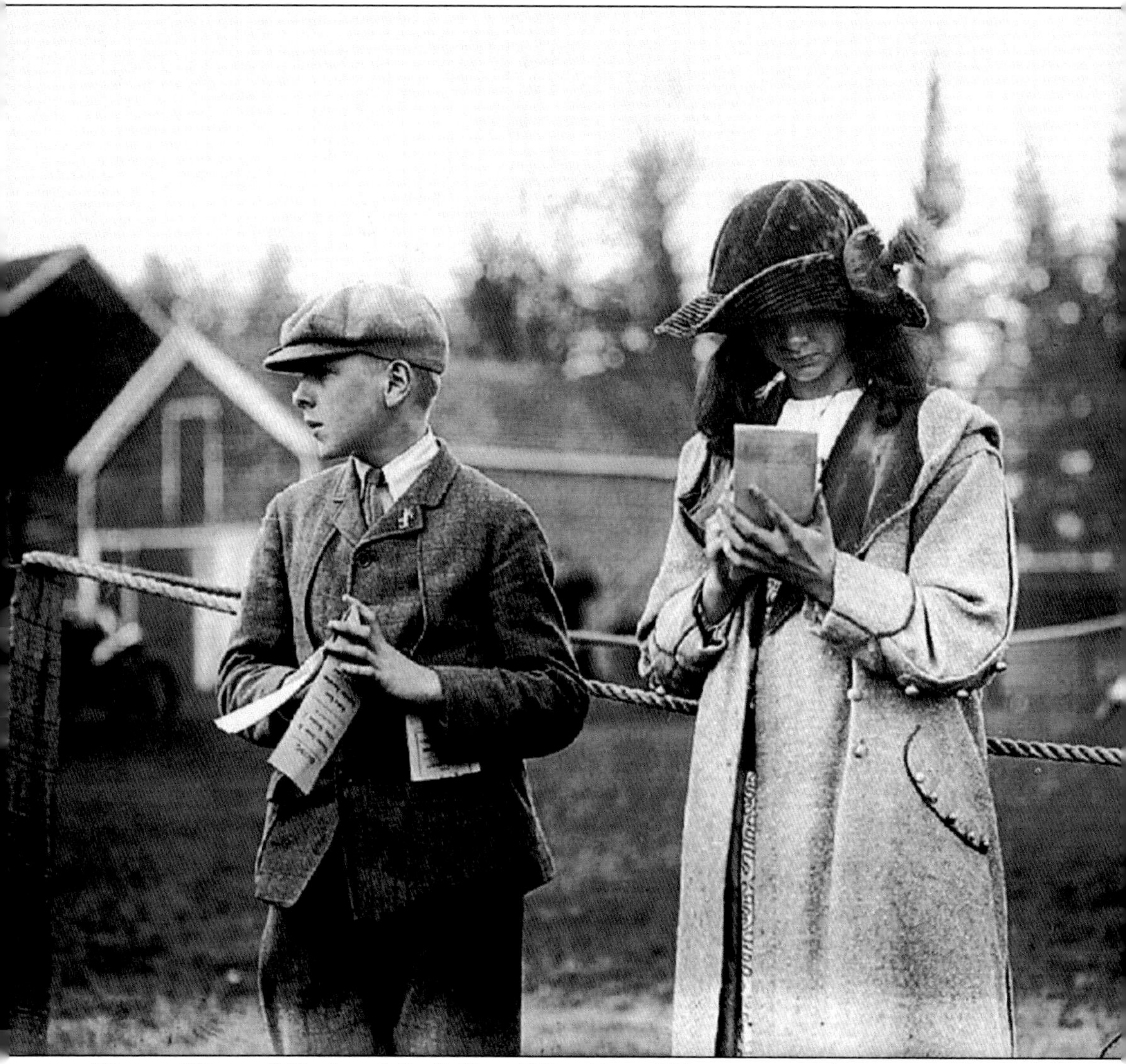

Thomas "Tommy" Hitchcock Jr. (left) and Flora Payne Whitney assess the race card for one of their fathers' Thoroughbred horse races in Aiken. This image of children embracing the sporting enthusiasm in Aiken captures the generational spirit that perpetuates this community. Tommy's life would later inspire one of the characters in F. Scott Fitzgerald's *The Great Gatsby*, and Flora's love letters to Quentin Roosevelt during World War I were featured in Edward Renehan's book *The Lion's Pride*, about Teddy Roosevelt's children. Often the legacies one leaves are found outside the gift of children and in the life led. (Aiken Thoroughbred Racing Hall of Fame.)

Six

Celebrating Aiken's Milestones

Sporting Events and Traditions Reach the Century Mark

Between 2014 and 2017, many of Aiken's traditions and organizations celebrate major milestones. Hitting the century mark are the Aiken Horse Show and Aiken Preparatory School, now merged with Mead Hall Episcopal School, both founded in 1916. In 2017, Aiken Polo Club will reach 135, Palmetto Golf Club will hit 125, and Aiken Tennis Club will be 115 years old. Aiken Hounds celebrated its 100th year in 2014, while the Hitchcock Woods Foundation logged its 75th year. Steeplechase started in 1930, the trotting track in 1937, and the Aiken Trials in 1942. Aiken Golf Club is the home of the first forward tees for ladies, which were installed in 1916.

Many of these institutions owe their longevity to their founders, but it is the current members and patrons who have sustained these venerable institutions. Hitchcock Woods Foundation and the Aiken Horse Show in the woods are the main landmarks celebrated in this book. With 2,100 acres of maintained pine forest and 70 miles of trails, the woods are a refuge from the pressures of modern life. From the Chalk Cliffs to Sand River and Black Gum Pond to Cathedral Aisle, Hitchcock Woods will continue to be Aiken's private playground that welcomes visitors and friends.

The pinnacle of the current Aiken season is the Aiken Horse Show, which concludes on the first Sunday in April. There is much to the spectacle: the children in lead-line, the creativity of the costume class, the thrill of the hunt teams, the technique of the handy hunters, the jumping rounds, and the pomp of the side saddle division. Since horse trailers are not allowed into the woods for the show, exhibitors pull together sharing tailgate space and supplies. In true Hitchcock form, the Aiken Horse Show brings out the competitive nature of the riders, but couples that desire to win with the humility of friendship.

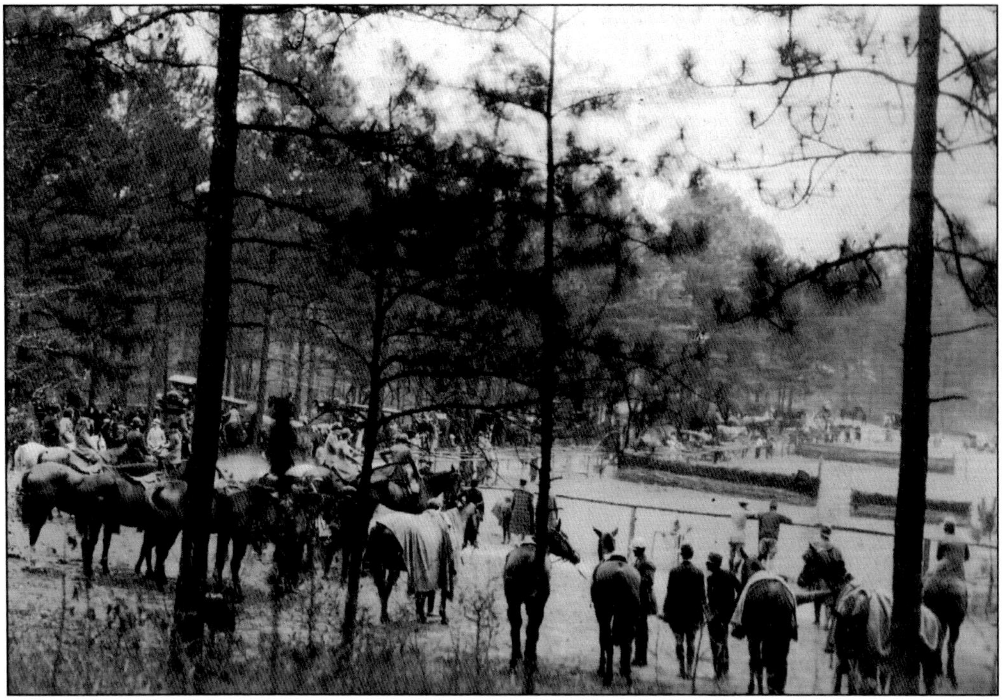

Before the official founding, competing horses in Hitchcock Woods was a tradition that the Aiken Horse Show recognized in 1916. Hope Goddard Iselin started the Aiken Hospital with earnings from a poker game, but needed to raise additional funds for supplies, so the show was born as a fundraiser. (Brainard.)

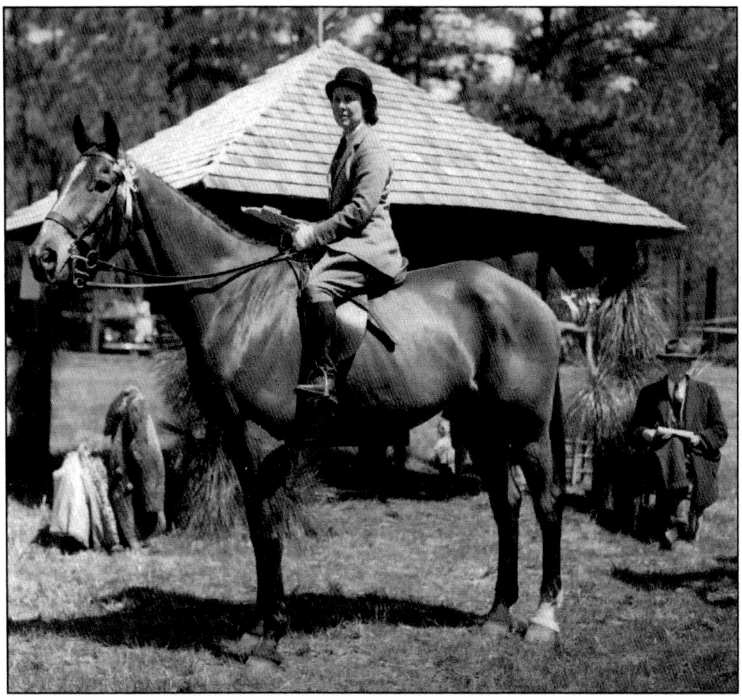

Being pinned as top of the class at AHS was quite an honor. Alix Dolan sports her blue ribbon with pride as a conscientious judge looks on. Originally, the secretary's hut was in the center of the ring with the American flag flying from the top. Today, the grounds are surrounded with additions—it has come a long way in 100 years. (Brainard.)

Thomas Hitchcock (left) and Louise Hitchcock jump an Aiken at AHS during the hunt-team class. The much anticipated conclusion of the horse show are the pairs and team classes, in which two or three riders barrel down the course to take the same jump at the same time. The thrill of that successful accomplishment is captured on Louise's face. (Brainard.)

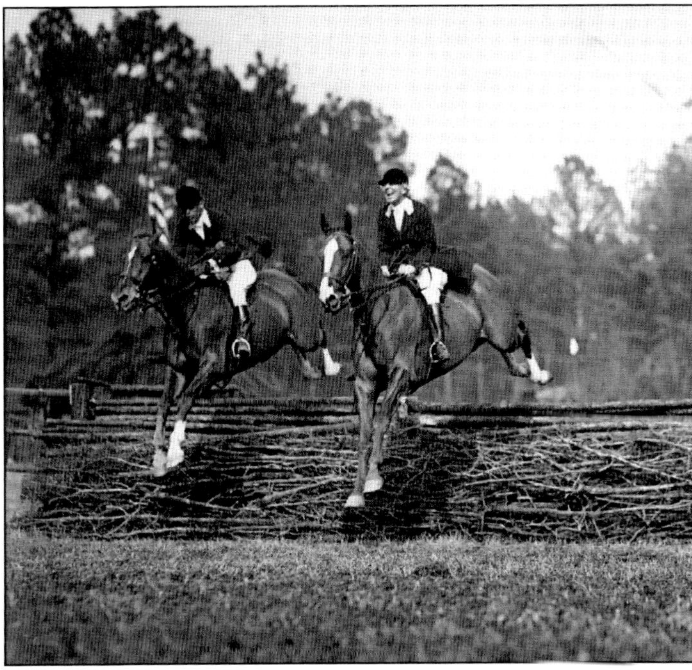

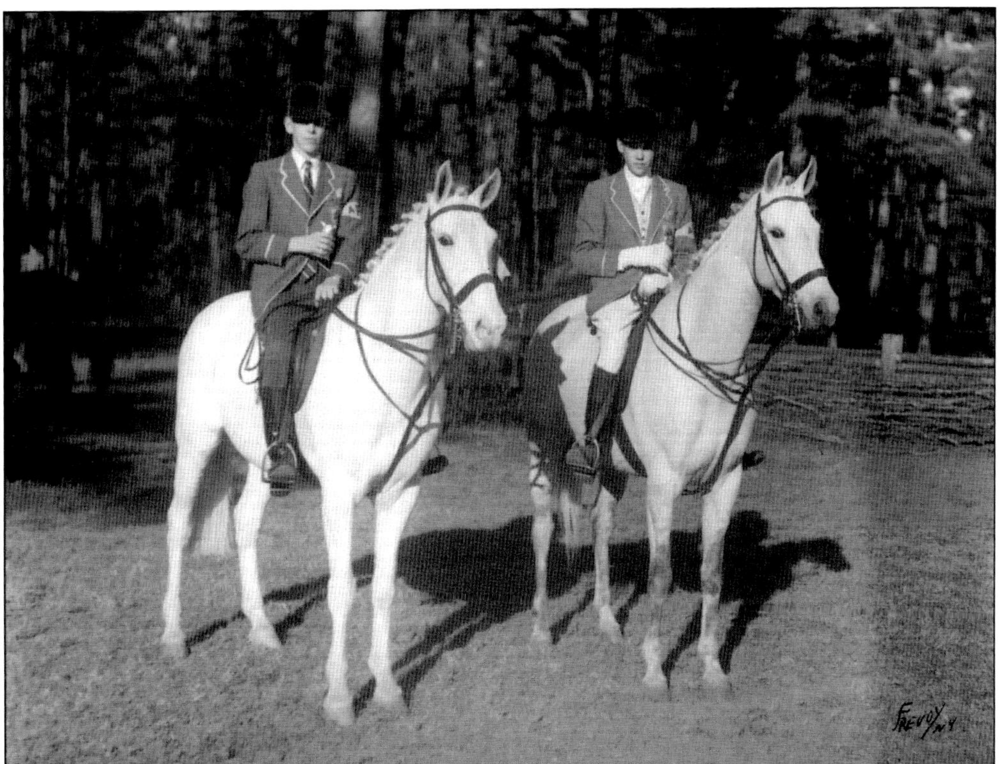

Aiken Prep School, also founded in 1916, has a longstanding tradition of providing whips and junior masters to the Aiken Hounds. Competing in AHS in the pairs class, the Toland boys on their matched grays sporting their winning trophies exemplify the seriousness of sport. (Brainard.)

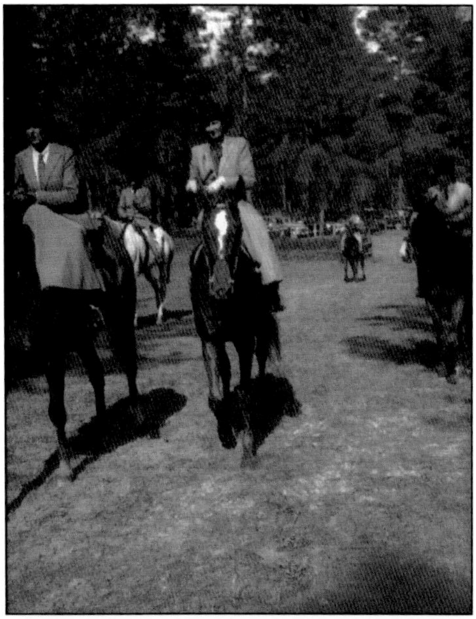

Betty Ruckelshaus (center) rides sidesaddle at AHS, no longer the convention; riding aside took a 40-year hiatus from the show but was brought back in 2007 with a sidesaddle division promoted by Aiken Ladies Aside organization and sponsored by Bettina, Betty's daughter, in her honor. (Ruckelshaus.)

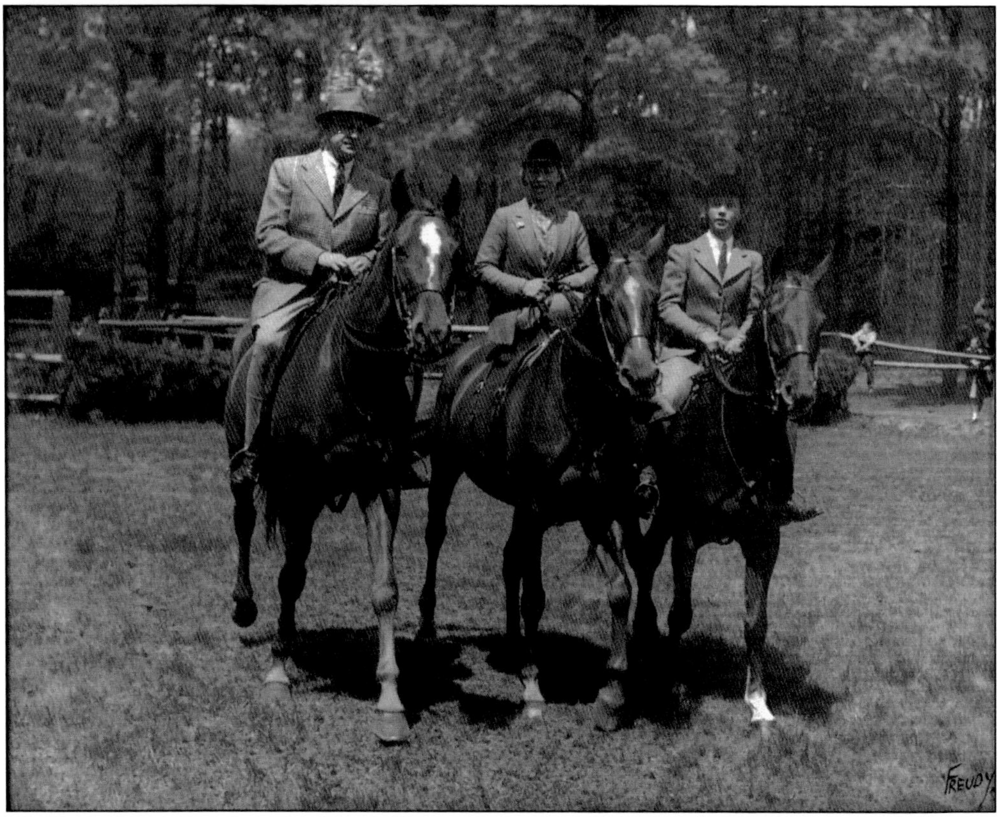

Families participating in the horse show added a bit of competitive flair to the family class. Pictured here from left to right are Bill Wood, Fran Wood, and Aileen Wood. Aileen Wood was on the cover of *Life* magazine in 1950 preparing for AHS. It was on this day of showing that the photographer snapped her cover shot. (Rucleshaus)

Tommy Ruckelshaus is pictured here in the lead-line class at the Aiken Horse Show. Many an Aiken child has been propped on a pony for this baptism of sorts. The clamor to borrow habits, saddles, and mounts prior to the show is almost as vigorous as a day of trading from the floor, one stockbroker father remarked. Many of those children have grown up to continue the tradition with their own children or to aid in the scramble for their friends. (Ruckelshaus.)

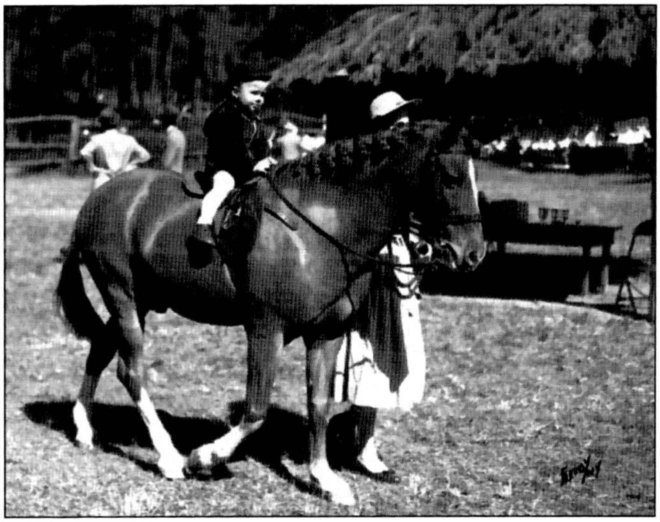

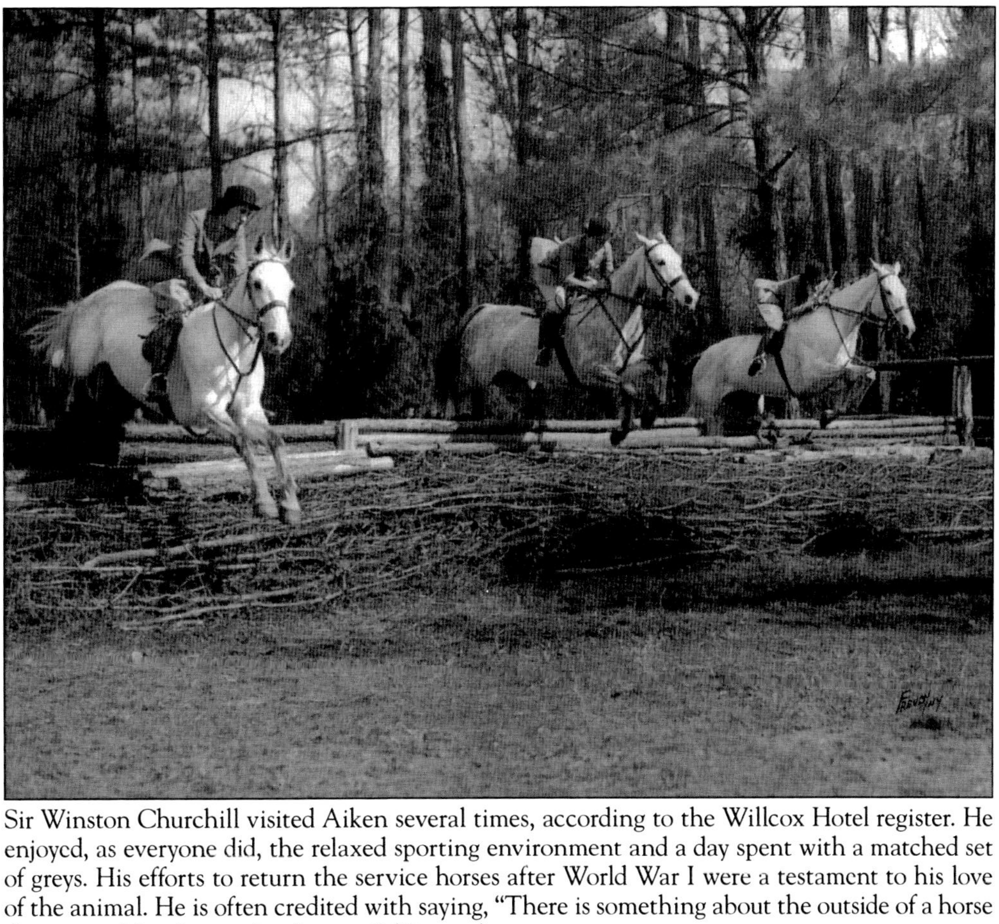

Sir Winston Churchill visited Aiken several times, according to the Willcox Hotel register. He enjoyed, as everyone did, the relaxed sporting environment and a day spent with a matched set of greys. His efforts to return the service horses after World War I were a testament to his love of the animal. He is often credited with saying, "There is something about the outside of a horse that is good for the inside of a man." (Conger.)

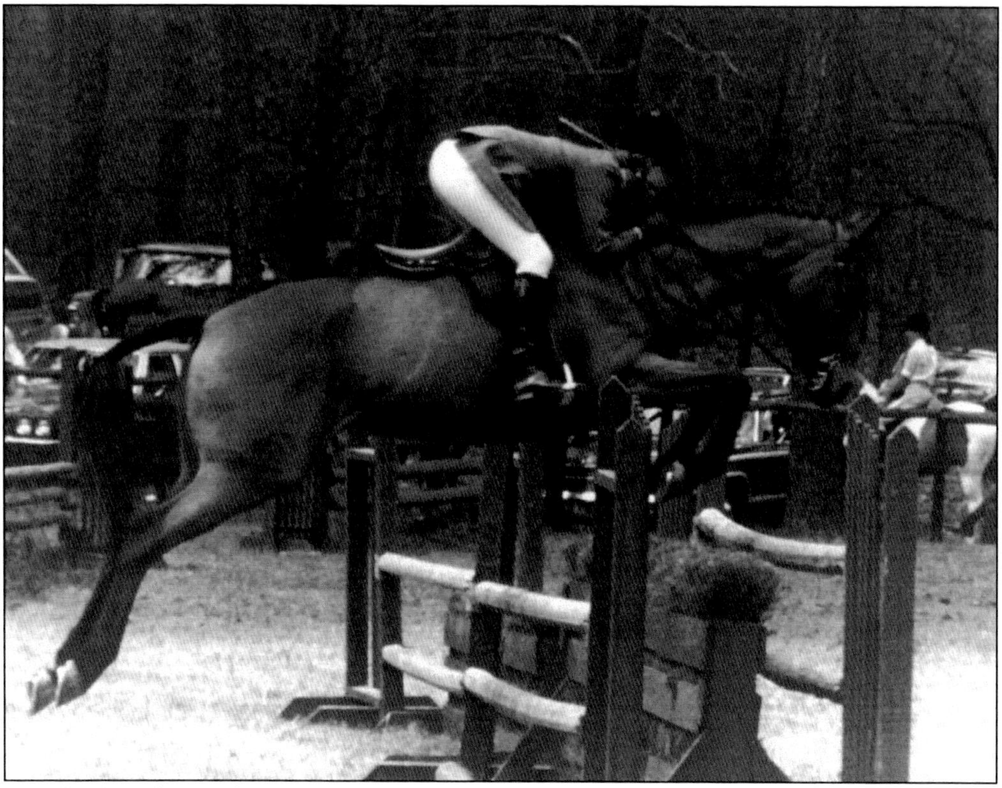

AHS has been known for its high jumps and tight course, making it a true challenge for a foxhunter. Beth Sauerborn shows great form over this Aiken at AHS. After the show one year, Frederick Prince suggested to Louise Hitchcock that they finish the course, ride up to the Ridge Mile Track and around the track, and back down to the show grounds and over the course again to see who could do it in the fastest time. She took his challenge and barely won. (Sauerborn.)

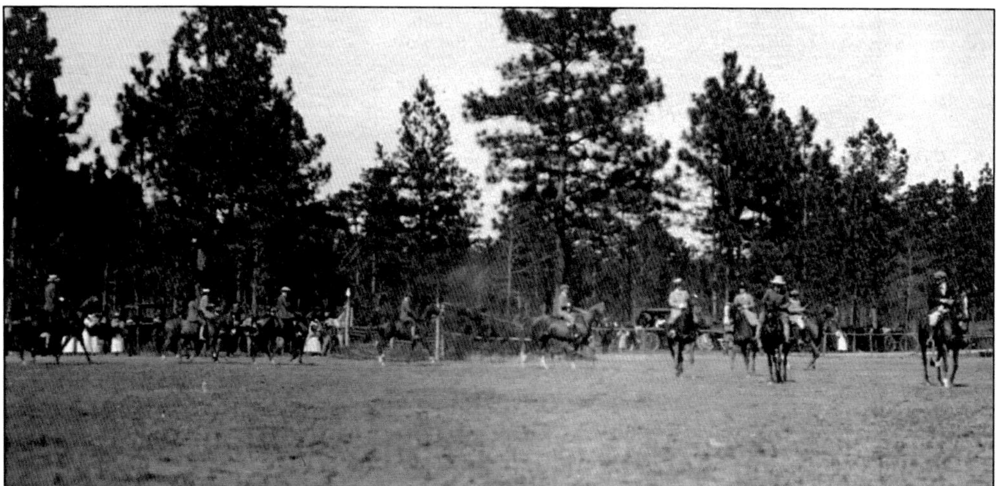

The classes at AHS have always been a testament to the support that riders give to the woods. In modern times, the entries have seen 35 horses in the hack classes alone. The funds raised from the horse show serve as the major fundraiser for the Hitchcock Woods Foundation.

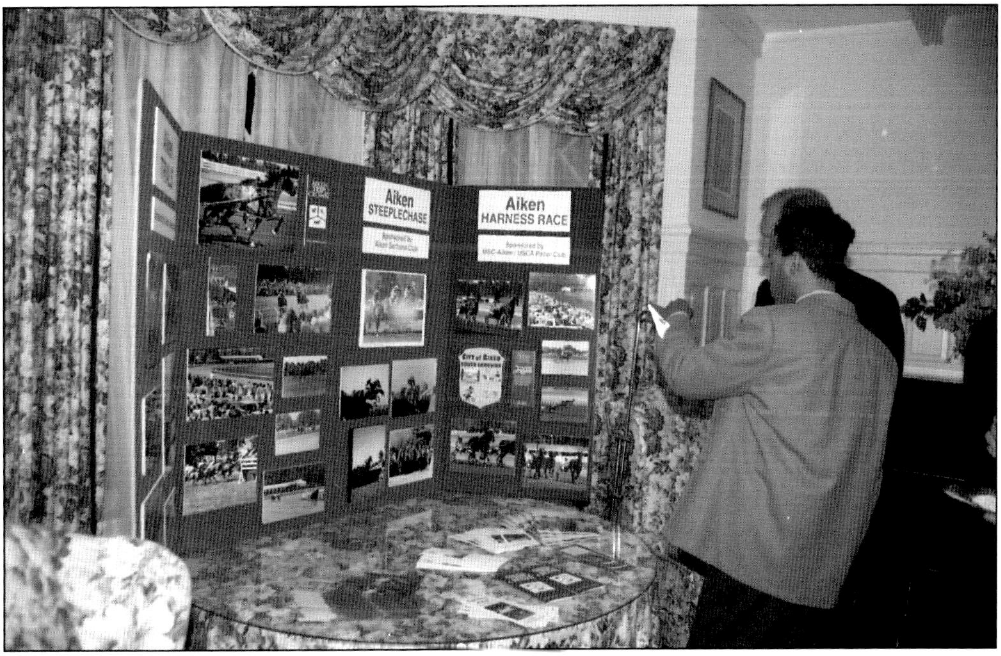

Aiken Triple Crown was coordinated to promote tourism; originally, it consisted of Thoroughbred flat racing, Thoroughbred steeplechase racing over jumps, and harness races, horses pulling sulkies. In the early 2000s, harness racing was replaced with polo. The Triple Crown of Aiken fills the calendar with three weekends of back-to-back horse activity. The following week is the Aiken Horse Show in the woods and then the Masters Tournament at Augusta National Golf Club, making six weeks in March and April very exciting in Aiken.

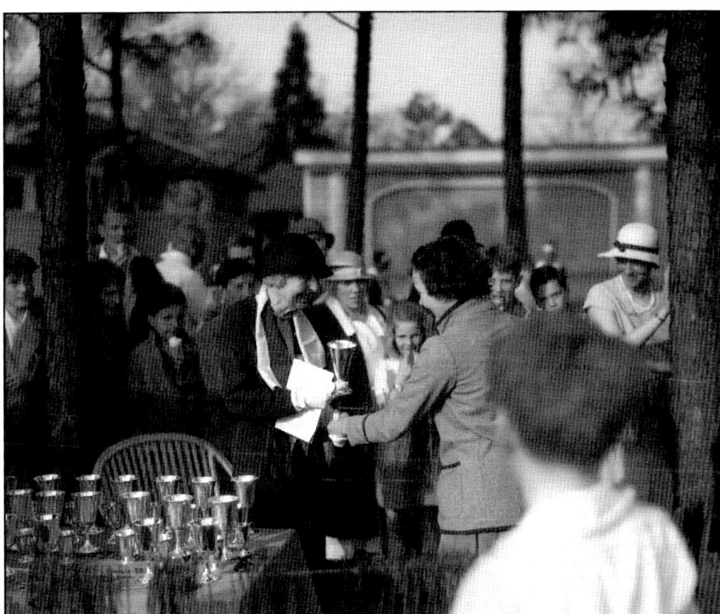

At Aiken Golf Club, Mrs. Hitchcock awards Patty Berg, who still holds the record for the most Majors won by a female golfer and member of the World Golf Hall of Fame, one of many trophies that she and fellow leader board occupant, Babe Zaharias, would win in their careers. Babe Zaharias played in Aiken often, and ESPN named her one of the Top 10 Most Influential Athletes in the 20th Century.

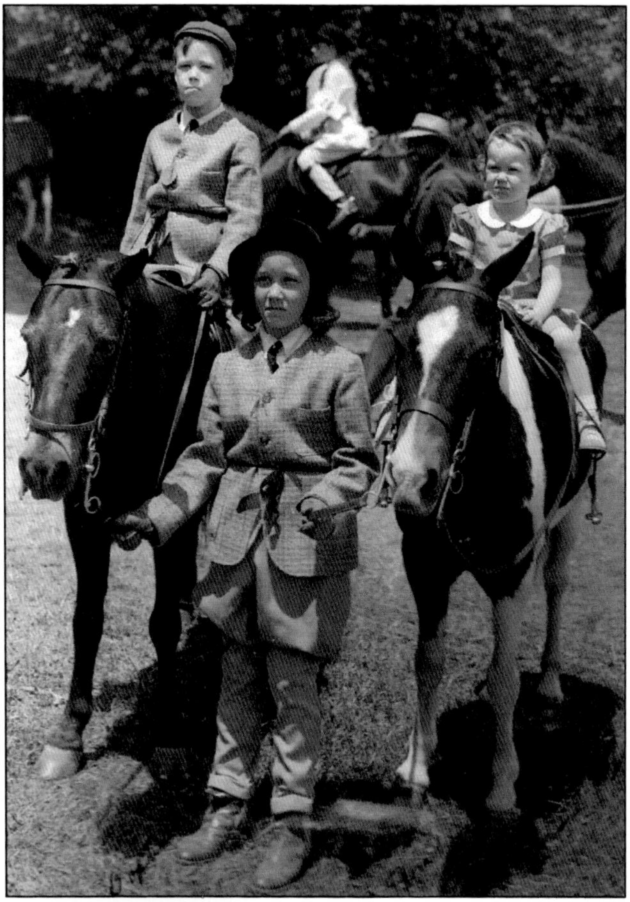

The Dolan children pictured here prepare for the family class at the horse show. The treasure trove of Dolan and Sellar photographs chronicles this family's love of horse sports, their time spent in the Hitchcock Woods, and their joyful days in Aiken. (Brainard.)

Aiken Preparatory School for Boys was founded in 1916 by Mrs. Hitchcock. In 2012, Aiken Prep and Mead Hall Schools merged. Mead Hall was founded in connection with St. Thaddeus Episcopal Church in honor of George Mead, who died in World War II. Fitting that the Mead family would start a school given that their commercial enterprises (Mead Paper) make most of the notebooks schoolchildren use today.

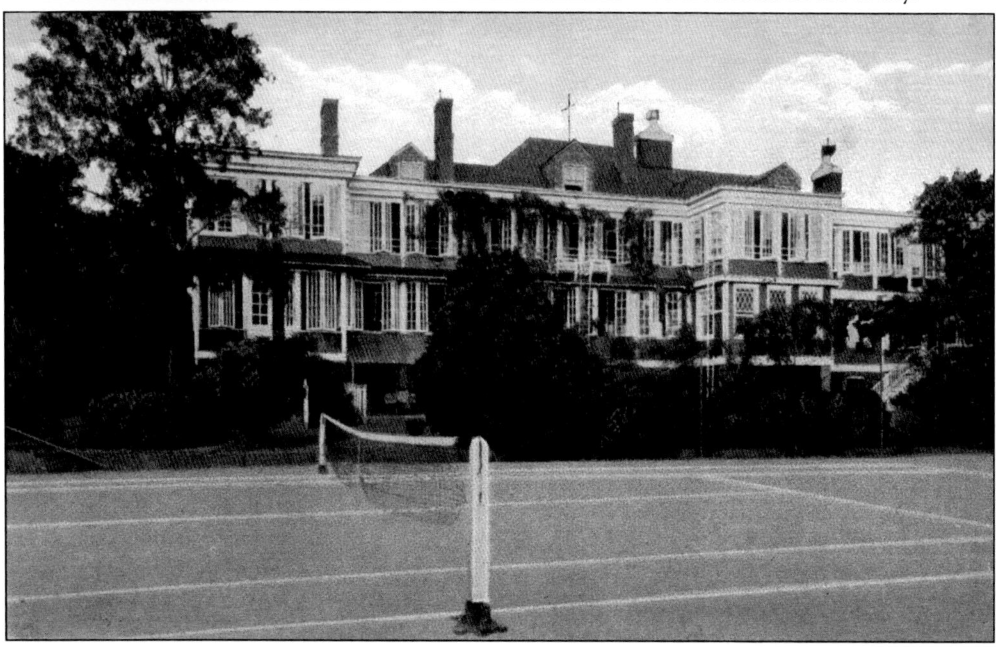

In the early days, like those seen here traveling to the show grounds to exhibit in AHS in 1919, a buggy would serve as one's grooming stall and picnic table. Now it is the bed of a truck or the tailgate of an SUV. Showing at AHS eliminates all of the fancy trappings of modern competition; no trailers, no big rigs, no stalls—just the woods and the horses. (Brainard.)

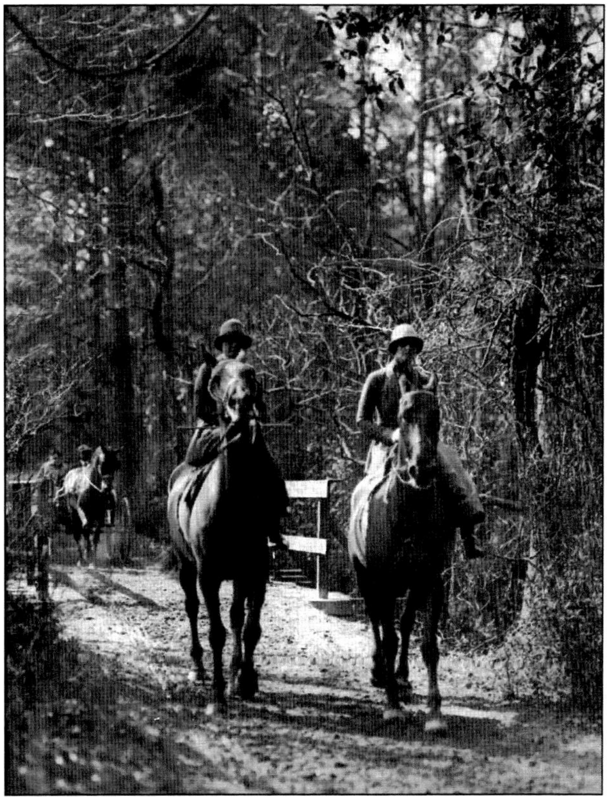

Aiken Prep School had a reputation for producing young boys whose minds were made clear by the art of sport. According to Mrs. Hitchcock, "Healthy bodies make for sound minds." This philosophy is why sporting activities were so enthusiastically offered to the students of both Aiken Prep and Fermata School.

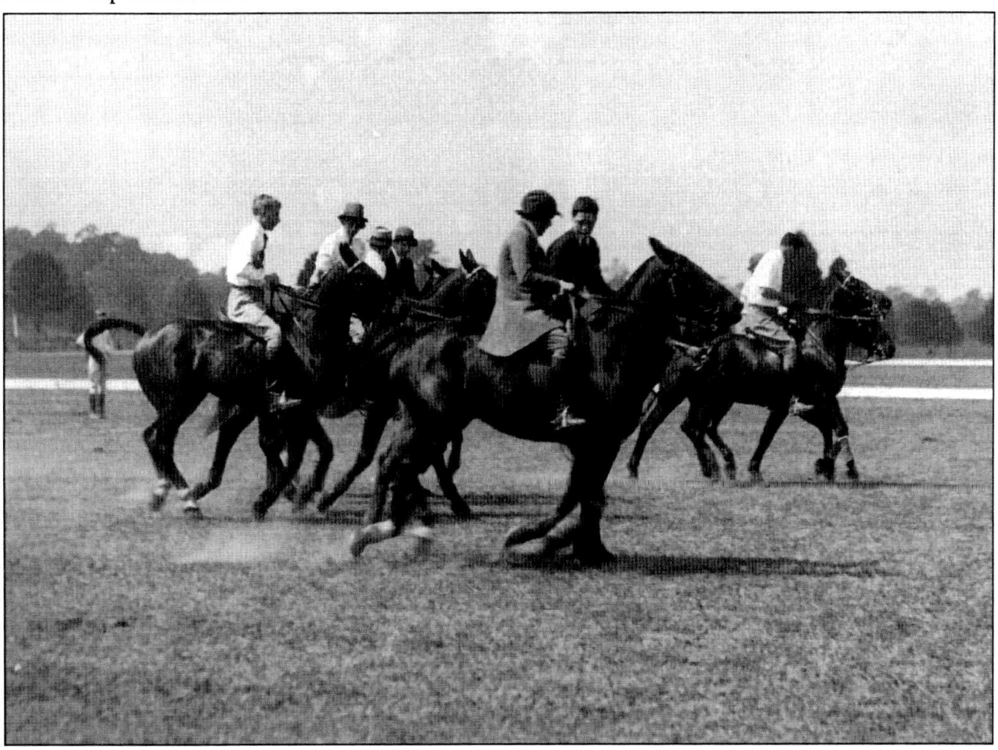

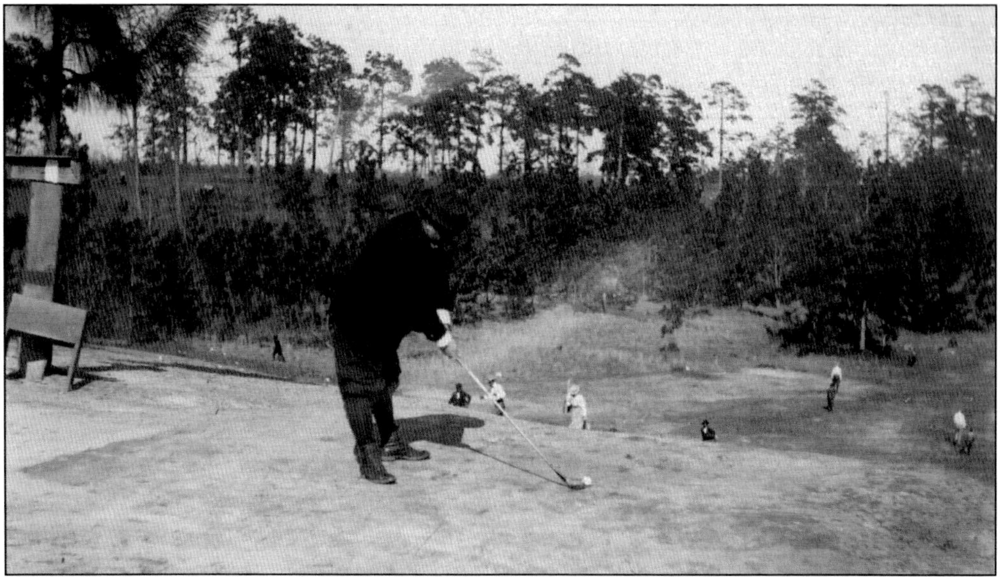

Golf was a burgeoning sport at the beginning of Aiken's sporting life. It has now become a scholastic sport. Aiken has a First Tee program, hosts the Palmetto Amateur, and has several young professional golfers on the PGA tour.

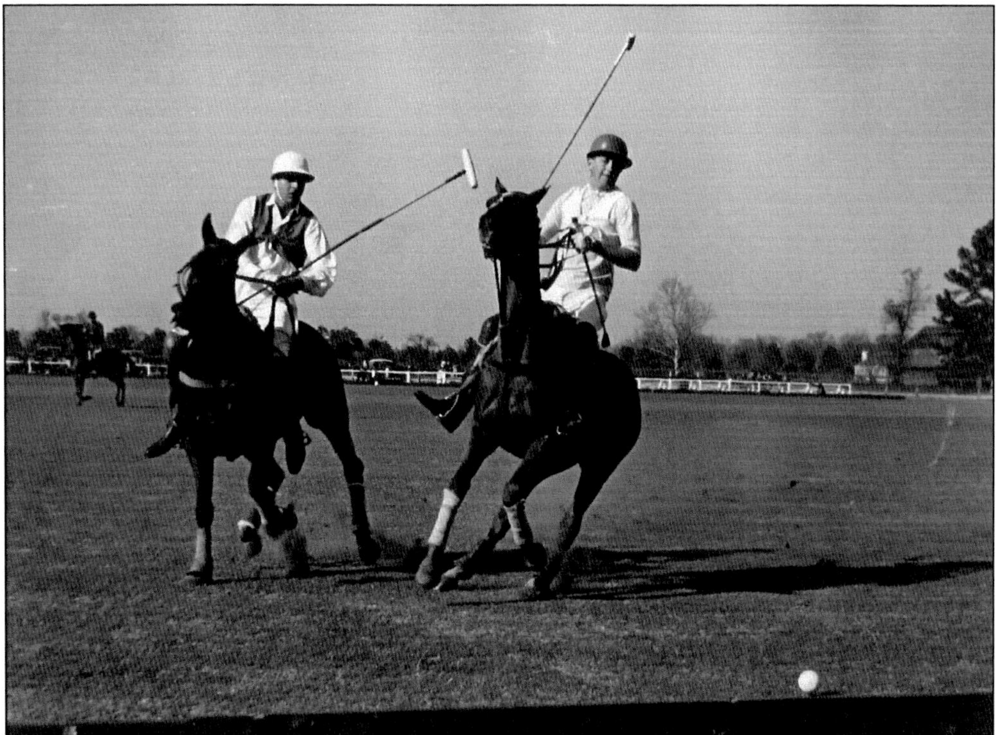

Polo, reaching its 135th year in Aiken in 2017, has been a mainstay of sport and social activity. The 125th year of polo was celebrated with a televised match on ESPN. Dunbar Bostwick, who founded the Aiken Trotting Track, and his brother Pete played polo and court tennis and later took up harness racing, proving that sporting at any age is possible.

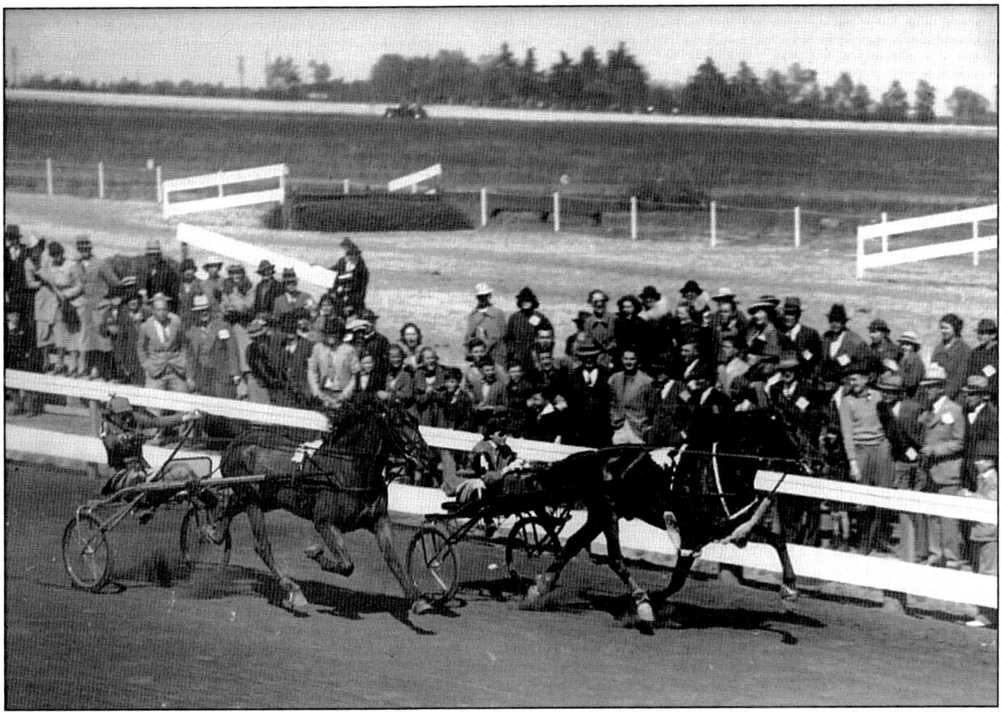

Aiken Trotting Track was installed where the old Hassler Polo Field had been. Pictured here is a trotting race in the 1960s. Bruz Ruckelshaus was in pursuit of horsepower of a different kind in his Indianapolis 500 racecars, but made an enthusiastic spectator. (Ruckelshaus.)

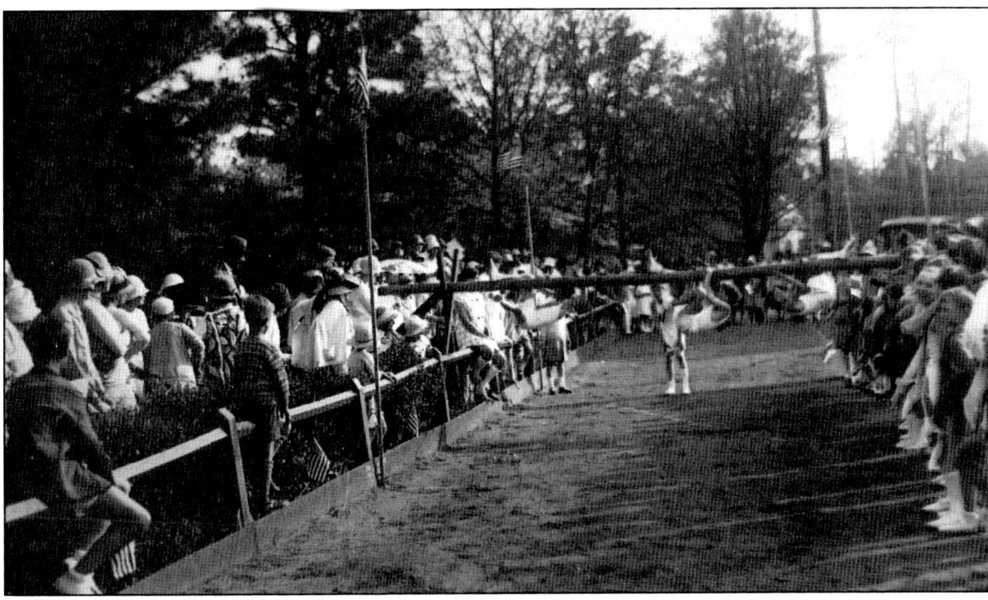

Aiken Prep Field Day was quite a contest, with many challenges that put the boys through their paces. The boys were not the only ones having to compete on field day; the mothers' foot race was always a highly coveted prize for the prevailing mom. Mrs. Fred Astaire set the course record for the 50-yard dash in 1947 and held it for several decades.

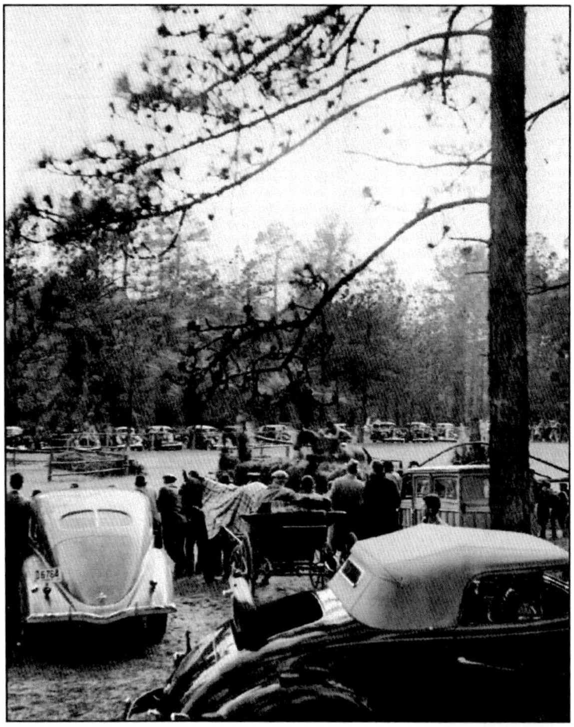

Under the sponsor tent at AHS, looking toward the ring, the view has not changed much in the last 100 years. With the wise stewardship of Gail Balding King, William Howard, Scott Riviere, Linda Knox Mclean, and Pat Corey over the last 20 years, the Aiken Horse Show entered its 100th year on solid footing.

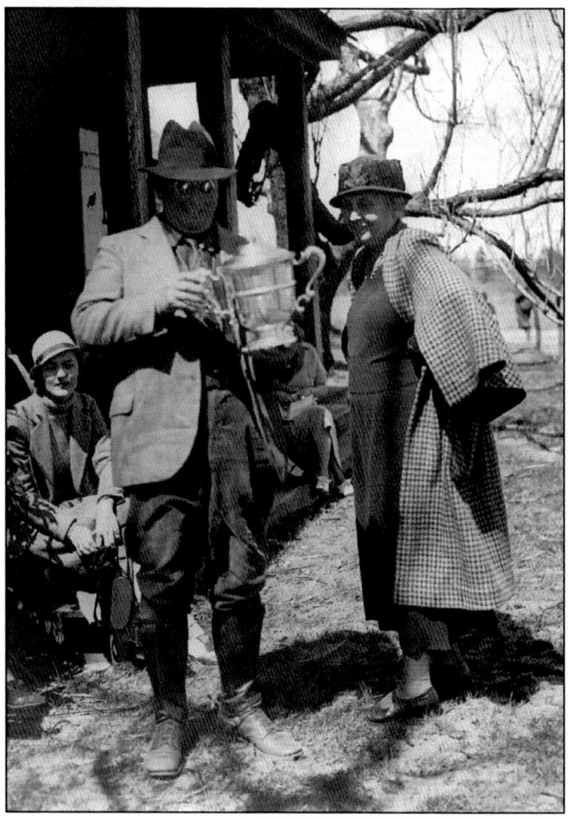

Trophy presentations in Aiken are a common occurrence, but there is no greater prize than that of having the Hitchcock Woods and its many trails and adventures as an award itself. One of the early medical doctors associated with Aiken reported to Paul Hamilton Hayne, "Aiken is particularly rich in provision for both one's spiritual and physical needs."

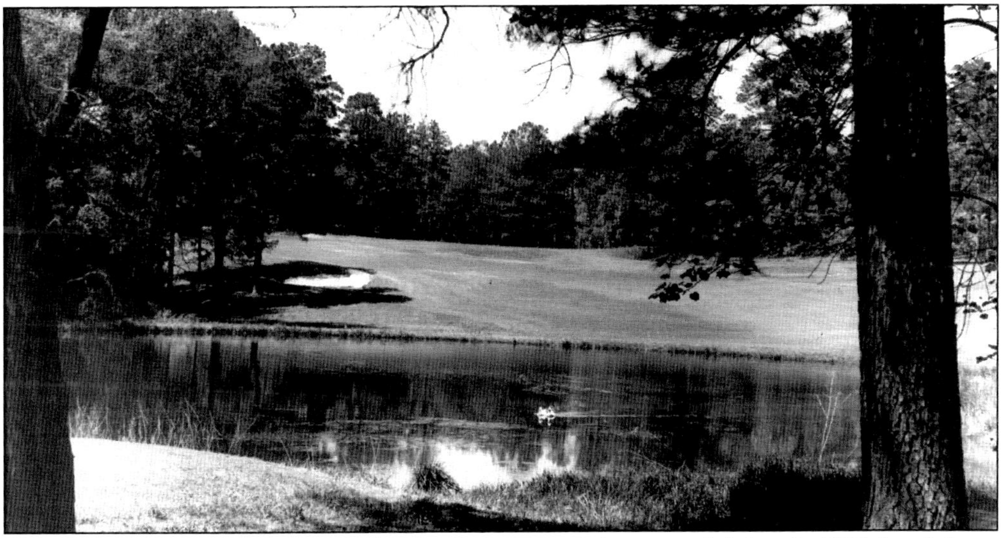

As women's tees celebrate their 100th year of existence, Palmetto and Aiken Golf Clubs celebrate their long history of golf in Aiken. The natural terrain and towering trees make for a challenging day on the links. Adding heritage to the challenge, Aiken's Hickory Shafted Golf Tournament makes for an interesting test of skill. The open and ladies' events bring out seasoned golfers and history buffs to enjoy the original game on original courses. The players dress in antique whites and knickers, looking like they stepped out of a 1911 photograph. (Lista.)

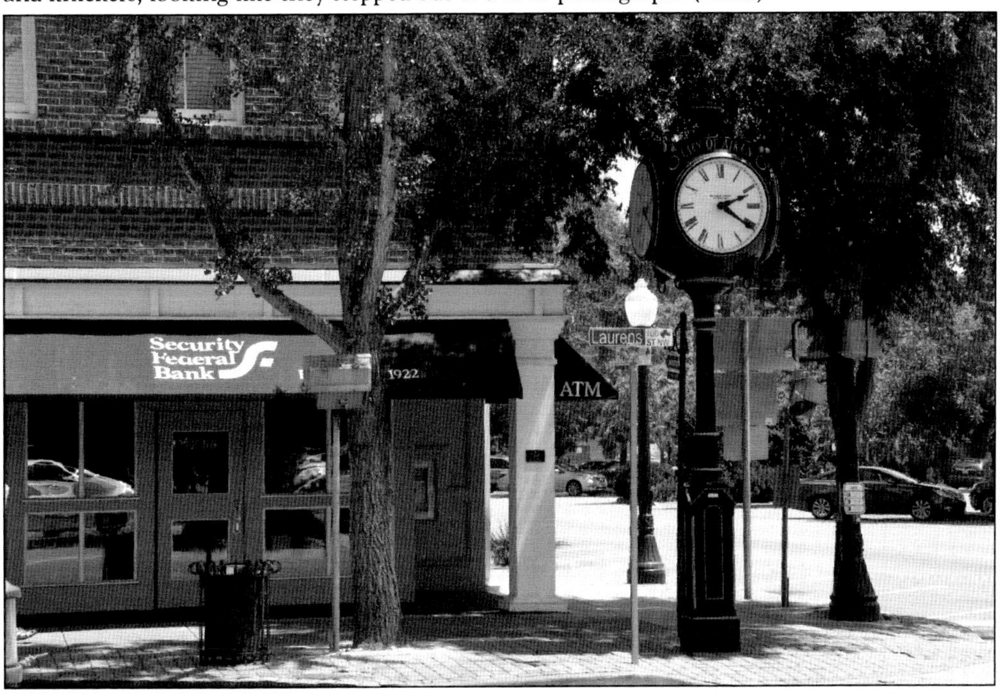

Sporting events in Aiken would not survive without the financial commitment of sponsors. Aiken's downtown is filled with professionals and chamber of commerce members who support sports. Businesses all over Aiken County provide monetary and volunteer support to the events that make Aiken special. One such bank, Security Federal, has been making Aiken dreams come true since 1922. (Lista.)

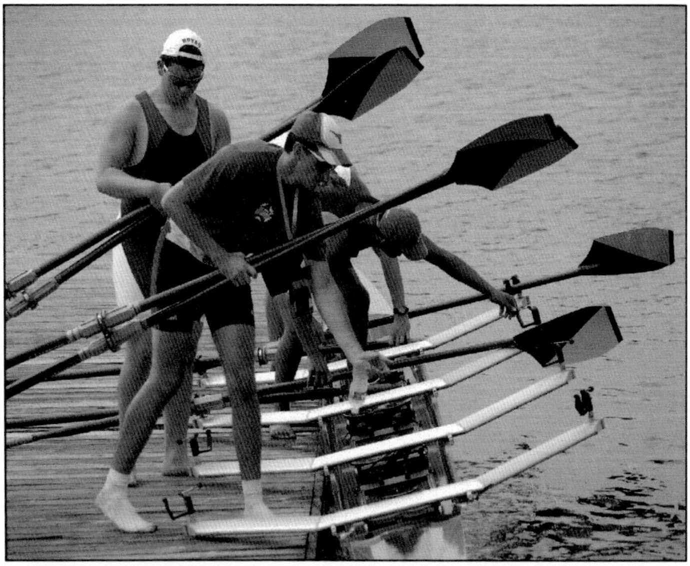

In 1996, members of the 1995 world-championship eight-man rowing team trained at Langley Pond, hoping to win a berth on the US Olympic team. Five of the eight went on to Atlanta to row for Team USA, capturing four medals in the overall rowing events. Langley Pond still serves as a training ground for regattas 20 years later. (The *Aiken Standard*.)

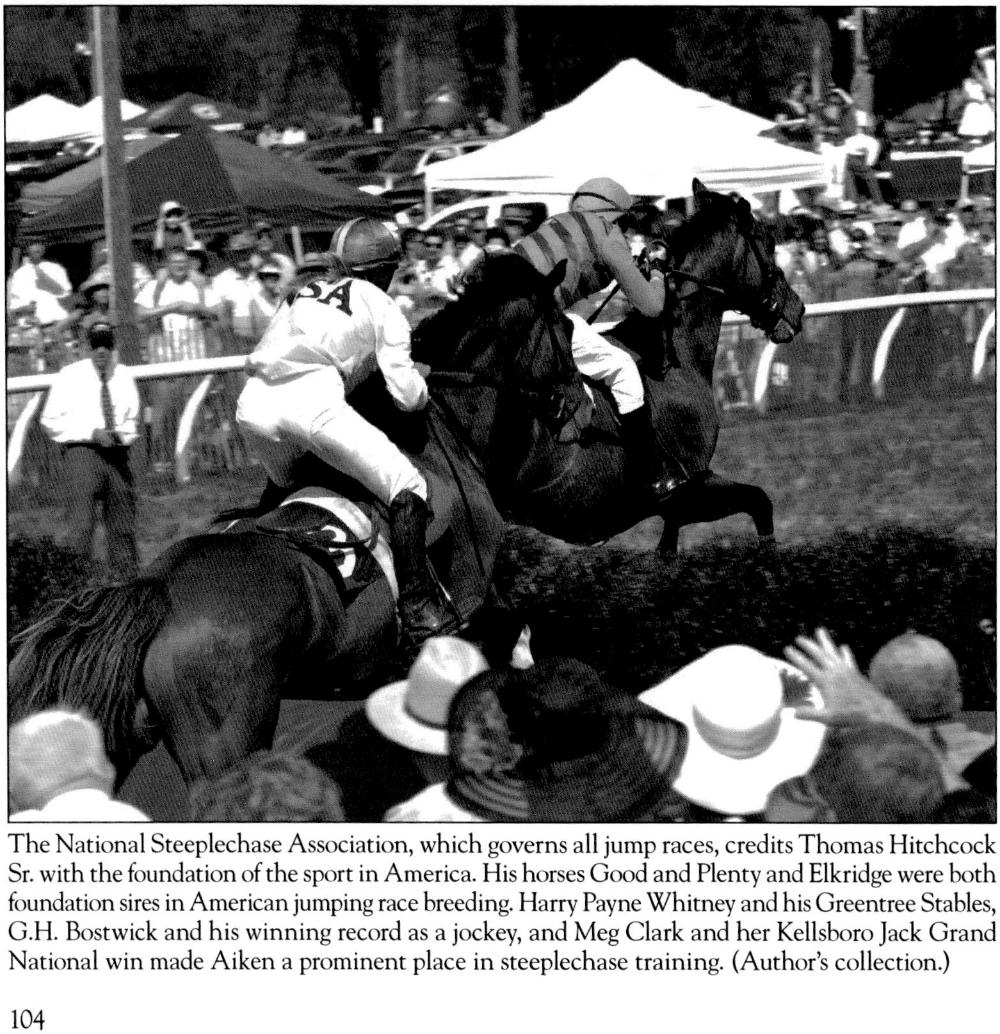

The National Steeplechase Association, which governs all jump races, credits Thomas Hitchcock Sr. with the foundation of the sport in America. His horses Good and Plenty and Elkridge were both foundation sires in American jumping race breeding. Harry Payne Whitney and his Greentree Stables, G.H. Bostwick and his winning record as a jockey, and Meg Clark and her Kellsboro Jack Grand National win made Aiken a prominent place in steeplechase training. (Author's collection.)

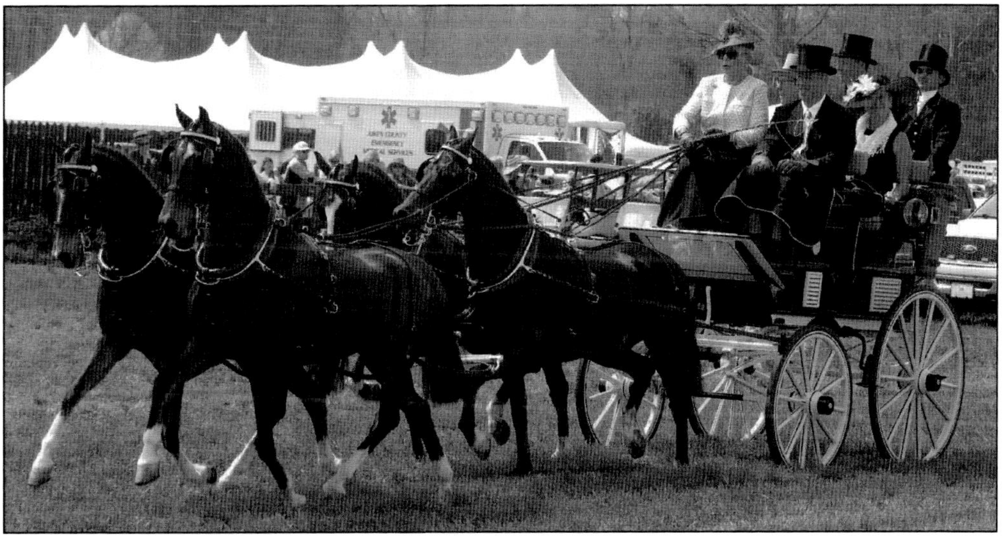

The carriage parade and the driving rally hosted on steeplechase weekend by Jacqueline Ohrstrom brings coaching enthusiasts to town and encourages elegant passengers on each equipage for the parade. Ohrstrom's mastery of driving skill is captured in this image as she maneuvers the matched team of four. Sporting a fashionable Folly hat, Jane Hottensen cuts an elegant figure for the parade. (The *Aiken Standard*.)

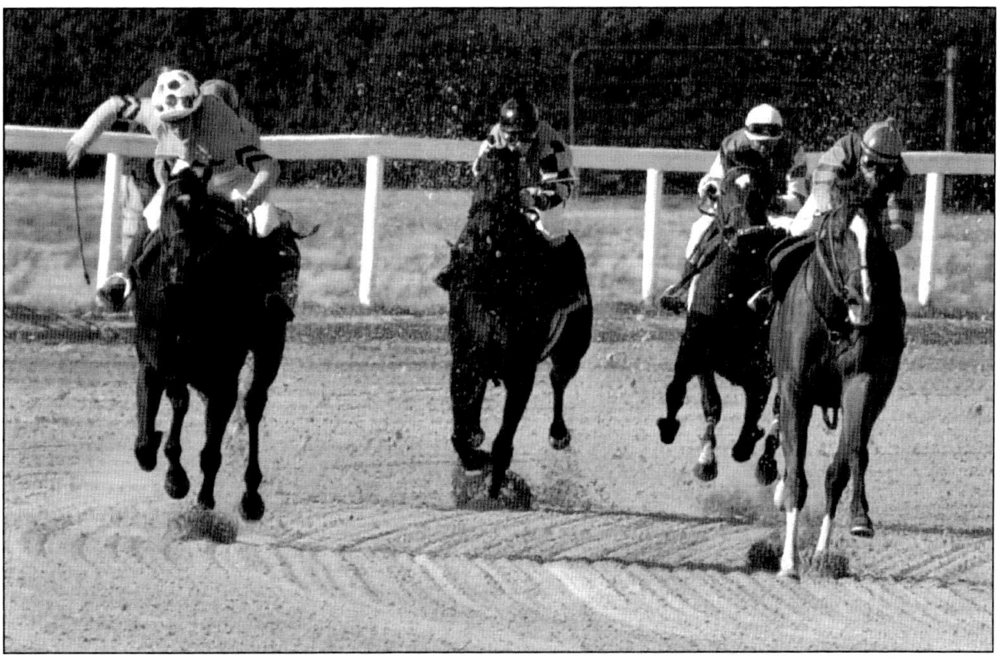

The Aiken Trials as an official event did not form until 1942; however, racing over fences and on the flat has been a part of Aiken since the 1880s. W.C. Whitney and F. Ambrose Clark were known for their flat-race training and Thomas Hitchcock for his jump racing, and since then, many trainers, riders, and owners have continued to keep training in Aiken a relevant enterprise. (Hall.)

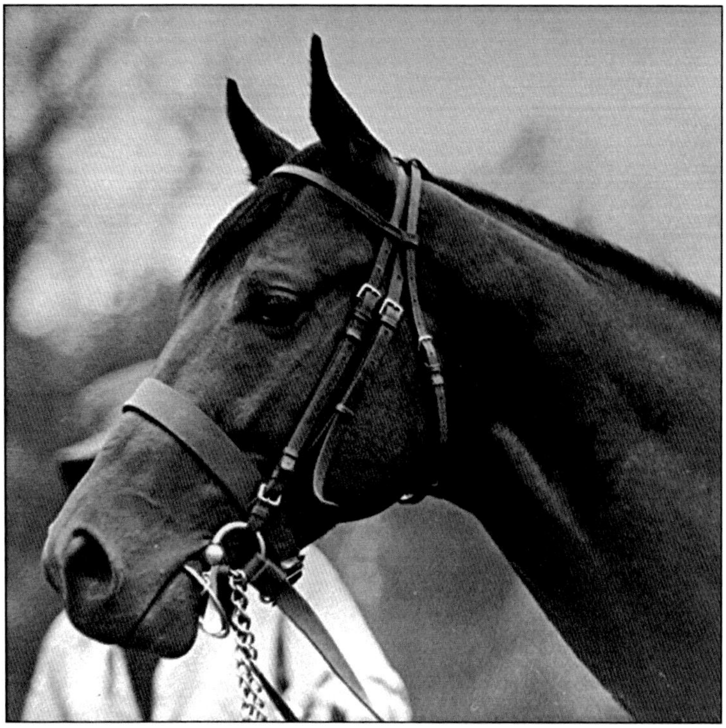

When Blue Peter died, the *New York Times* ran his obituary. His owners buried him in a coffin under the live oak in the middle of the Aiken Training Track. Blue Peter was a Thoroughbred of unique promise whose career ended too soon. Inducted into the Aiken Thoroughbred Racing Hall of Fame in 1977, Blue Peter's sire was War Admiral and grandsire Man o' War; he was out of Carillion and in 1948 was America's champion two-year-old. (Aiken Thoroughbred Racing Hall of Fame.)

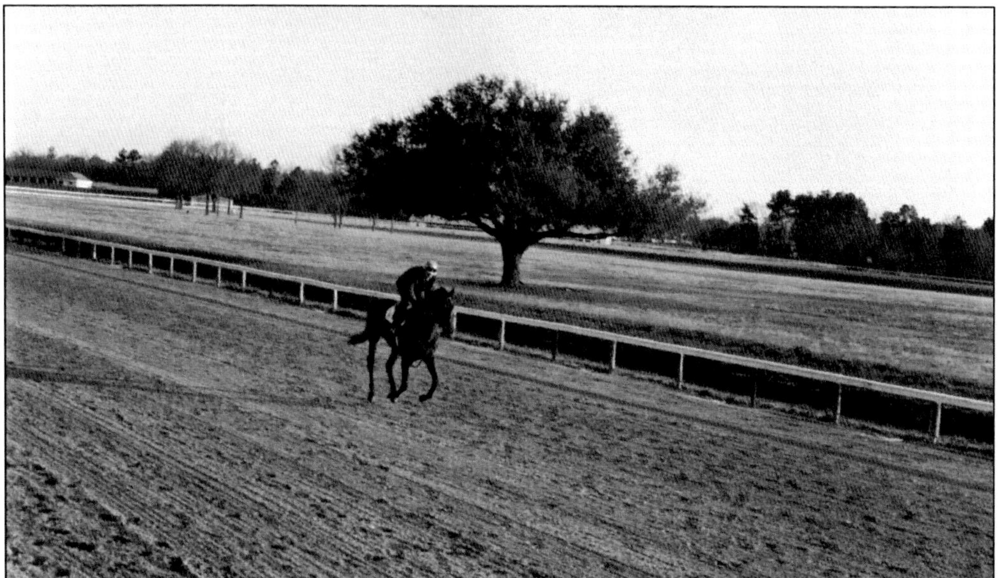

John Gaver Sr., Flint "Scotty" Schulhofer, and MacKenzie "Mack" Miller, all National Racing Hall of Fame inductees, were the backbone of Aiken's racing heritage from 1950 to 2000. Gaver graduated from Princeton and went to work making Greentree a legendary race stable. Schulhofer, born into an Aiken racing family, is best known for Colonial Affair's 1993 Belmont win, ridden by the first woman to win a leg of the Triple Crown, Julie Krone. Miller trained for several great Thoroughbred organizations. The most prominent was Rokeby, Paul Mellon's racing stable. (Aiken Thoroughbred Racing Hall of Fame.)

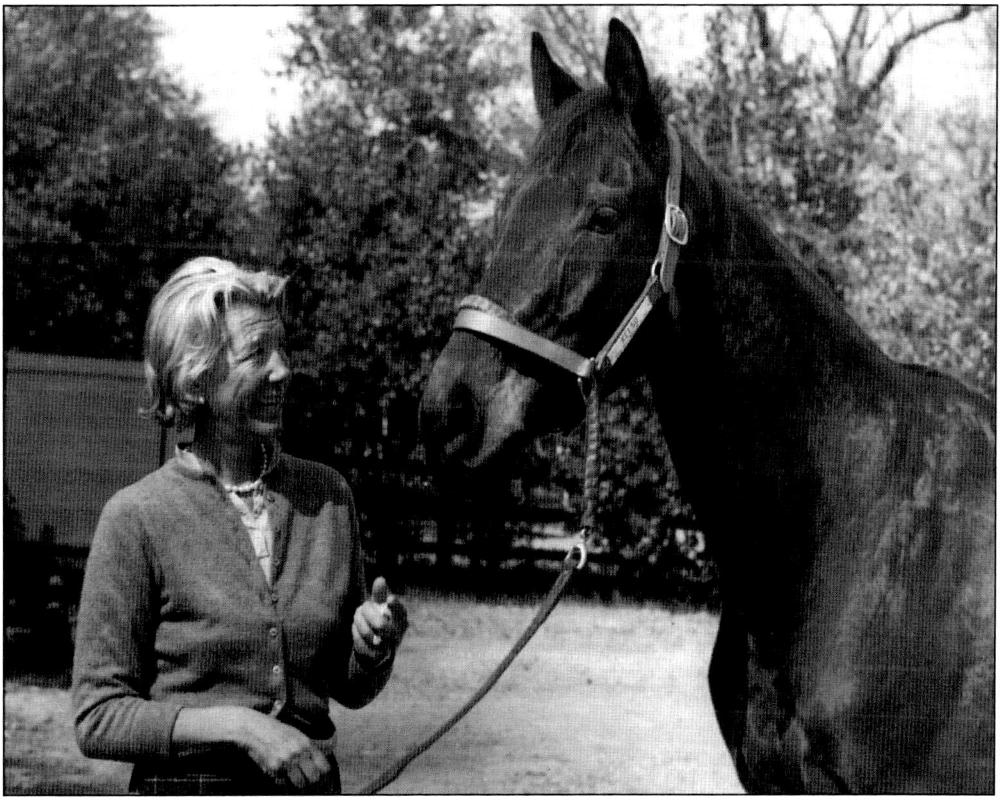

Kelso was named Thoroughbred Race Horse of the Year five times and retired as a foxhunter. Trained in Aiken with Bohemia Stables during the winter season, Kelso was owned by Allaire DuPont, who in her own right was a remarkable sporting woman in shooting, tennis, and piloting gliders. Kelso is in the National and Aiken Racing Halls of Fame. (Aiken Thoroughbred Racing Hall of Fame.)

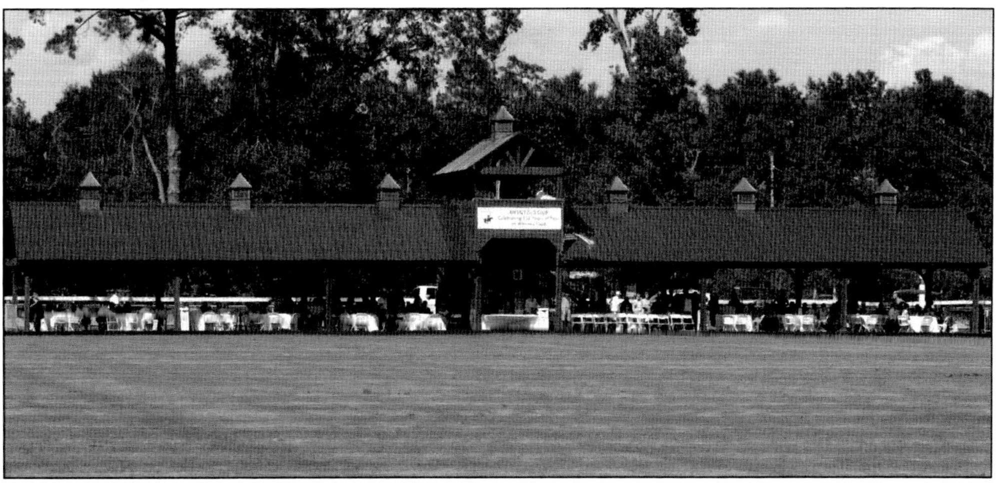

Alan Corey was a founder of Star Riding Program and the leading force for Aiken Polo Club. Building the pavilion at Whitney Field was of paramount importance to Corey. Keeping the new construction in character with its surroundings was a triumph of diplomacy, and the structure will serve the club well. For more information, go to www.aikenpoloclub.org. (Bossard.)

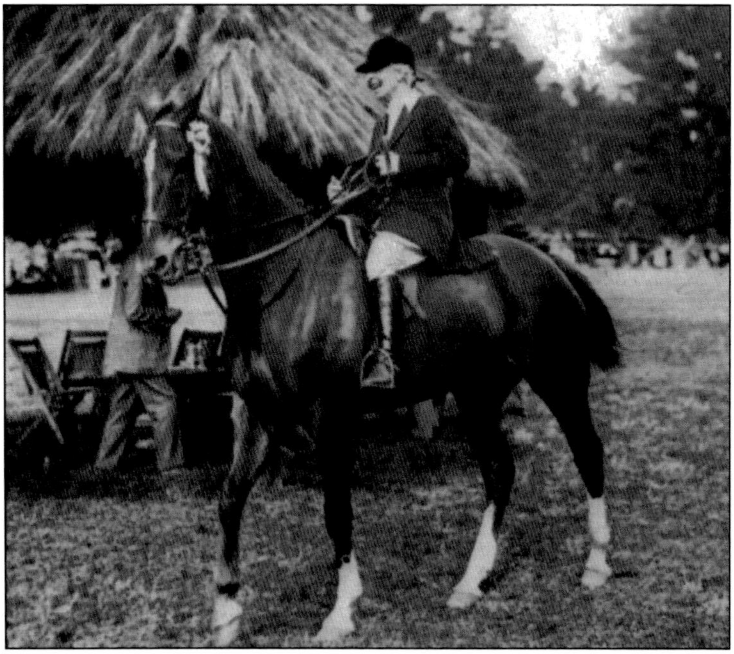

The 100th anniversary of AHS in 2016 and the centennial celebration of Aiken Hounds in 2014 inspired the collection efforts of photographs and anecdotes about Aiken's sporting life. Many of those images and stories are captured on these pages, and everyone who has enjoyed the living that Aiken offers has been a champion in their own way, as Louise Hitchcock is in this photograph at AHS. (Brainard.)

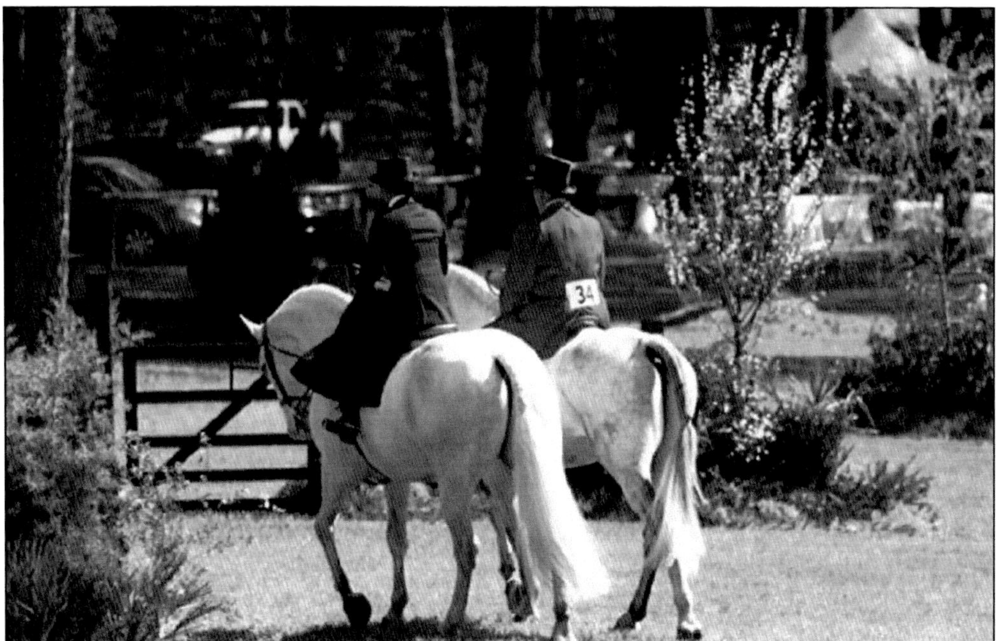

AHS will continue on into the future so long as those people who enjoy the experience continue their support. Exhibitors, volunteers, sponsors, and spectators, along with the hardworking staff of the foundation, make this annual fundraiser an enchanted step back in time. The dedication and commitment of everyone involved is so appreciated and a true gift to Aiken's greatest legacy. Taylor Myers and Arnold Bloom cut a classic swath in the pairs class on their matched greys. (Author's collection.)

Seven

Aiken and the Next 100 Years

The Faces Change but the Sporting Remains

Aiken's sporting life into the next century is secure so long as those who love the city continue to safeguard its traditions and character. In changing economies and fluctuating demographics, some things change, others remain the same, and some are lost forever. With community and business support, many of the traditions that have made Aiken special for the last 100 years will continue to draw visitors and residents alike for the next 100 years.

New entities will rise up to help foster these traditions in the future as they have in the past. The universal themes that make up the fabric of Aiken may manifest in unique or different ways, linking to the past but defining the future. The thrill of speed has been floating in the air for decades, so new sports like the Southern Nationals speedboat racing on the Savannah River and the drag-race challenges on Drag Strip Road will match the thundering hooves of polo and steeplechase. The fluid elegance of regattas on Langley Pond or the thrill of landing a big one while sportfishing may be the future title sports for Aiken. The past heritage games will remain and continue through polo, court tennis, golf, and all things equestrian; even the Western brethren will join with English riders and bring barrel racing to the fore.

New technologies from the Savannah River Site, new corporate and business sponsors, and new residents will bring renewed vitality to the sporting life. As a community, Aiken celebrates many of the sports that other communities have—cycling, marathons, and football—but residents also embrace the odd or archaic sports that allow for individuality. World champions walk the streets unnoticed, Olympic athletes dine at restaurants without being asked for an autograph, and national titleholders practice their skills without press scrutiny. As it was in the past, Aiken will remain a relaxed playground for those who seek sport at its highest level without intrusion from the rest of the world. Aiken will always be the Sporting Capital of the South and the Queen of Winter Resorts.

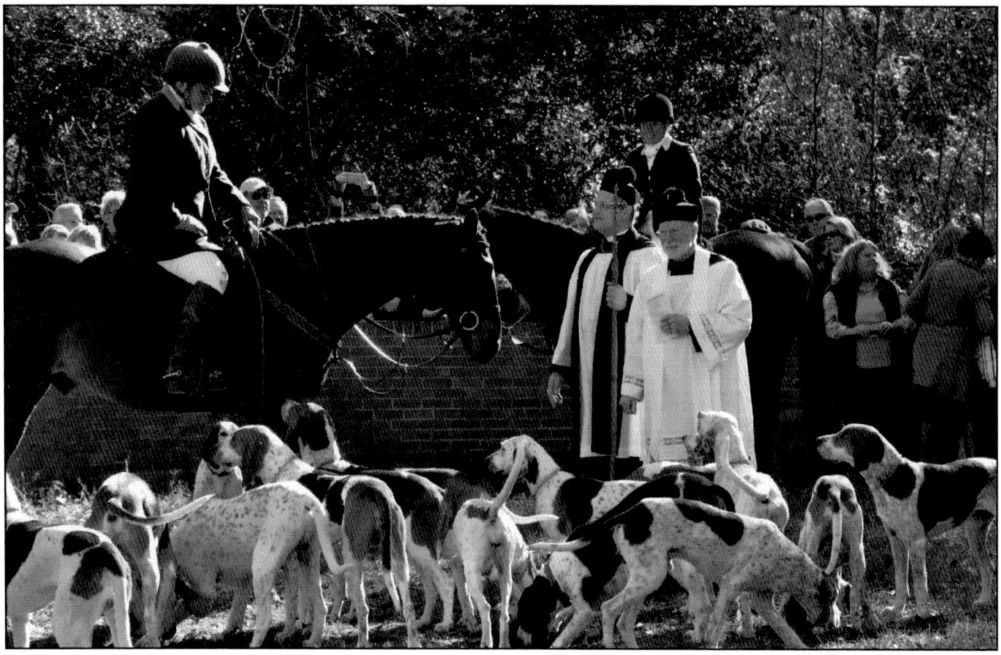

Aiken Hounds' annual blessing on Thanksgiving morning brings together the next generation of hunt personnel and the community to celebrate the bond between man and beast. Huntsman Katherine Gunter (mounted at left) and Arden Wildasin, junior whip and a nationally ranked event rider who sent her horse to compete in the London Olympics (mounted at right), bring the hounds together at Memorial Gate for the blessing. (Lista.)

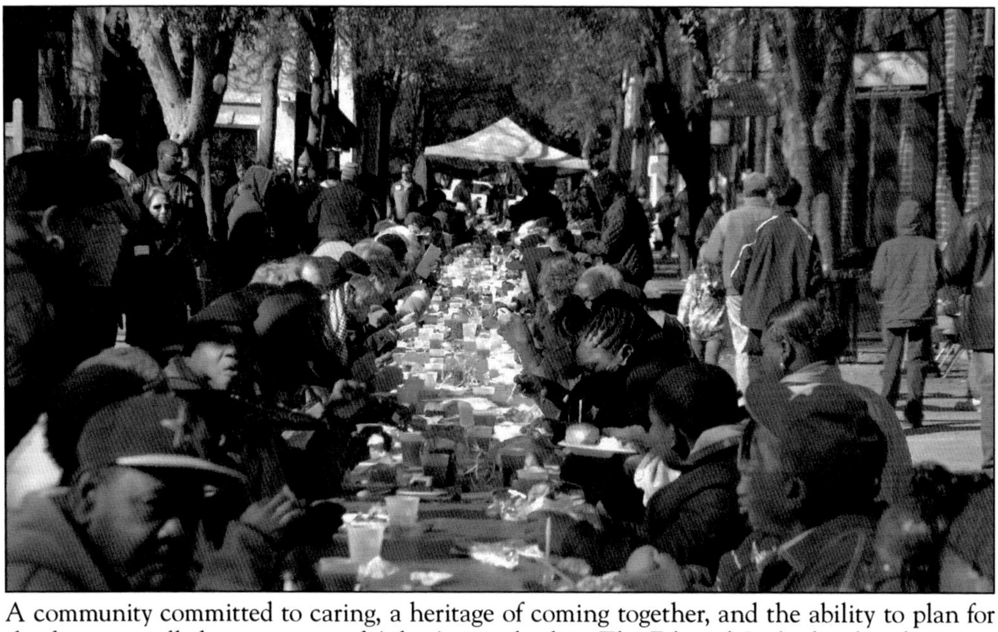

A community committed to caring, a heritage of coming together, and the ability to plan for the future are all characteristics of Aiken's civic leaders. The Erb and Sacks families, longtime hospitality-industry leaders in Aiken, started a One Table event in the Alley on Thanksgiving Day, bringing people of all walks of life and backgrounds together to enjoy the spirit of community. (The *Aiken Standard*.)

Juilliard in Aiken, now Joye, is a winter arts festival of music, dance, and theater arts started by Steven Naifeh and the late Gregory Smith of Joye Cottage. Concerts and workshops offer citizens world-class performances by Juilliard students, professors, and alums. Connie Darden and Jesse Colin Young, of the Youngbloods, have helped bring the Juilliard workshops and concerts into the elementary and middle schools and have organized jam sessions for high school and college students. (The *Aiken Standard*.)

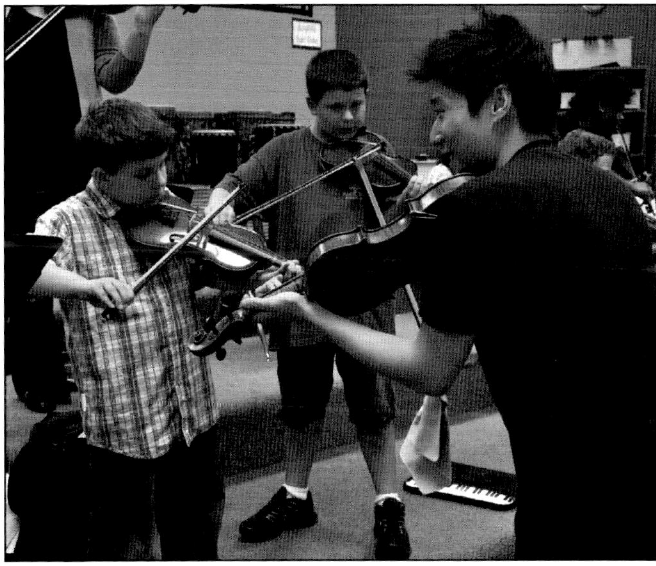

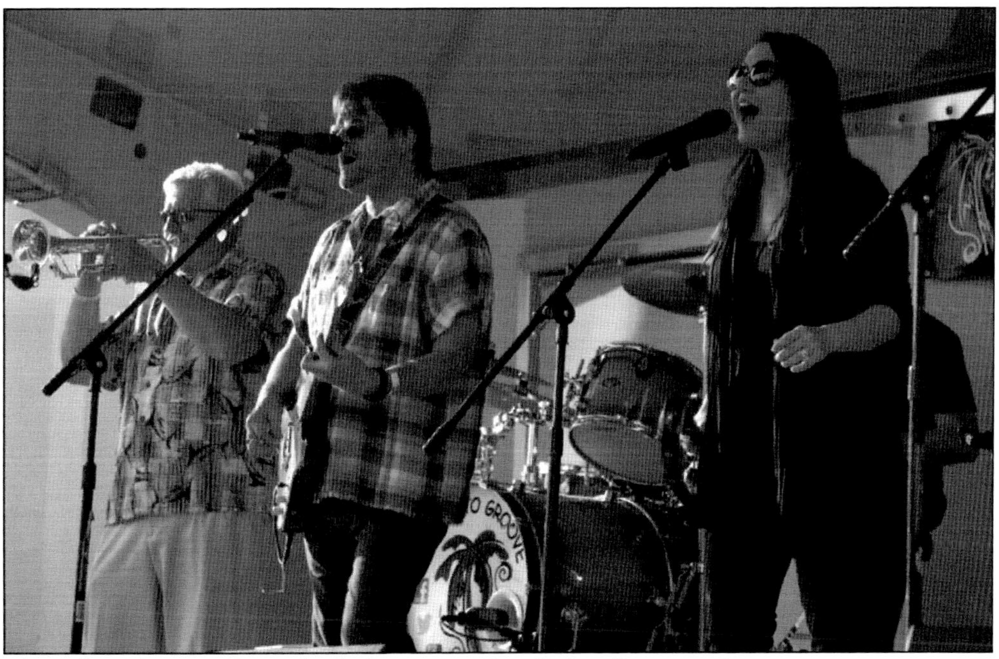

The Aiken Bluegrass Festival, which supports Star Riding Program, therapeutic equine services in cooperation with Aiken Tri-Development Centers, is a highly anticipated event. Combining the community's love of the arts culture and its equine heritage, this event draws crowds from near and far in both spring and fall. Pictured here is the Palmetto Groove Band performing at Highfields. (Cram.)

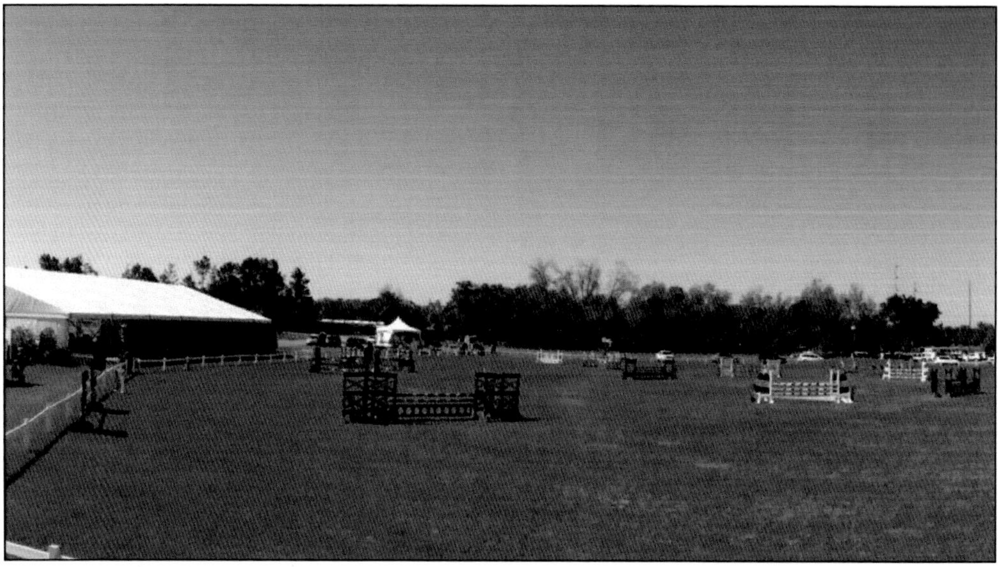

Progressive Show Jumping Inc. owners Cathy and Rick Cram have brought A-rated shows back to fashion in Aiken. Having hosted the Aiken Spring Classic at Highfields and at the Aiken Horse Park, shows for hunters and jumpers are a boon to the local hospitality industry. Their facility also hosts many charity functions without horses. (Cram.)

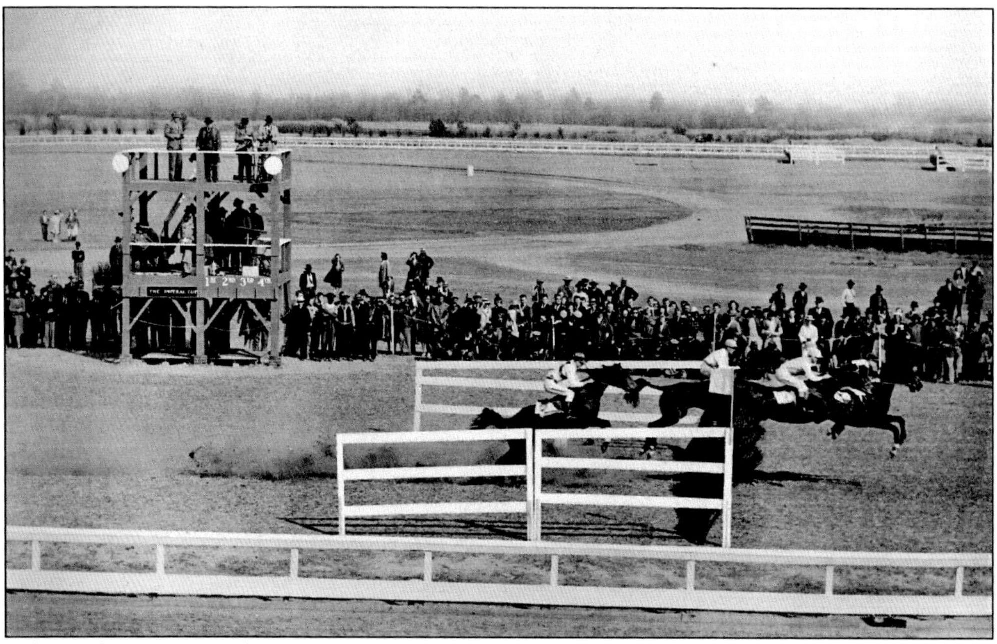

Aiken's dirt streets and equestrian traffic lights will always remind drivers whose roads these really are—king horse. The Winthrop family and their donation of Winthrop Field and Aiken's historic preservation organizations will ensure that the barns at Whitney Field and the charm of the Aiken Training Track and the Track Kitchen remain due to the importance of Aiken's Horse District. (Ruckelshaus.)

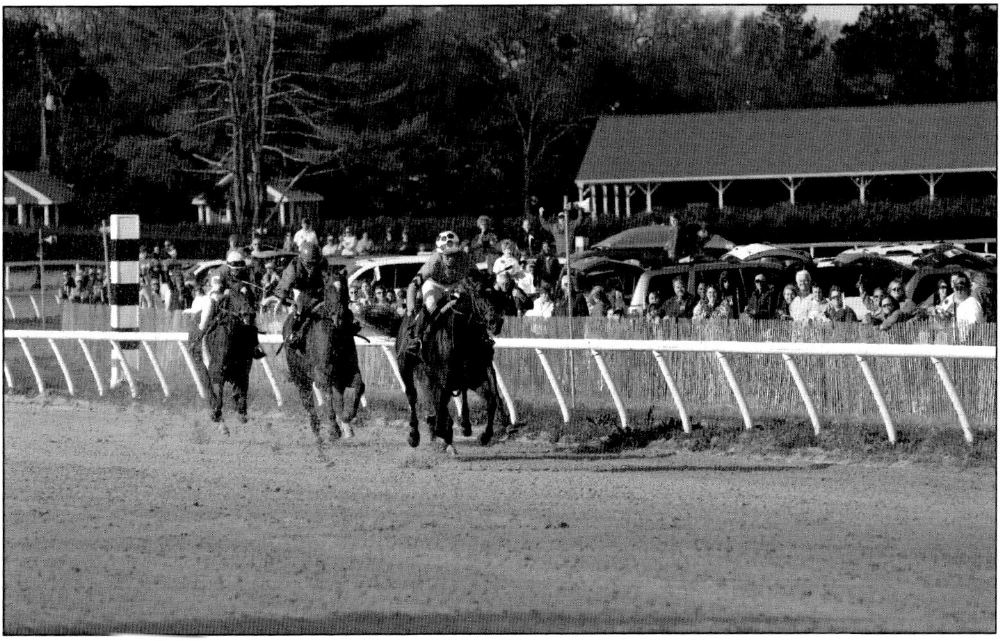

The first leg of Aiken's Triple Crown, the Trials, have expanded their appeal to the public. The sponsor tent, with a raised viewing deck, various ticket options, and an expanded parking area, has attracted more spectators for the coming years. For more information, see www.aikentrainingtrack.com. (Conger.)

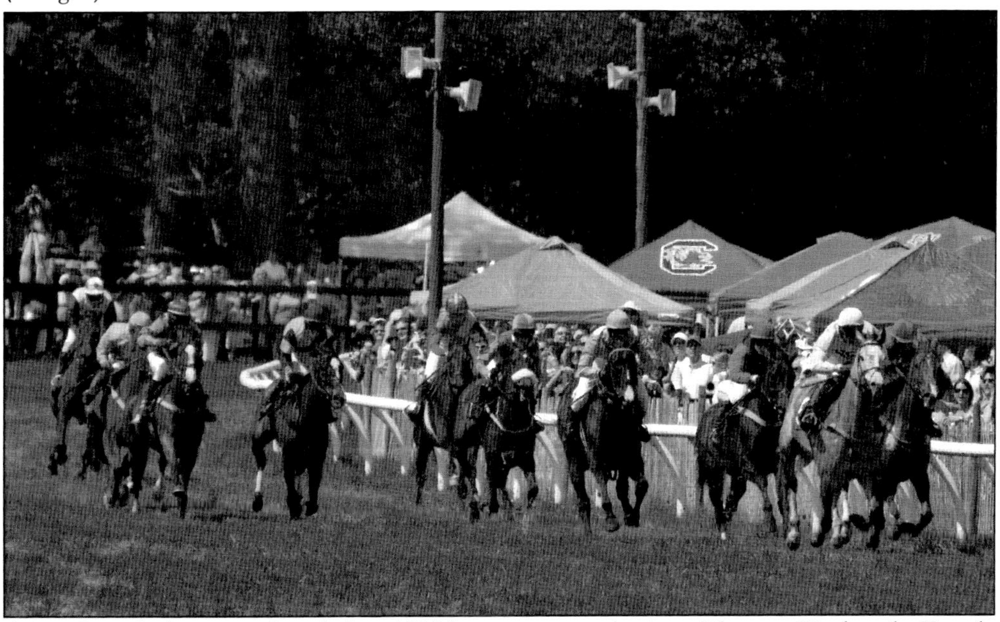

Aiken Steeplechase was founded in 1930 by sporting enthusiasts Thomas Hitchcock, Temple Gwathmey, and Harry Worchester Smith. In times of war and civic development, continuing the races seemed almost impossible, until in 1967 the efforts of Charlie Bird III, Pete Bostwick, MacKenzie Miller, Willard Thompson, Ford Conger, and Paul Mellon revived the tradition. In 2015, Bruce's Field at Aiken Horse Park was founded to honor late Aiken horseman Bruce Duchossois, who had a love of both racing and showing horses. (Author's collection.)

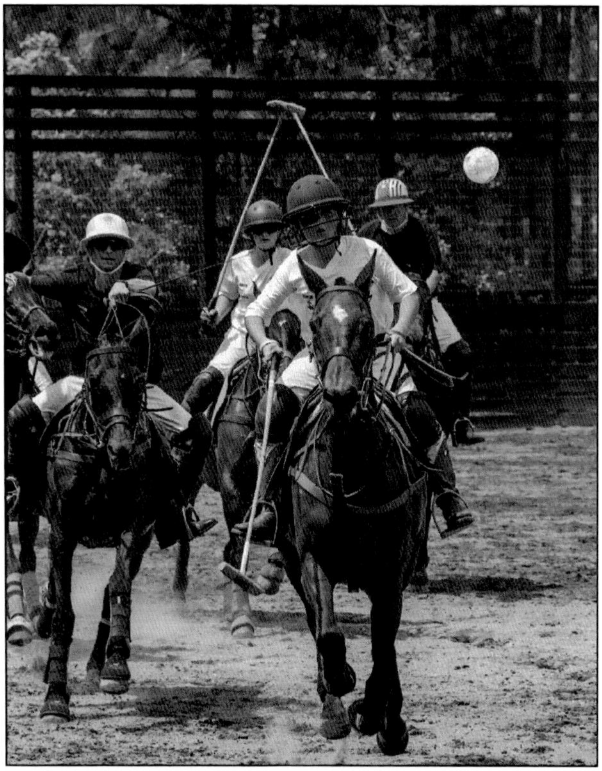

Aiken Youth Polo has been active for the last decade, with arena polo championships played at Hilltop Farm and youth leagues started at Aiken Polo Club sporting full field play. The Sunday youth skirmishes at Whitney Field make polo a popular sport among the under-16 set. (hoofpics.com.)

As much as youth sports are a focus of activity within the community, the chalk cliffs are a focus within the woods themselves. The various ecosystems and abundant flora and fauna attract hobbyists and scientists to study the biodiversity. Without the efforts of the foundation, one of the largest urban forests in the United States would have been lost to mining, timbering, and residential development. (Lista.)

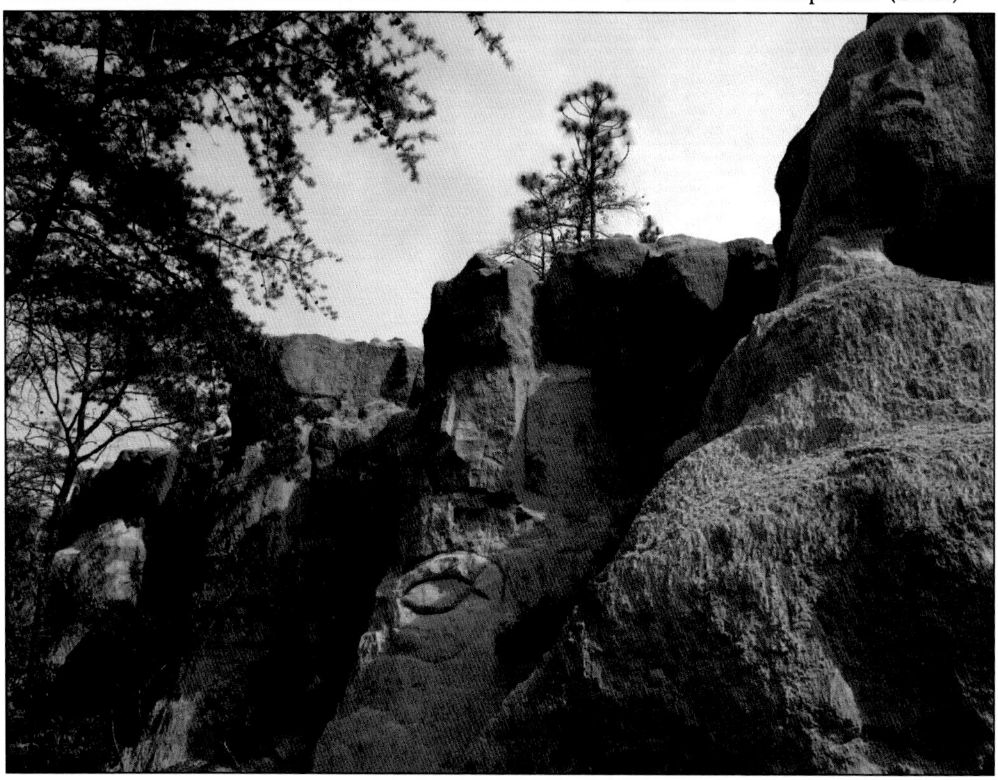

The Hitchcock Woods have played host to many great announcements, whether the birth of a child, or, in this case, the announcement of a marriage: Biz Carey and Ted Gregory took the leap into wedlock and announced it to their friends with this photograph. Many weddings have taken place in the woods; the favorite day is Thanksgiving at Memorial Gate. (Carey.)

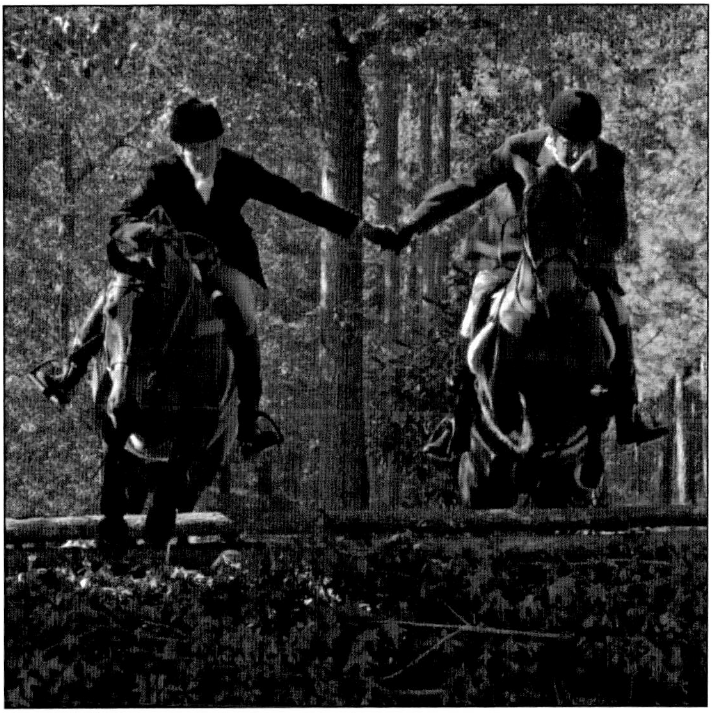

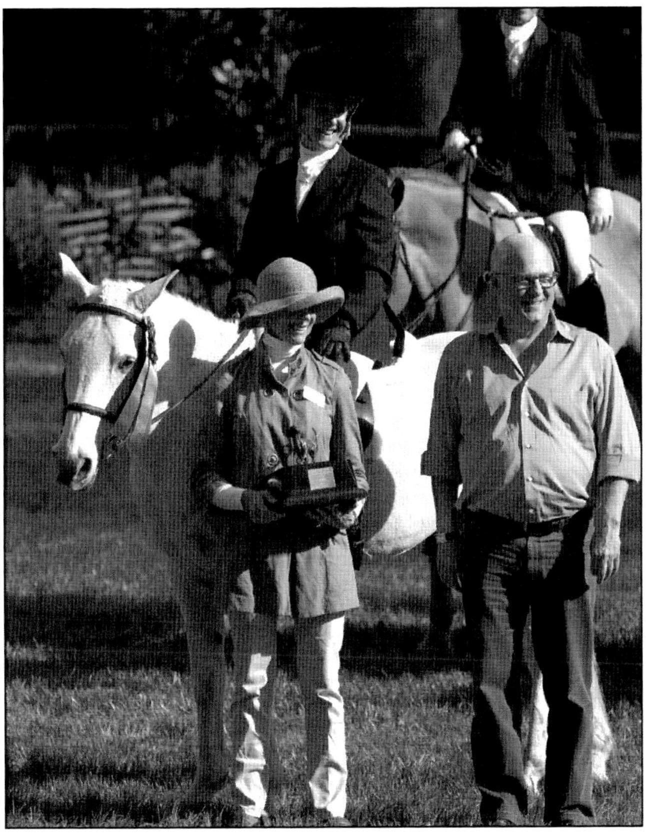

AHS has been a cultivator of those who will carry on the mission of Celestine Eustis, Francis Hitchcock, and Louise Hitchcock and their love of the pinelands and its preservation. Hitchcock Woods Foundation ensures that several of its trustees foxhunt, show ride, or play polo. Foundation trustees Sara McNeil, mounted, and Nancy Francis, presenting trophies, and Rich McNeil, right, are examples of the commitment that trustees show for the woods. (Bossard.)

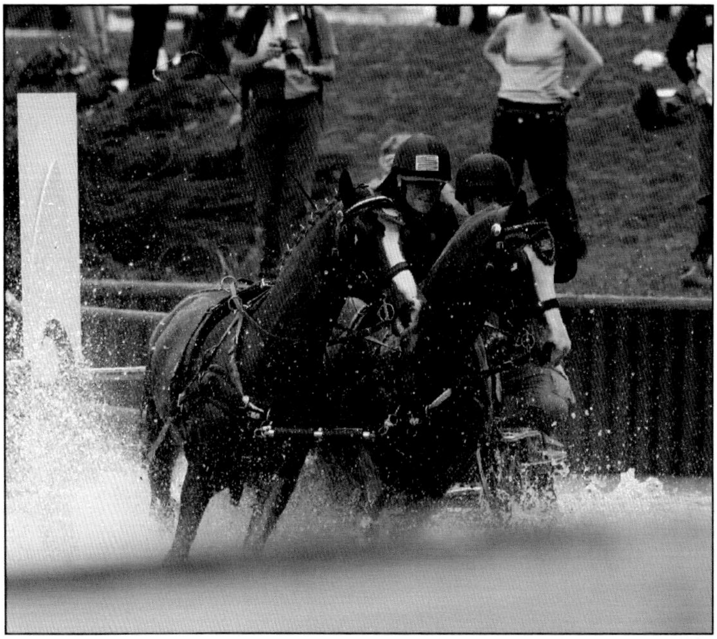

World-champion driver Wendy O'Brien calls Aiken home and was attracted to the area through Katydid Combine driving events hosted by Katrina Becker and Jennifer Matheson. The Aiken Driving Club hosts many events for drivers of all levels. The US Driving Society held its 2014 National Annual Meeting in Aiken. (Ruckelshaus.)

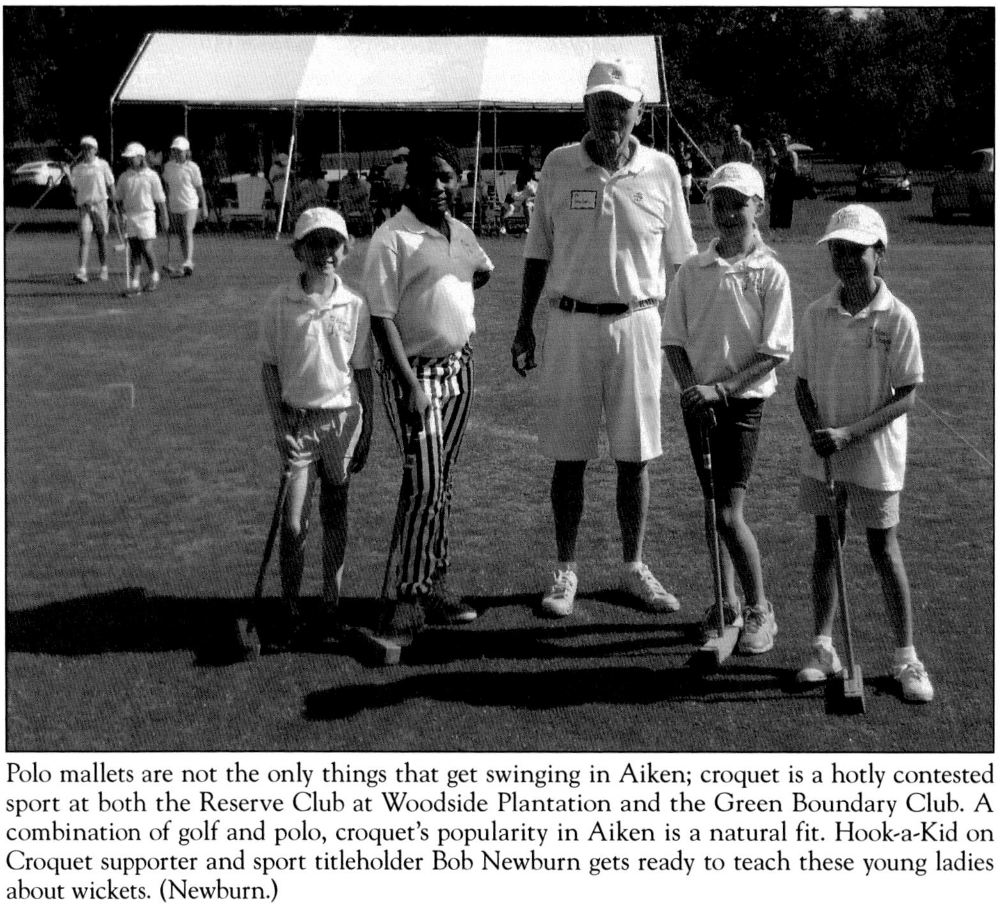

Polo mallets are not the only things that get swinging in Aiken; croquet is a hotly contested sport at both the Reserve Club at Woodside Plantation and the Green Boundary Club. A combination of golf and polo, croquet's popularity in Aiken is a natural fit. Hook-a-Kid on Croquet supporter and sport titleholder Bob Newburn gets ready to teach these young ladies about wickets. (Newburn.)

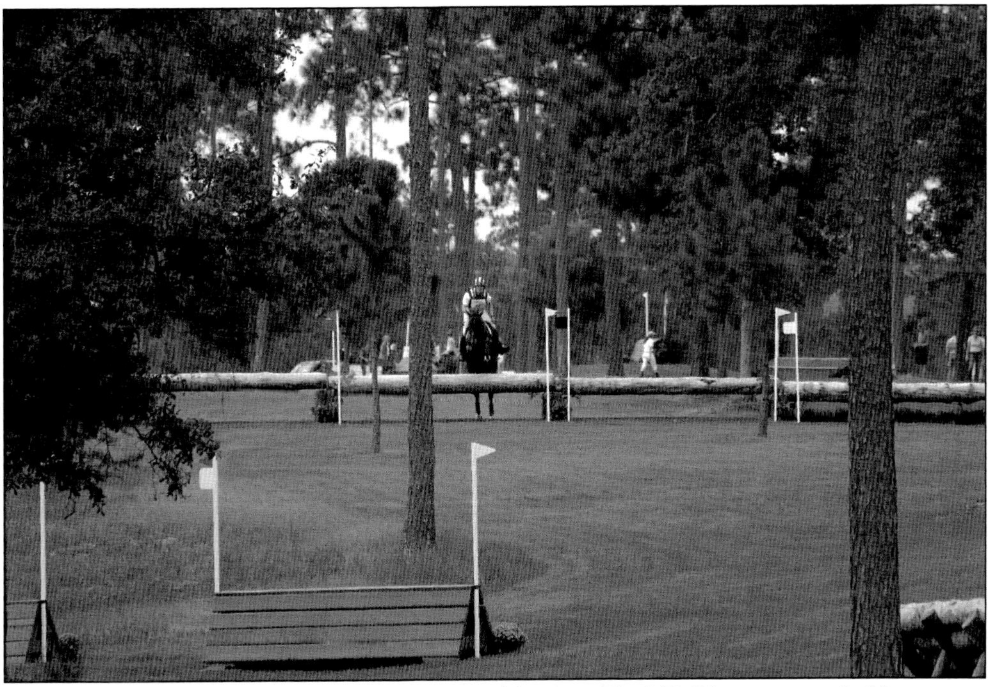

World-class eventing has a home in Aiken at Stable View. The US Olympic team holds training sessions, international eventing greats such as Phillip Dutton and Boyd Martin offer clinics at their farms, and numerous three-day eventing venues make this an ideal area for the winter season. Sporting Days, Three Runs Plantation, Full Gallop, Old Tory, Jumping Branch, Quintynne Hill, Black Forest, Bridle Creek, Hopeland Farms, and Paradise Farm have all played a critical role in the resurgence of eventing in Aiken. (Olliff.)

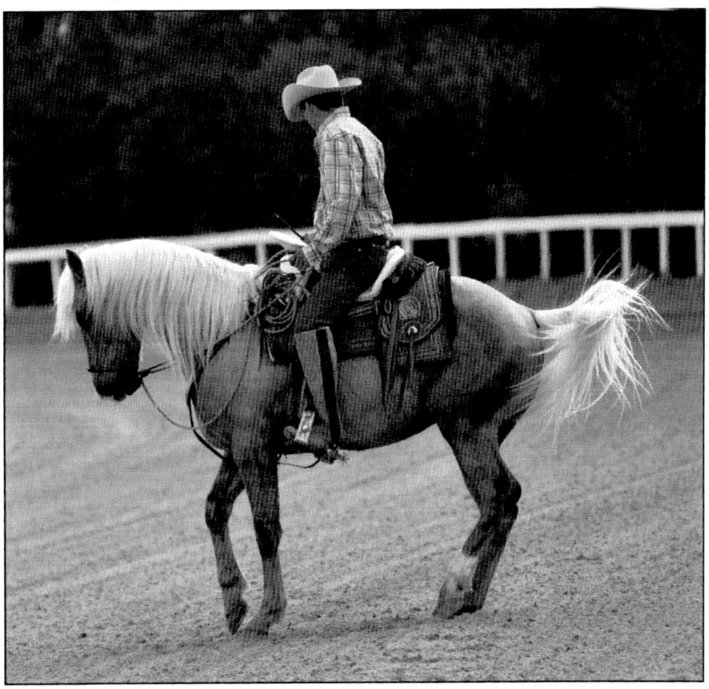

Western riding has deep roots in nearby Augusta, Georgia. Devotees of Western game riding, reining, halter breeding, and pleasure riding are active members of the Aiken equine community. Barrel racing and reining have strengthened in the equine vernacular, and in coming decades should rise in popularity locally as they have nationwide. (Author's collection.)

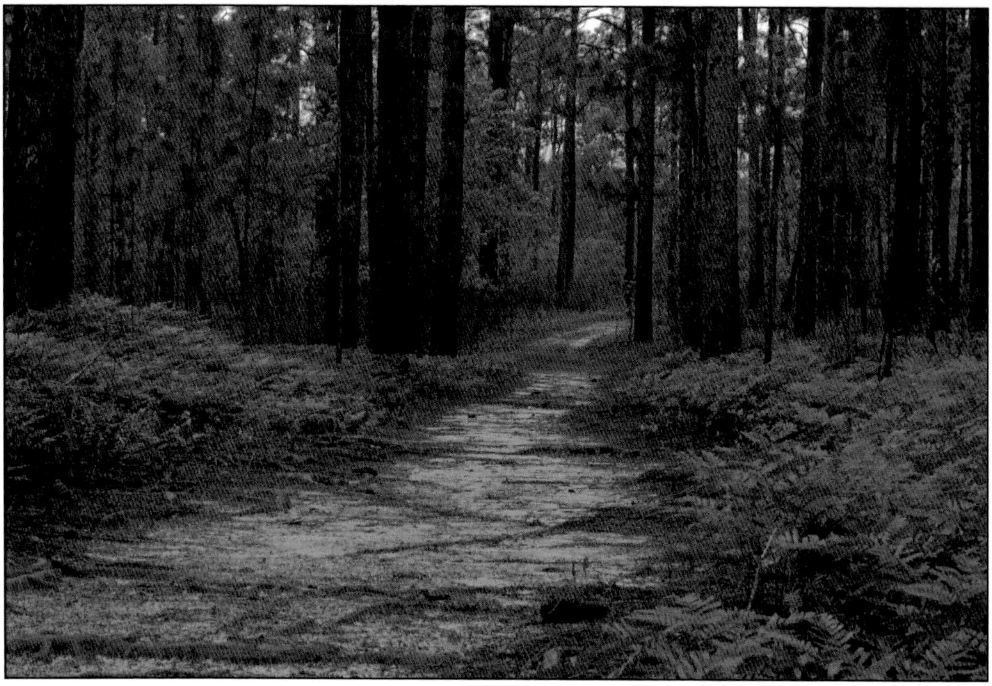

The Hitchcock Woods Foundation works to preserve the woods with prescribed burns, land acquisition, and community education. The foundation trustees work to promote their mission through the Celestine Eustis Prize Essay Contest and the Fall Festival of the Woods. Dr. Harry Shealy's educational and ecological tours discussing the 1,664 various plants that grow in Aiken County, among other things, are an integral part of the foundation's outreach. (Bridges.)

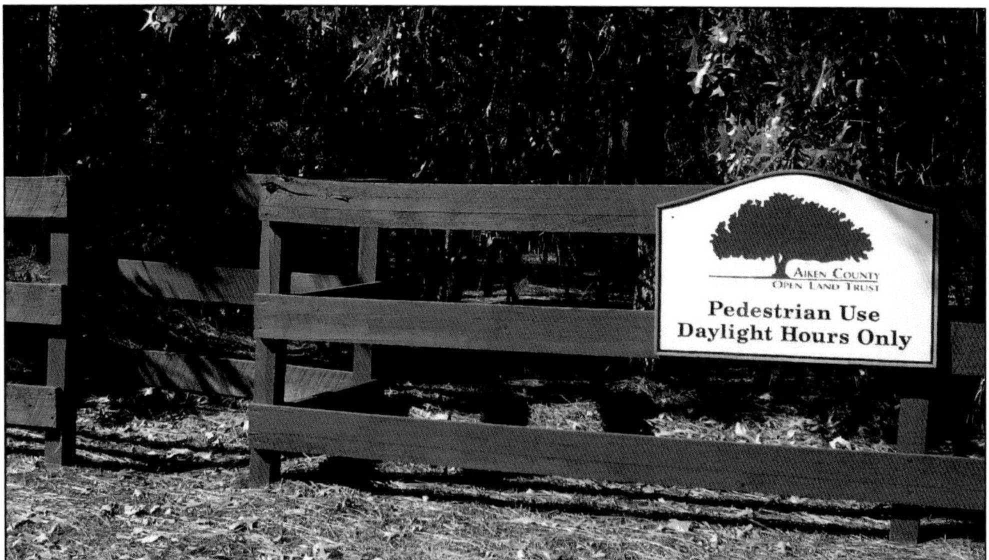

The Aiken County Open Land Trust, now the Aiken Land Conservancy, works to secure wetlands, grasslands, trailways, and woodlands for all types of use. Their partnership with the Greater Aiken Integrated Trail Foundation has been the culmination of decades of thinking, planning, and doing. (Author's collection.)

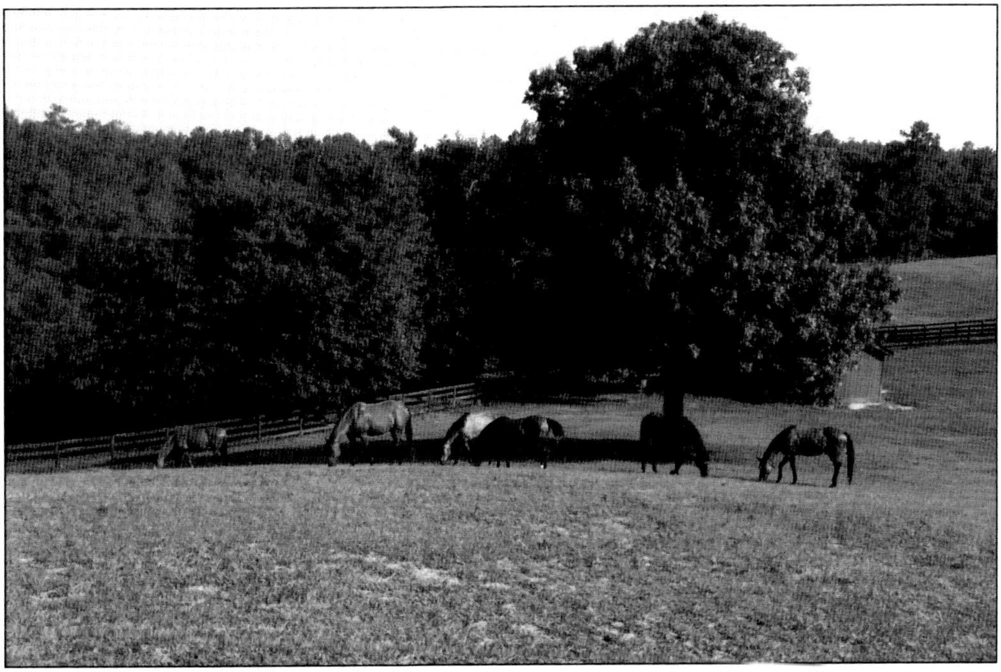

Aiken Equine Rescue has become a vital part of the community. Providing a safe haven for at-risk equines from across the country, Debbie and Jim Rhodes have managed to cultivate many new horse owners through their efforts. Nonprofits like these are essential to the community. (Rhodes.)

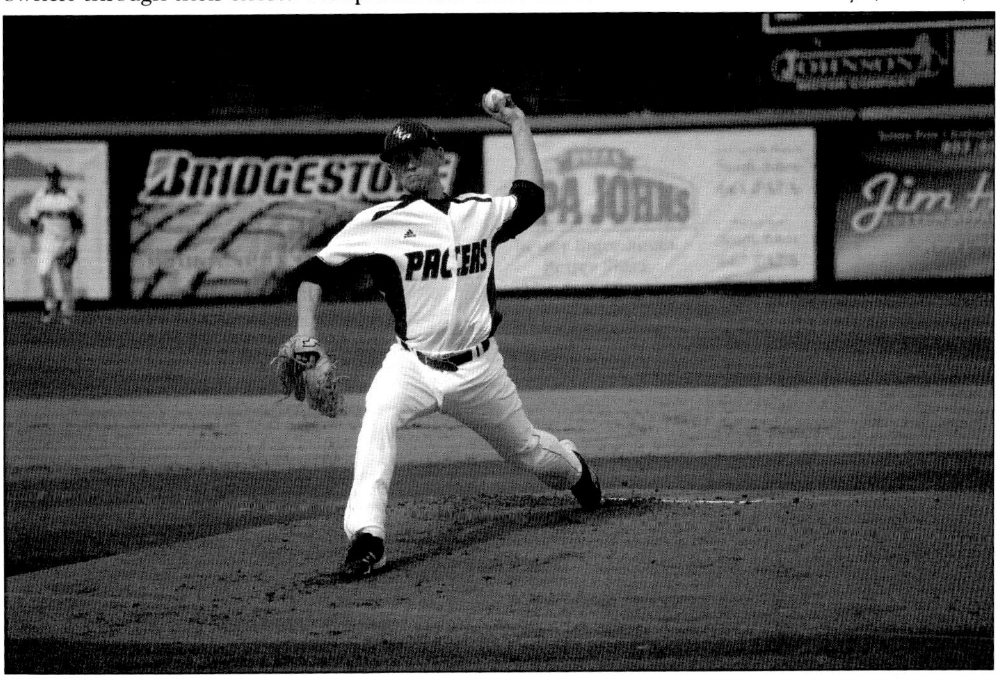

University of South Carolina–Aiken and its baseball team have a great fan base in the sports-loving people of the community. Continued success for the USCA baseball team and the other teams such as polo, basketball, golf, and soccer should figure prominently in the decades to come. (The *Aiken Standard*.)

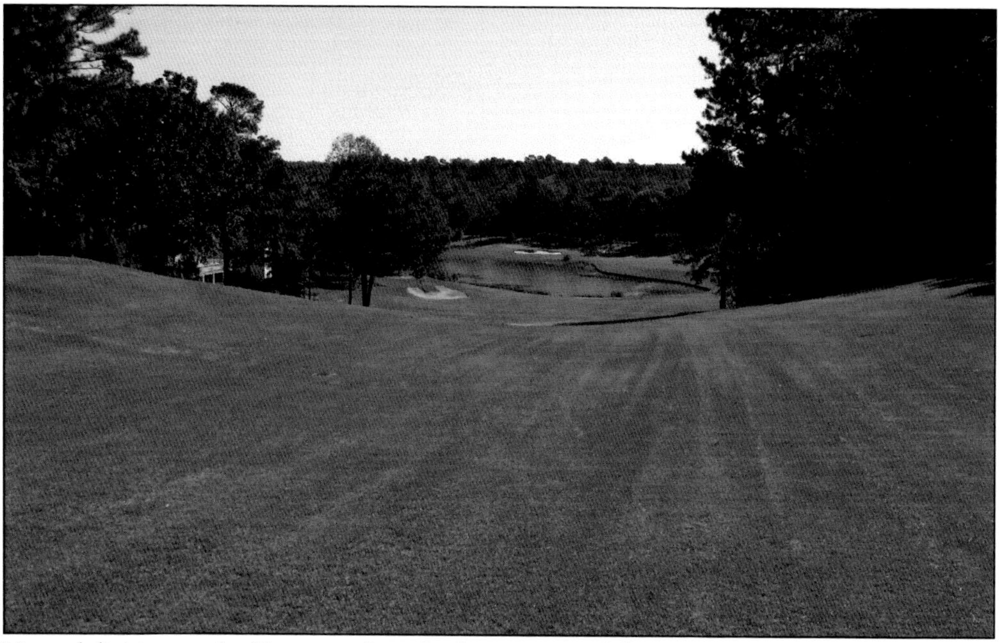

New subdivisions and golf courses also take their space in Aiken County. Houndslake Golf Club, bordering the woods, Woodside Plantation, built on the old Burden Hunting Preserve, and Cedar Creek have added a new dynamic to Aiken over the years, and residents will continue to be the supporting volunteers and activists that give Aiken heart and character. (Seawell.)

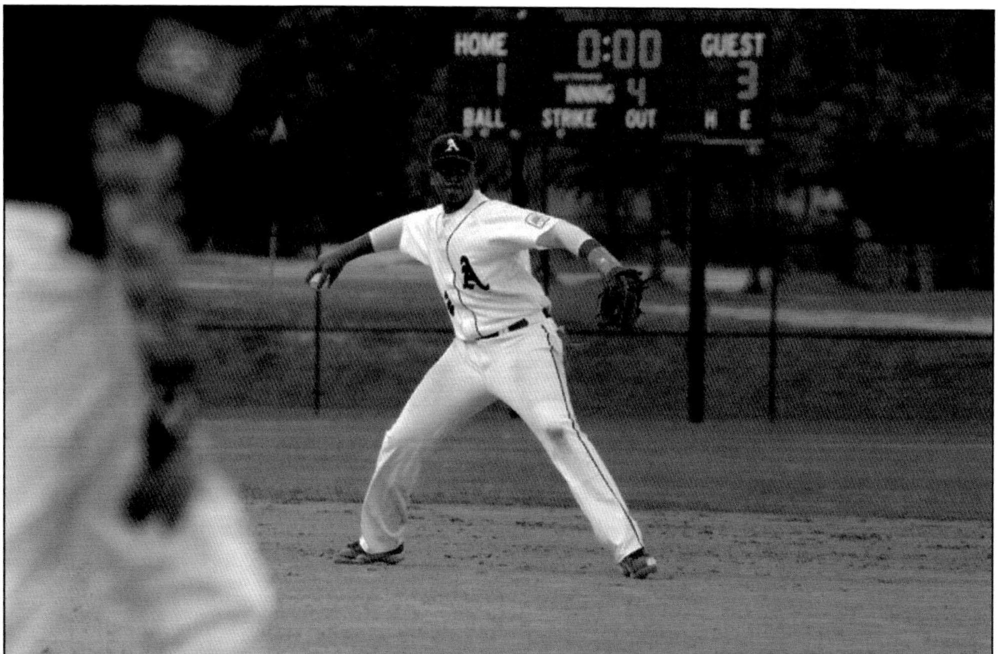

With the infrastructure of parks, fields, and courts, Aiken County is sure to be a future host of the Little League Regional Championships, as it is for the North Augusta Peach Jam for basketball coaches to preview players from across America. Citizens Park alone has nine lighted baseball diamonds and four soccer fields. (The *Aiken Standard*.)

Many of Aiken's traditions would not be possible without the ground crew. These are the dedicated volunteers, family members, friends, spouses, and participants who forgo riding to distribute trophies, set up tables, and fix jumps—the ground crew in Aiken is the backbone of its sporting life. Pictured here are Larry Byers, Paddy Ann Burns, and the late Latham Burns preparing to present trophies. (Bossard.)

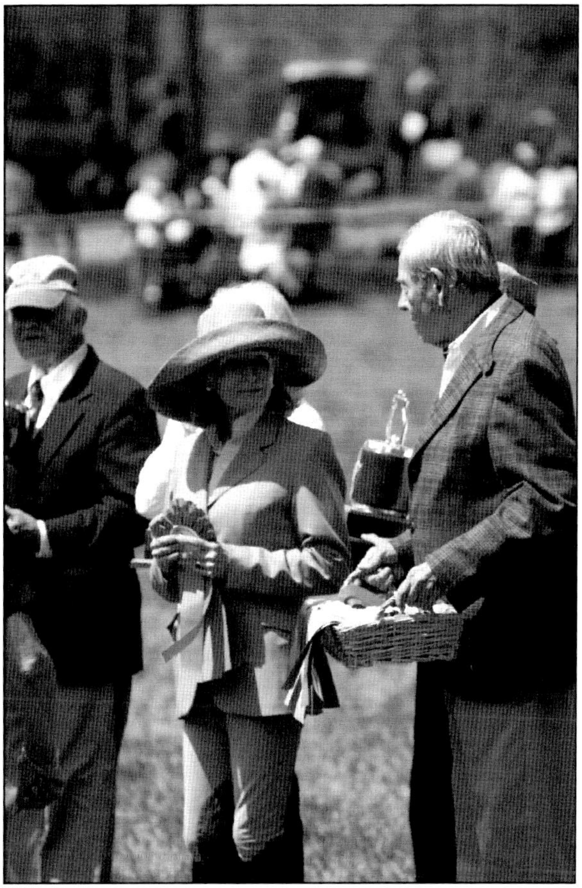

Drag-racing cars and trucks at the Carolina Dragway is a thrill a minute, or more like a thrill in 6.2 seconds. Micro sprint races at the speedway and Western Carolina State Fair Demolition Derby are also a part of the sporting menu in the area. (Author's collection.)

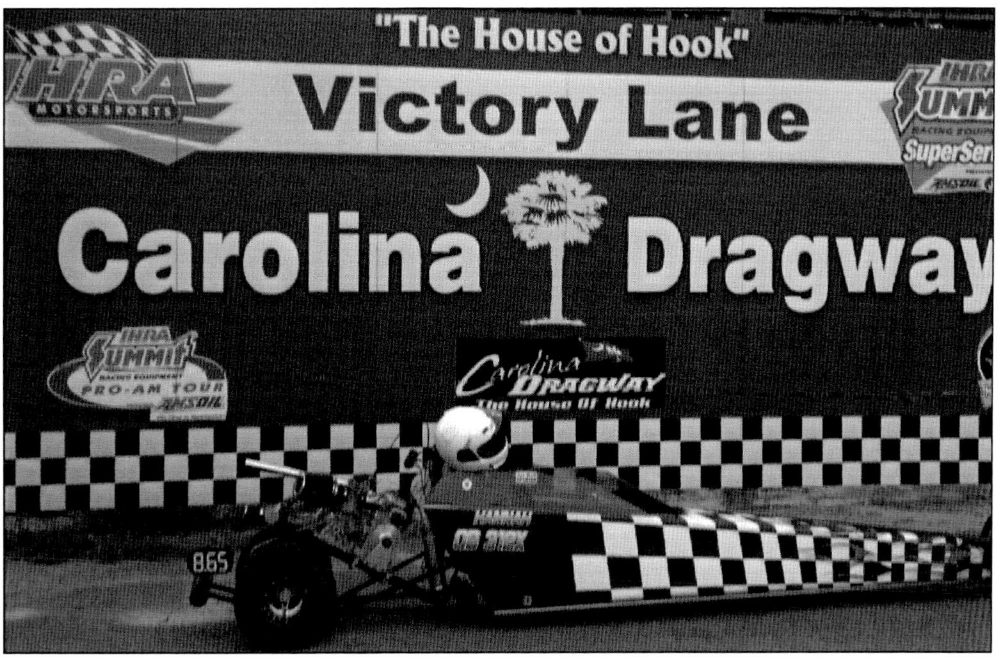

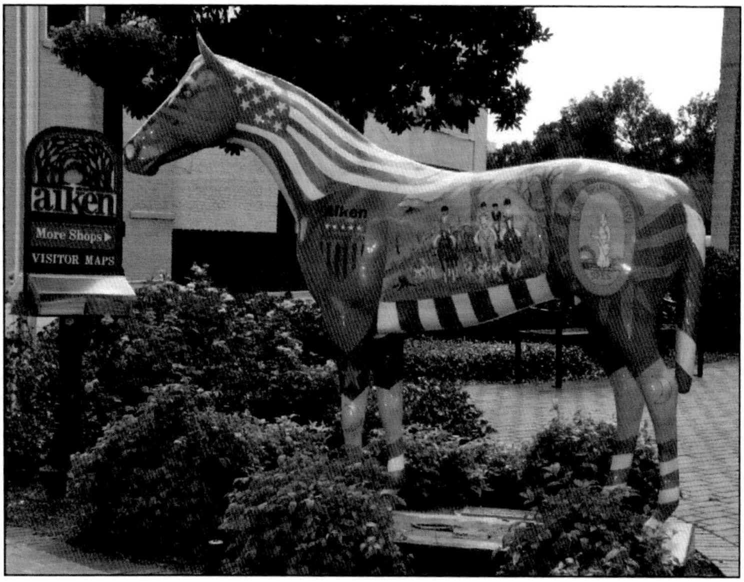

Visitors become quickly aware of the prominence of the horse culture in Aiken. Horseplay statues are positioned in key areas around the county. Many people recognize the artistic endeavors that these quarter-size equines represent, as they were auctioned to benefit the Aiken Center for the Arts. (Lista.)

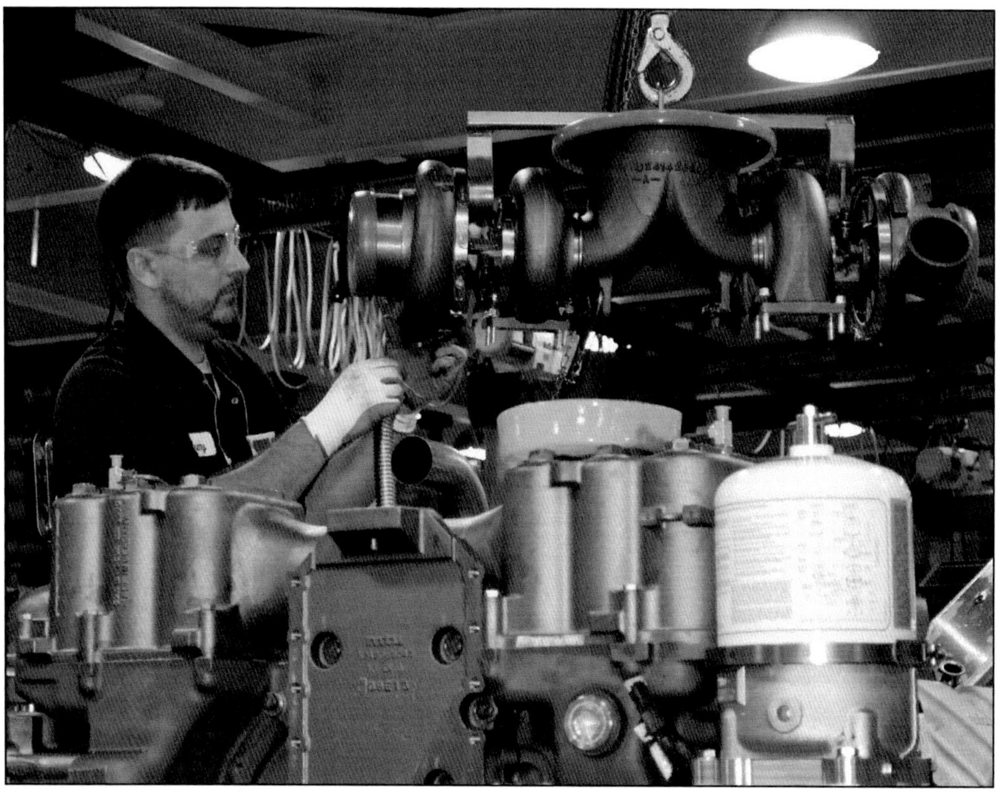

Corporate partners such as AB Beverage, Holley Tractor, MTU Diesel, Bridgestone, Zeus, Hutson Etherredge, SRS Companies, Autoneum, ASCO, Aiken Regional Medical Centers, Dumpster Depot, and many others will continue to support Aiken sporting traditions that enhance the area quality of life through jobs and recreation. (The *Aiken Standard*.)

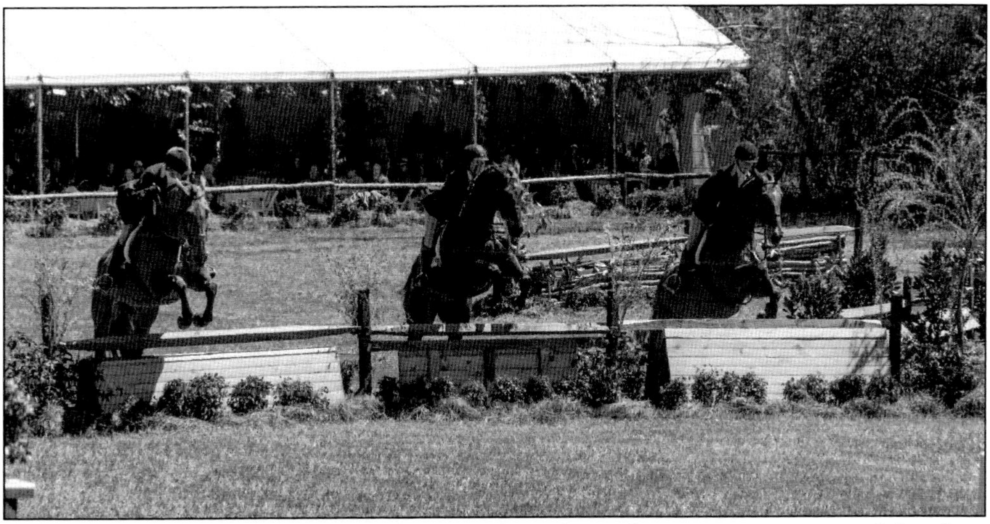

Hunt teams at AHS often practice at their own farms for weeks prior to competing while others join up that day and create blue-ribbon wins. From left to right, Gretchen Wintersteen, Maggie McGovern, and Emily Smith take the last jump together. (Bridges.)

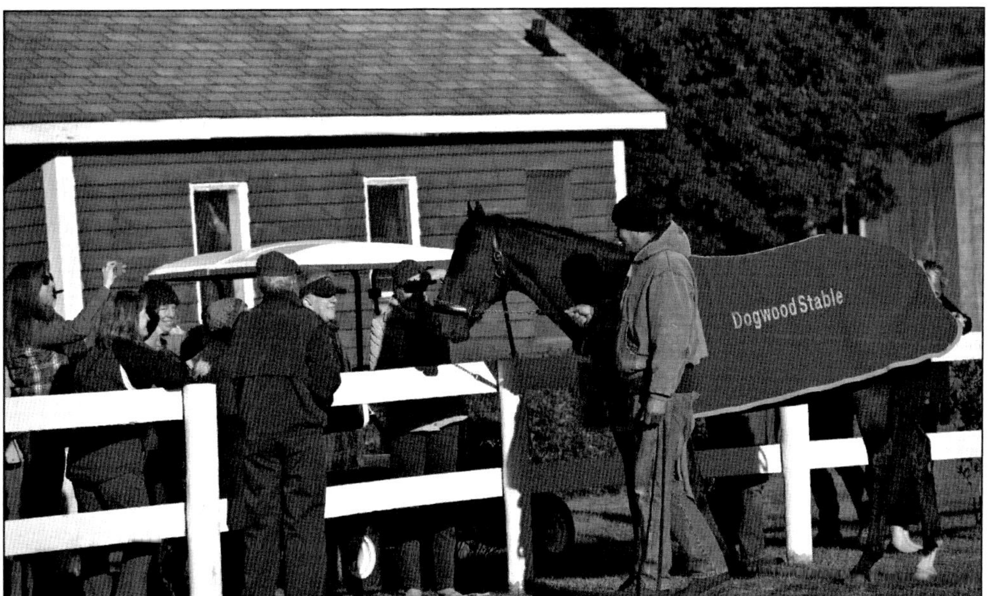

Aiken is sure to have a few more Belmont winners in its future. Dogwood Stable's Anne and Cot Campbell and Palace Malice created a national stir when he won the 2013 Belmont Stakes. Cot Campbell told reporters: "They'll be dancing in the streets in Aiken tonight." When Anne and Cot returned to Aiken the Sunday after the race, yellow and green balloons lined the road from the airport to their home and a can-can line of dancers kicked to Belmont's theme song, "New York, New York." When Palace Malice wintered in Aiken, there was standing room only at the rail for his morning jog. Aiken knows how to celebrate its horses. (Lisa Hall.)

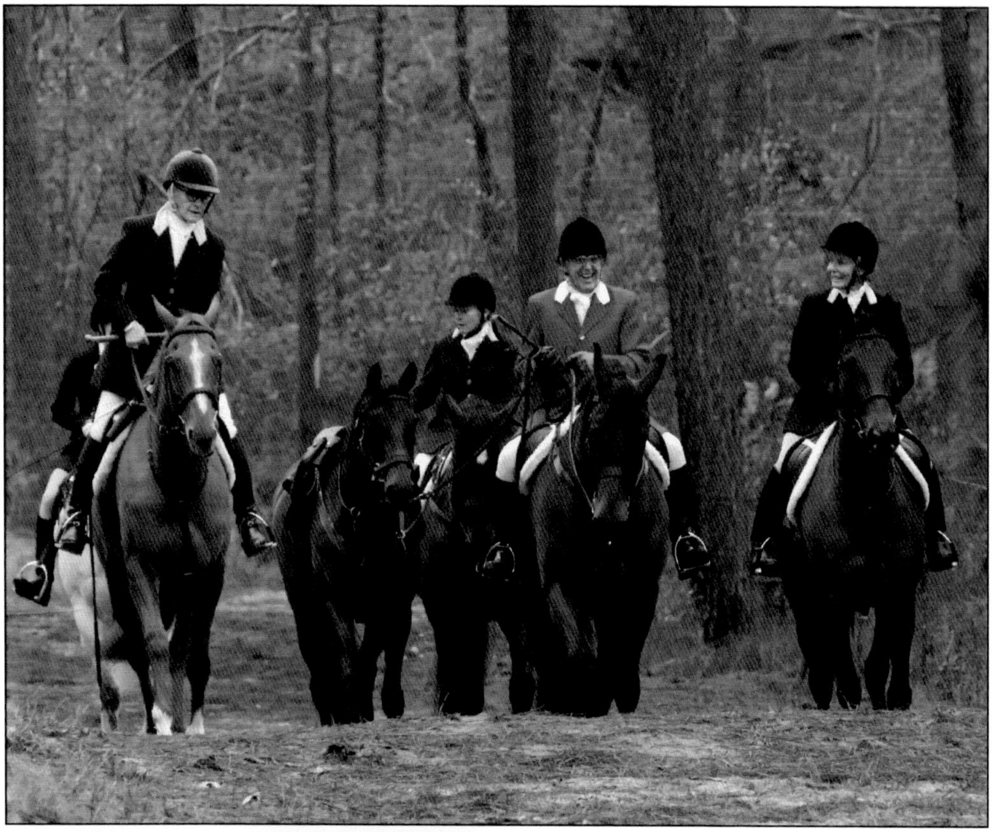

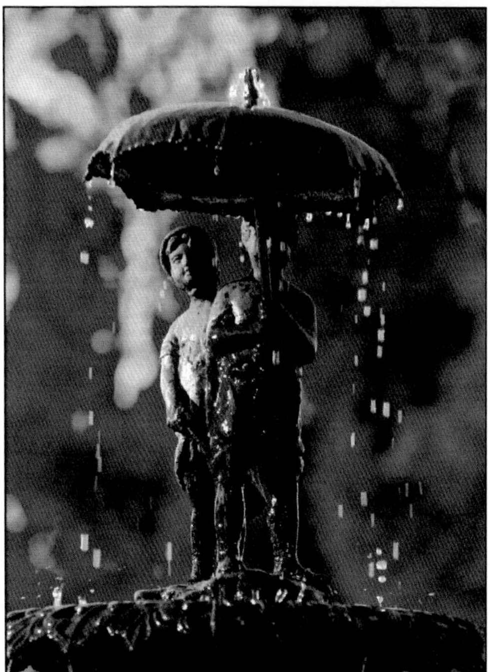

Aiken Hounds has welcomed its second century. Master Joey Peace and whippers-in Gina Salatino and Gene Kneece discuss where the draglines were laid with Carolyn Rees-Potter, usually the fox. The activity in Hitchcock Woods could not happen without the work of Namon Corley and Bennett Tucker, who have been the superintendents for the last 60 years. (Bridges.)

Aiken icons include painted horses, the live oaks on South Boundary Avenue, and Morgan Fountain at the circle on Laurens Street and Park Avenue. Thomas Redman Morgan was the mayor of Aiken in 1899, when the plan for the remaining parkways and civic plantings were implemented. Civic engineering, railroad engineering, nuclear engineering—it seems as much as Aiken's character lies in horses and botanicals, so too has it been shaped by engineers. (Lista.)

Southern Nationals drag-boat racing, held on the Savannah River, is the world's richest drag-boat race. The power of the drag boats makes Aiken County a place for fast fun, even without a horse. (The *Aiken Standard*.)

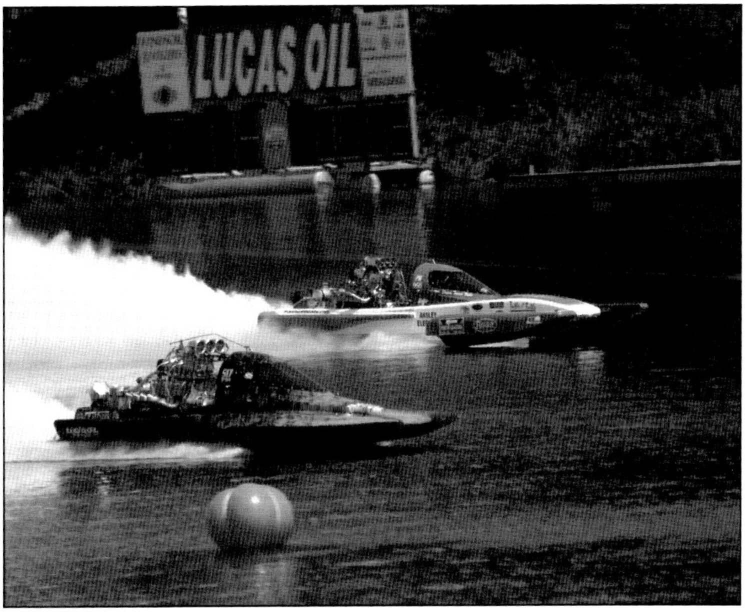

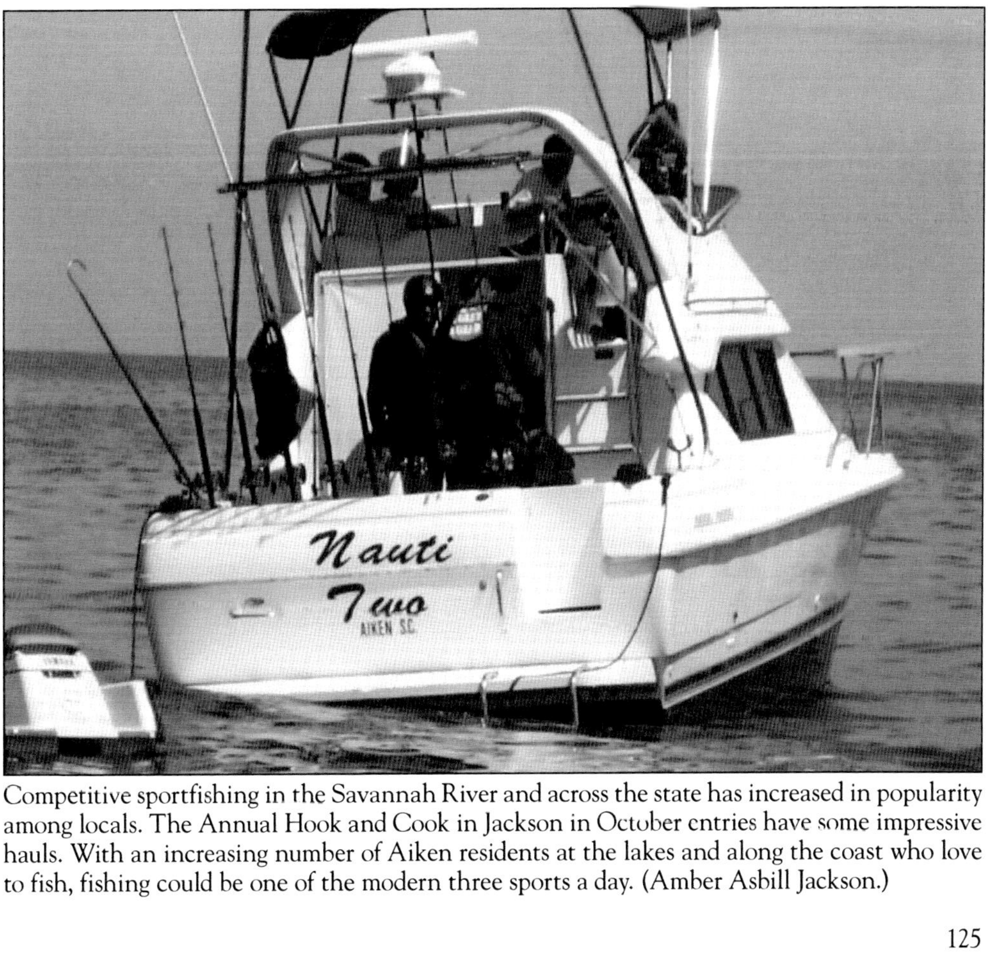

Competitive sportfishing in the Savannah River and across the state has increased in popularity among locals. The Annual Hook and Cook in Jackson in October entries have some impressive hauls. With an increasing number of Aiken residents at the lakes and along the coast who love to fish, fishing could be one of the modern three sports a day. (Amber Asbill Jackson.)

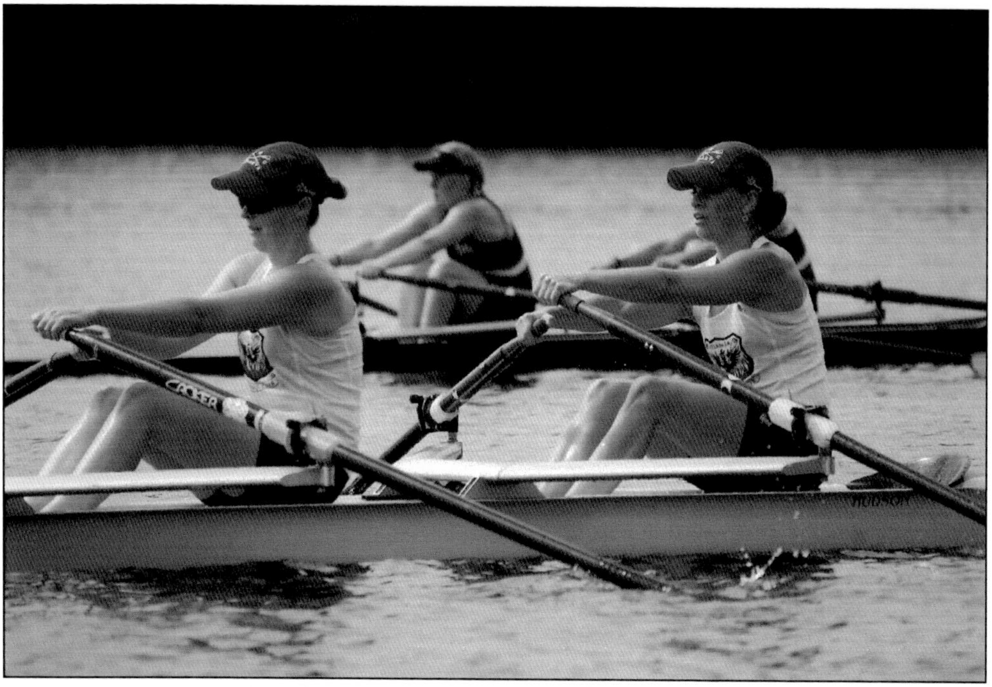

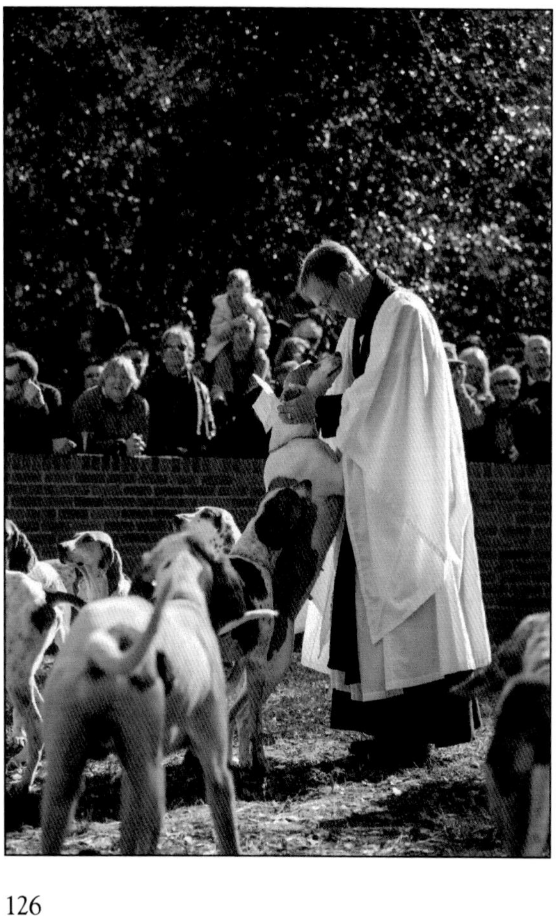

Regattas on Langley Pond have brought collegiate rowers to the area to train. As Aiken County Parks, Recreation and Tourism improves the pond, competitive regattas and an expanded viewing season may add an Aiken Triple Crown of Water Sports to the annual calendar. (The *Aiken Standard*.)

Father Grant Wiseman of St. Thaddeus Episcopal Church blesses the hounds on Thanksgiving Day, reminding us that always at the heart of Aiken is the Hitchcock Woods. The communion of family and the support of friends bring people and animals together in a meaningful way that touches generations. Locals are blessed for having the Hitchcock Woods in Aiken, South Carolina. (Lista.)

About Hitchcock Woods

Hitchcock Woods in Aiken, South Carolina, is among the largest urban forests in the nation, with about 2,100 acres of forestland resources. Once owned and enjoyed by Louise and Thomas Hitchcock, this longleaf pine forest has retained its natural character and cultural heritage. Today, equestrians, hikers, dog walkers, and joggers enjoy the 70 miles of sandy trails that provide access to the stunning variety of ecosystems in the Hitchcock Woods. Hitchcock Woods is open to the public on horseback or on foot from dawn to dusk 365 days a year. Admission is free of charge, thanks to donor support.

The mission of the Hitchcock Woods Foundation is to protect and preserve the Hitchcock Woods in a natural and ecologically healthy state, maintain and manage historic and traditional equestrian and pedestrian uses, and foster education and research on the history and resources of the woods. The vision of the Hitchcock Woods Foundation is to maintain and restore the ecological integrity of the Hitchcock Woods and serve as a model for sustainable urban forestry, balancing stewardship of forestland natural resources with compatible human uses. For more information, visit hitchcockwoods.org.

Hitchcock Woods
FOUNDATION

Consistent with our mission to preserve history on a local level, this book was printed in South Carolina on American-made paper and manufactured entirely in the United States. Products carrying the accredited Forest Stewardship Council (FSC) label are printed on 100 percent FSC-certified paper.